AF770060

The Authorized Insider's Guide to ACT!®

The Authorized Insider's Guide to ACT!®

Douglas J. Wolf

Windcrest®/McGraw-Hill

New York San Francisco Washington, D.C. Auckland Bogotá
Caracas Lisbon London Madrid Mexico City Milan
Montreal New Delhi San Juan Singapore
Sydney Tokyo Toronto

FIRST EDITION
FOURTH PRINTING

Published by Windcrest, an imprint of McGraw-Hill, Inc.
The name "Windcrest" is a registered trademark of McGraw-Hill, Inc.

Library of Congress Cataloging-in-Publication Data

Wolf, Douglas J., 1956-
The authorized insider's guide to ACT! / Douglas J. Wolf.
p. cm.
Includes index.
ISBN 0-8306-2455-4 ISBN 0-8306-2454-6 (pbk.)
1. Time management—Computer programs. 2. ACT! (Computer file)
I. Title.
HD69.T54W65 1992
650'.0285'5369—dc20 91-28712
CIP

Acquisitions Editor: Ron Powers
Book Editor: Andrew Yoder
Director of Production: Katherine G. Brown
Book Design: Jaclyn J. Boone
Paperbound Cover: Sandra Blair Design
and Brent Blair Photography, Harrisburg, PA.

WPT1
3856

Contents

Dedication

I dedicate this book to the outstanding Senior Class of 1974 of Le Center High School, Le Center Minnesota. Those I wish to personally honor are: Jeffrey Gibbs, William Krenik (deceased) Craig Bartelt, Timothy Kelly, Diane Jerrow, Debbie Steinbach, and Colleen Claffey.

Acknowledgments

The following people helped make this book possible: President Pat Sullivan and Karen Hart of Contact Software International, Matt Wagner of Waterside Productions, and Ed Wright of Amazing Bytes Computers.

Special thanks go to Intel's Randy Burress for getting me an Intel SatisfaXtion board for testing purposes, and to Reference Software for the use of their product, Random House Webster's Electronic Dictionary and Thesaurus. both are fine products that worked flawlessly.

Introduction

"To understand is hard. Once one understands, action is easy."

SUN YAT-SEN

This quote seems appropriate as it applies to computer software. Many new computer users have thrown up their hands in despair in trying to figure out how to integrate a "user-friendly" piece of software into their working lives.

ACT! is different. From the moment you begin working with ACT!, you see the elegant structure that the designers intended. ACT! was designed by two men whose work depended on keeping track of meetings, calls, and things to do. They approached the problem from a salesman's standpoint. The result is ACT!, a fun way to use a computer effectively in your work.

In this book, I am assuming that you own ACT! version 2.0 or 2.1 and that you have purchased this book for one of two purposes: either you are new to ACT! and therefore need a step-by-step approach to how to get started or you are an experienced user and want to learn how to get more out of ACT! than you already do. The first few chapters are for the beginning user: entering contact information, editing and so on. After covering the basics, the more elegant uses of ACT! are explored.

The principal designers of ACT!, Pat Sullivan and Mike Muhney, used the name ACT! with the obvious allusion to taking action!

I was introduced to ACT! version 1.0 in 1988, by a friend. He was insistent that ACT! was the best product on the market for keeping track of all the activities that come from working with people. At the time, I was writing computer books, and working as a mortgage broker.

The book writing business does not require a tool like ACT!. But the mortgage business does. Considering that in a typical home purchase there are the following players:

- The seller
- The seller's real estate agent
- The buyer (usually my client)

- The buyer's real estate agent
- The escrow officer
- The title insurance representative

On top of these players, because I was the mortgage broker, I was searching 20–30 different mortgage companies for the best loan for my client. Plus, I normally had 7 to 10 clients at a time; therefore, the list above was repeated for every client.

At my friend's urging, I started using ACT!. In a short period of time, I found that I started to control my work flow rather than the other way around. No more lost phone numbers, forgotten calls, or misplaced priorities. I could document for myself and others how many times I had called a certain agent or escrow company. My credibility as being a person who did what I said I would do increased, making life much less stressful.

Then, in the spring of 1990, I was asked to help develop the documentation for ACT! version 2.0. In your hands is a book that grew out of that experience. The goal is to give you a book that progresses in ACT! as you would in day-to-day usage: from simply entering people's names, addresses, and phone numbers to creating customized reports. The ideas detailed here spring from many sources: the folks at Contact Software, the San Diego ACT! user's group, and from me.

ACT! 2.0 and 2.1

This book is intended for users of ACT! versions. 2.0 and 2.1. The two products differ. When appropriate, a notice is included in the text to alert you that the example or explanation applies to only version 2.1. I urge you to upgrade to 2.1 as quickly as possible. However, if you have not, this book will still be very useful in expanding your use of ACT!. Some of the new features in ACT! 2.1 are:

- The integration of a software program, *Books, Cards and Labels*, designed to produce highly customizable calendars, Daytimer formats (such as FiloFax and Day Runner), laser Rolodex cards, and a whole host of other types of printed output from your ACT! database.
- Direct output to a fax board. If you have purchased an INTEL SatisFAXtion board or a HAYES JT fax board (or one that is compatible), you can send ACT! documents directly to the fax. You can even fax a single document to multiple fax locations!
- Improved data merge capability. Suppose that you are the sales manager of a company and all of your salespeople are required to use ACT!. Keeping a current and accurate company database can be a pain because the contact information is distributed and changing constantly as your salespeople do business. ACT! now makes it a breeze to not only upload the information from a laptop or notebook computer, but also to determine what information from which contact has changed and how you want to handle it.

- Graphic representation of your contacts. It might be a cliché that a picture is worth a thousand words (most clichés are true), but wouldn't it be great to be able to see where your contacts are located by overlaying their addresses on a map? Well, with ACT! and MAPLINX, you can create a Contact map and print it or create a color transparency.
- Easier dBase importing and exporting. Many software users come to ACT! with a database already created in a program that produces a dBase file format. Maybe they would like to be able to export their ACT! database files to dBase format. Although ACT! has always allowed for this, the 2.1 version makes it much less cumbersome.
- The ability to record frequently used keystrokes. In computer jargon, a series of recorded keystrokes that can be played back is called a *macro*. Suppose that your work involves frequently sending follow-up letters to contacts, and the letter is identical, except for the recipient's name and address. You can record the keystrokes needed to access the word processor, open the correct letter and print it and the envelope.
- Passwording your databases is now possible. If you choose to do so, you can create a password lock to a database so that only you (or those you give the password to) can access the database.
- Snooze-All option. If you have recorded one or many critical calls, you can select the Snooze-All option so that the ACT! pop-up screen reminders do not reappear until you tell them to.
- Enhanced mouse support. If you have become addicted to using a mouse, the mouse driver is much better.

Final note

I would appreciate hearing your ideas on how ACT! helped you to do business, solve a chronic problem, or made you a fortune, at the following address:

P.O. Box 160
Poway, CA 92074

or via CompuServe 73607,665.

At the beginning and end of each chapter, I have selected quotations which, in my curmudgeonly opinion, have some sort of connection to the material. Have fun with ACT! and as they say in show business, "break a leg."

"The business of America is business."

CALVIN COOLIDGE

1
CHAPTER

How ACT! works

"Nothing in the world is so powerful as an idea whose time has come."

VICTOR HUGO

In today's business world, the overwhelming task is management of time. Keeping track of appointments, calls to make, and the things that you promised to do has become a full-time job in itself. When personal computers arrived, people assumed that the computer would become the personal assistant that everyone needed. Unfortunately, the software was not up to the job. It was either too hard to program or too task specific.

Contact management

Out of the frustration with database software packages and hand-written methods, ACT! was born. By entering all of the people with whom you come in contact or want to be in contact, ACT! will make it possible for you to increase the amount and quality of work you do. Thus, *contact management* is the ability to control your time by controlling your activities instead of activities controlling you.

ACT! is:

- a multipurpose database
- an electronic appointment book
- a phone dialer
- an electronic address book
- a word processing system, including a form letter generator

. . . and more.

Getting started using ACT! does not require that you invest a tremendous amount of time entering all the people you have contact with before using the program. I don't recommend that you begin using ACT! that way.

Begin your normal working day with ACT! running on your computer. As you work, simply start entering the names, addresses, and phone numbers of the people that you are calling, going to meet with, or who require you to complete a task. If your contact with that person requires a follow-up call, meeting, or task, enter it into ACT!. Very quickly, you will have entered the majority of contacts that are critical to your work. At your leisure, you can enter the contacts that are less frequently a part of your day-to-day activities.

Getting started

Before you can begin using ACT!, you must install the program. The installation information (version 2.1) is in chapter 2 of the *ACT! User's Guide*.

In this screen play, the following conventions are used. When a key press is needed, the key to be used will be presented in this style of type:

Enter, Escape, F1 . . .

When it is necessary for you to type characters, they will be presented in this type style:

123, ABCDE . . .

If you have not already turned on your computer, do so now. When the C:> appears, type: CD\ ACT! and press Enter. This takes you into the ACT! subdirectory. Next, start ACT! by typing: ACT and press Enter. The ACT! opening screen appears and asks you to type any key to continue. The blank Contact Entry screen appears as in Fig. 1-1.

What you see in Fig. 1-1 is the first of two contact entry screens. The Contact Entry screen is similar to a recipe card in that it is a two-sided screen. As you can discern, the screen has several distinct sections.

The top section is where the basic information is entered regarding the contact. The company, the contact (the person you interface with), the phone number, and so on. In the middle of the screen is the activity section, which contains calls, meetings and to-dos.

The next section of the screen contains fields for entering results, the Status/ID of the contact, and the referral source. The final section on this first screen is a series of nine user-definable fields. That is, these fields are for you to design any way you please. Across the bottom of the screen is the program information: the directory where the ACT! database is located and the date and time indicator.

Using the F6 key

The Contact Entry screen has two sides. To see the reverse side of the Contact Entry screen (Fig. 1-2), press the F6 key.

Contact management usually involves more than just a single contact at a single location. So, the top section of the second Contact Entry screen has space for you to insert secondary information on the contact.

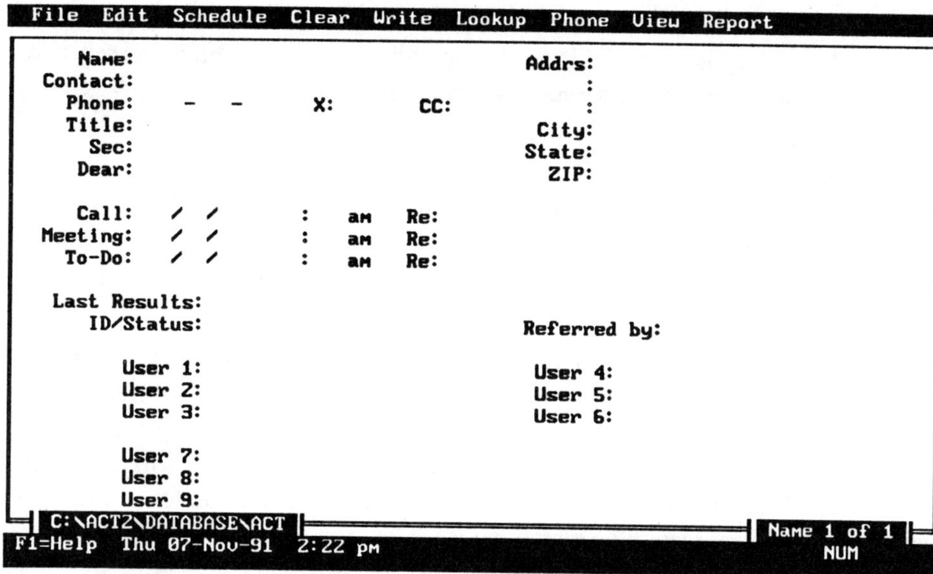

Fig. 1-1. The Contact Entry Screen.

Next, space is provided to enter names of the people you can contact if the primary contact is unavailable. After that are more user fields.

The bottom section of the screen includes a record keeping section of the messages sent, how and when, calls made and completed, and the person in charge of working with the contact. The E-Mail section is used to record the contact's electronic mail and fax numbers.

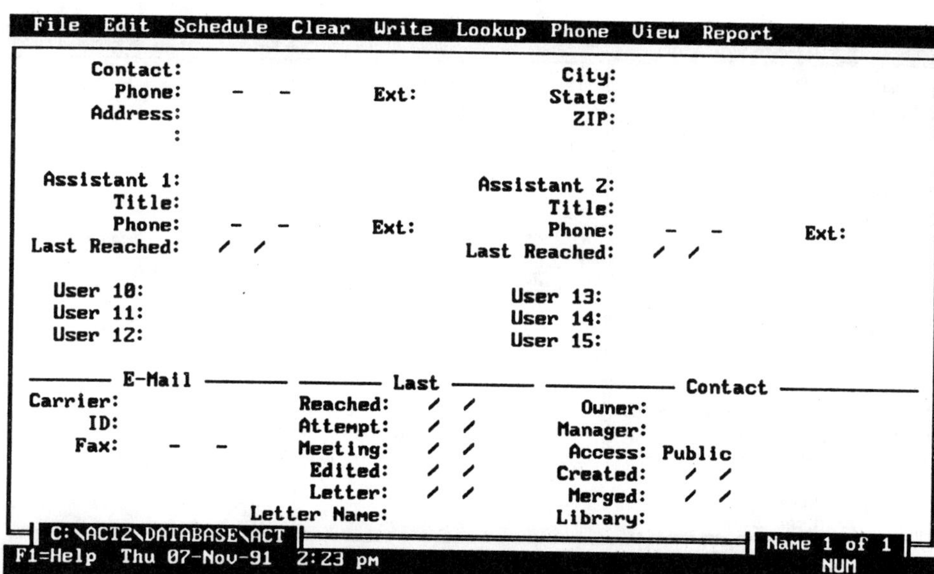

Fig. 1-2. The Contact Entry Screen 2.

Press the F6 function key again. You are back at the front Contact Entry screen. The F6 key is a toggle. Press it once and the Contact Entry screen is reversed; press it again and the screen is reversed again.

Accessing the ACT! menus

At the very top of both the front and reverse Contact Entry screens is the menu bar. At the far left is the first menu, *File*, and across to the right is the last menu, *Report*. ACT! uses "pull-down" menus. That is, when you access to a menu, it is pulled down over the Contact Entry screen.

How to open a menu ACT! menus can be opened in four ways. If you have a color monitor, the first letters in the menu names are displayed in a different color than the rest of the letters. For example, in the menu name "File" the *F* is a different color. If you have a monochrome or LCD monitor, the letter *F* will have a distinct shading. So, the first way to open a menu is to press the letter in the menu name that is different from the rest, the *access letter*.

1. Press F now. The File menu pulls down as in Fig. 1-3. Look at the File menu. The list of words on the menu, beginning with retrieve, are called *menu options*. Notice that each option has a letter that is displayed in a different color or shading. Each option on the File menu and on the other menus, has an "access" letter, too.
2. Now, press the right arrow key once. The Edit menu is now pulled down and the File menu is closed. Continue to press the right arrow key, and each menu in turn will be pulled down from the menu bar.

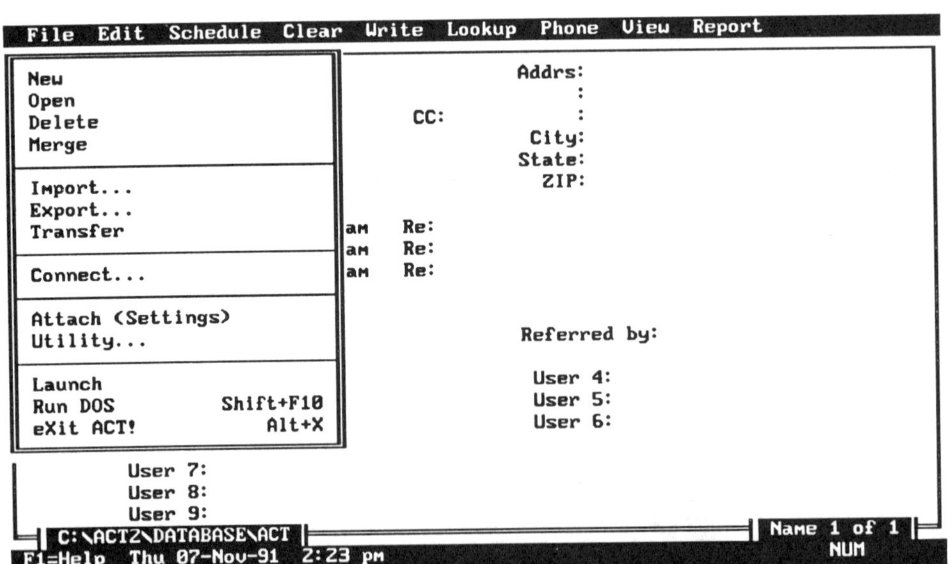

Fig. 1-3. The File Menu.

So, now you know of two ways to pull down a menu: using the access letter or pressing the left or right arrow key when a menu is already open, opens the adjoining menu.

Closing a menu Press Escape. Any menu that was open is now closed. The Escape key is used for a variety of tasks, one of which is closing menus. ACT! has menus, submenus, and submenus of submenus, from which you can select menu options. When you have opened a menu, a submenu, and another submenu, you can close the menus by pressing Escape repeatedly.

A good rule of thumb is, "When in doubt, Escape out." You can cancel virtually any ACT! operation by pressing Escape, without doing any harm.

Using the highlight to open a menu With the menus closed, a highlight or reverse color is visible on one of the menu names in the menu bar. Use the right or left arrow keys to move the highlight from menu name to menu name. At any menu name, press Enter. That menu will be pulled down from the menu bar.

Using the ALT key to open a menu Pressing the ALT key followed by the menu name access letter also opens a menu. For example, to open the File menu, you can press and hold the ALT key followed by the letter F. It does not matter which method you use to open menus. In a short time, you will find a method that is comfortable for you and your hardware.

Entering owner/manager information

When you installed ACT!, you were asked to enter the Owner's Name and the Manager's Name. The distinction is that the owner of the database might be different from the person (manager) who actually works with ACT! during the day.

When you create a letter in ACT!, the name that you entered as the Manager of the database is inserted in the signature line automatically. In many cases, the Owner and the Manager are the same person. Suppose that you are an insurance agent. You probably brought ACT! to handle your client database and when you send a letter, you want your name in the signature line. In another circumstance, if you manage a large insurance agency, your secretary might be the person who creates and sends letters. If so, the name of the secretary should be the manager entry.

If you did not enter the Owner/Manager information correctly when you installed ACT!, it is easy to make the change.

To enter the manager information:

1. Open the Edit menu.
2. Use the down arrow key to move the highlight to the Manager Information option.
3. Press Enter. The Manager Information window appears, as in Fig. 1-4.

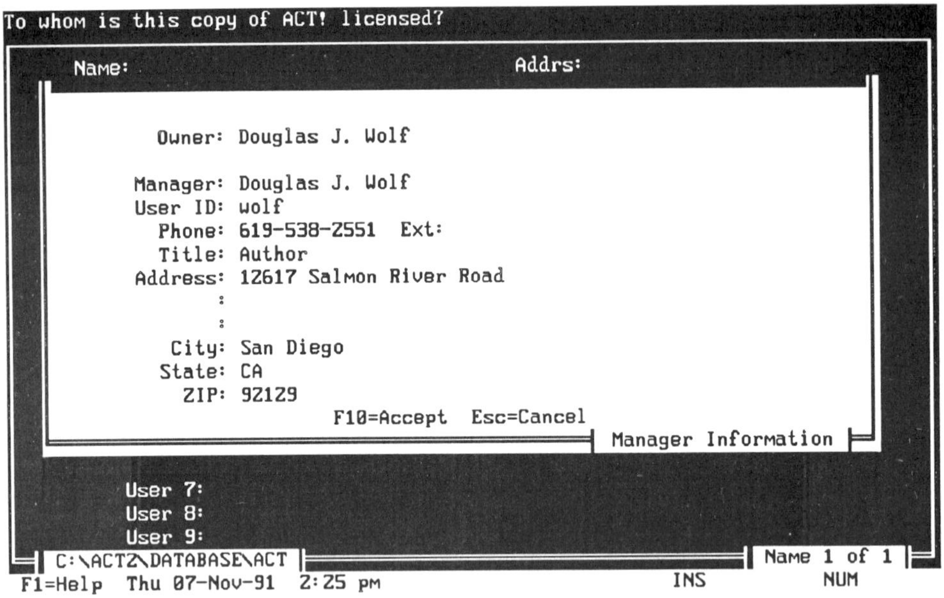

Fig. 1-4. The Manager Information Window.

Owner The entry in this field and in the Manager field depends on your working arrangement. If you are self-employed, you are likely to be the owner of the database. On the other hand, if you are an employee, it is likely that you will enter the name of the organization as the owner. The owner is considered to be the person who paid for ACT!.

Manager The entry is this field will either be yourself, as the person working with the contacts in the database, or it will be blank if you are self-employed and have entered your own name as the owner. If merged with a different ACT! database, the manager field can be used to identify the contact's manager.

User ID The user ID (identification) is used by ACT! to identify which person made an entry in the Notes of a Contact. Or, if a person sent a letter to the contact, it is recorded in the History file. If you are using ACT! in a stand-alone situation (not on a network), the value of this feature might not seem apparent. However, on the network version of ACT!, many people might be undertaking contact activities. When the contact is accessed, anyone can see who has been doing what with that contact.

Note: The user-ID feature is not editable. If you did not include an ID during installation, ACT! demands an entry when you initially start the program.

Phone Enter your phone number.

Title Enter your job title.

Address Enter your mailing address.

4. Press F10 to save the information. The entry screen closes and you are returned to the Contact screen.

Setting screen type

ACT! tries to determine the type of screen your computer has to best display itself. If your screen is hard to read, you need to make an adjustment.

1. Move the highlight to the Edit menu and press Enter. The Edit menu pulls down over the screen.
2. Move the highlight to the options choice and press Enter. A submenu appears.
3. Move the highlight to the Color Settings option and press Enter. The submenu appears (Fig. 1-5).

   If you have a color screen, you can select the preset color combinations with Color Set 1 or Color Set 2, or use the Edit Color option to design your own screen colors.

If you decide to create your own color scheme, follow these steps:

1. Select the Edit Color option. ACT! displays a color palette including a list of the attributes that can be modified.

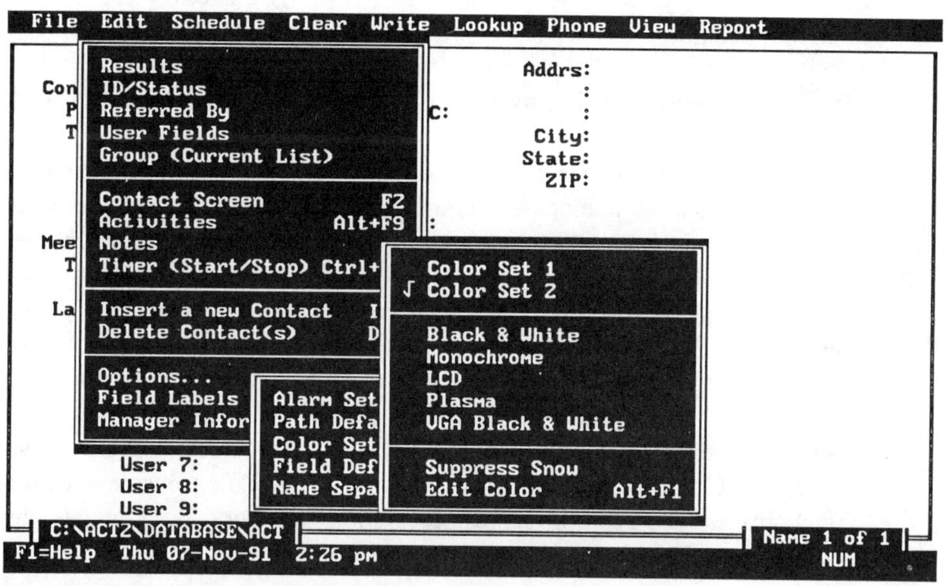

Fig. 1-5. The Edit, Options, Color Settings sub-menu.

2. Use the up or down arrow keys to move the highlight to the attribute you want to change.
3. Press the Tab key or F2 to begin the color edit. A box appears in the palette at the current color setting.
4. Use the arrow keys to move the box over the color combinations. As you do, the screen reflects the new color setting.
5. Press F10 to accept the new colors or press Escape to cancel the change.

Noncolor screen options:

- Black and white
- Monochrome
- LCD
- Plasma
- VGA black and white

To select any of the other options, move the highlight to the item that matches your hardware and press Enter. The ACT! screen immediately reflects the new setting and remains as the default until changed again.

Entering a Contact

Now that you have a grasp of the basics of ACT!, you can insert a contact. I am assuming that you have not yet entered any contacts into your ACT! database, and that you are entering the contact information described in each step. If you have entered contacts, simply read through the steps; you might discover capabilities that you are not using.

1. Press the Insert key. This causes ACT! to display the Insert Contact message window (Fig. 1-6).

   There are three variables in deciding on how to insert a new contact. The Default option includes the field entries, such as the area code or state that you have indicated. Setting up the field defaults is covered in chapter 7. The Primary item is used when you are entering a contact that is similar to the current on-screen contact, in terms of the address and the phone number. So, the Primary item duplicates those entries and blanks the rest of the fields. Last, the All option duplicates all of the entries in every field, except contact. You will use the Default option 90% of the time. In order to use the Primary or All options, you must have entered a contact, from which ACT! can copy field entries. So, if you are doing business with a company and you need to record information on several key contacts, the Primary or All entry options accelerate the data-entry process.
2. The highlight is on the Default option. Press Enter.

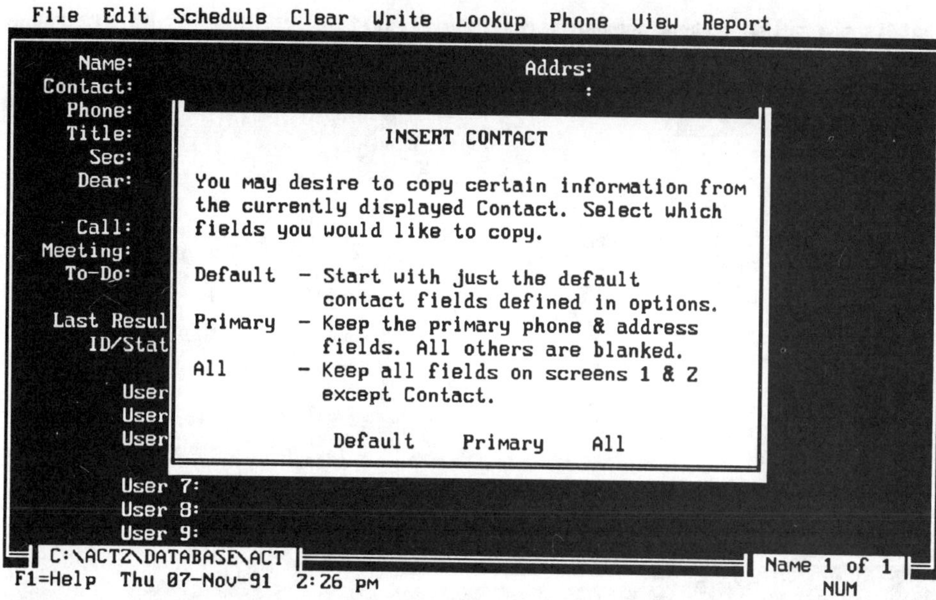

Fig. 1-6. The INSERT CONTACT window.

3. The highlight is now in the Name field. Type ABC Company and press Enter.

4. The highlight moves to the Contact field. Type Sam Jones and press Enter.

   Take notice that ACT! has automatically inserted into the Dear: field the first name of the contact, Sam. ACT! assumes that the first name is used in the salutation for correspondence. ACT! has moved the highlight to the Phone: field.

5. Press the F2 function key. This key opens the Area Code Popup window (Fig. 1-7). ACT! comes with area codes already included in this Popup window. The number is entered, followed by the city that is associated with the area code. You can add more at any time. To add an area code, read the section at the end of this chapter called "Modifying user-defined popups." For now, assume that ABC Company is located in Dallas.

   Note: As you are entering information, in the upper left corner of the screen, ACT! provides a prompt that guides you as to what type of entry is expected. For example, when the highlight is in the Phone field, ACT! displays the message, "What is the primary phone number (area code first)?". The prompts make it easy for a new user to quickly understand what to enter.

6. Press the letter D key. ACT! inserts the area code for you, and closes the Popup window.

7. Finish typing in the number 222-4567 and press the down arrow key. The

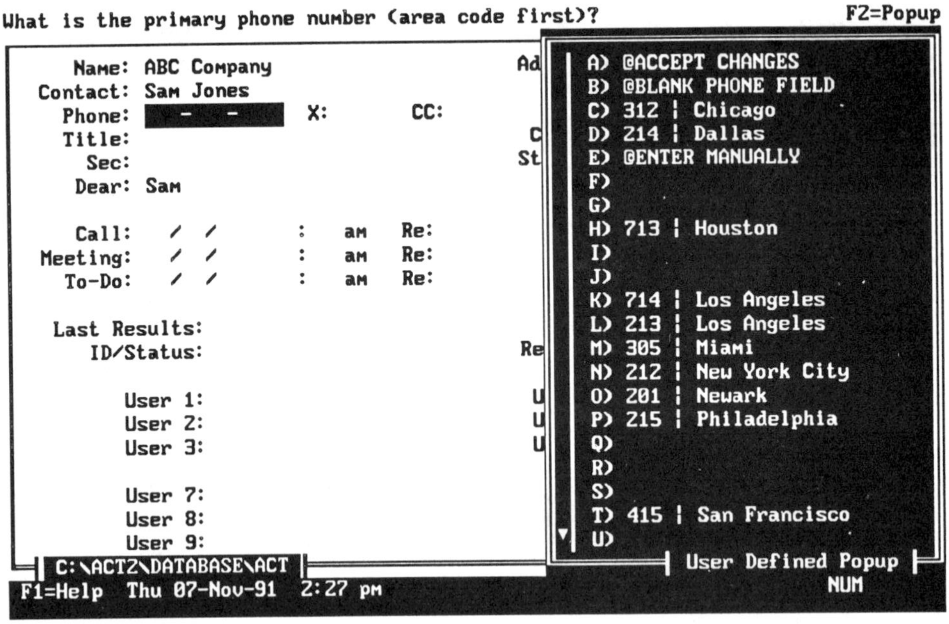

Fig. 1-7. The Area Code Popup window.

highlight moves to the next field, as it does when you press Enter. If you need them, ACT! includes two extra fields, the X: field for the extension of the contact, and the CC: field to enter a country code if the contact is overseas.

8. Press the down arrow or Enter until the highlight is in the Title: field. ACT! includes the title in any letters you create, so press the F2 key to see the ACT! list of titles (Fig. 1-8).
9. Highlight President, and press Enter (typing P works, too). ACT! includes a field for the name of the most important person you'll probably need to speak to, the secretary. The field label is abbreviated to Sec:. The entry in this field is not printed anywhere; it is for your information only. However, you can find contacts if you only remember the secretary's name!
10. Type June and press Enter.
11. Press Enter again to skip the salutation field. The highlight is now in the Addrs: field. Type 114 Wharf Drive and press Enter.
12. Press the down arrow or Enter key again until the highlight is in the City: field. Press the F2 function key. Up pops the City Popup window.
13. Use the down arrow keys to move the highlight so that it is on the word Dallas and press Enter. ACT! inserts the city name for you. Press Enter.
14. ACT! also includes a Popup window for the State: field. Press F2 and select the TX entry.

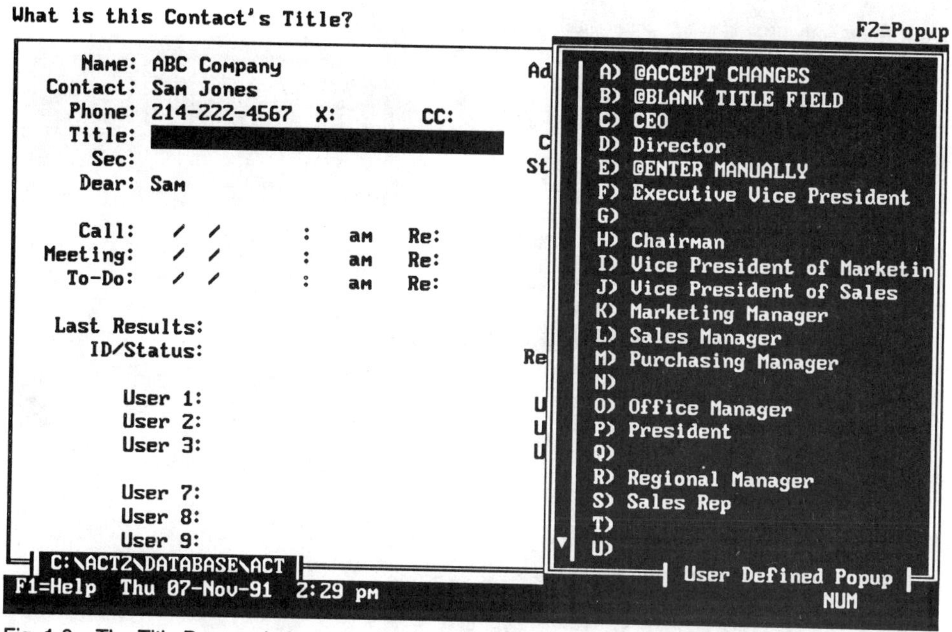

Fig. 1-8. The Title Popup window.

15. The final address field entry is the zip code. Type 75060. Now, all of the basic address and phone information is entered.

16. Press the Tab key twice. The highlight moves to the Last Results: field. Press the F2 key. The Popup window is displayed in Fig. 1-9. The idea of the Last Results entries is that in addition to scheduling an activity, such as a definite time to call, to meet, or to do something, you can make an entry to record what happened in your last activity.

17. Insert the entry labeled L, Left Message to call me back. Many ACT! users access the calendar by pressing F4, then Enter to insert the date after the Last Results text entry (i.e., Left Message to call me back 3/16/92.

    The next field, labeled ID/Status:, is used to identify your contacts by type. Pressing F2 opens the Popup window, into which you can enter your Status/ID types. In this example, Sam Jones is a prospective client.

18. Type Prospect and press Enter.

    The ID/Status field is particularly important. You should think carefully about how you wish to categorize your contacts. Consistent and well-planned identifications make finding your contacts much easier.

19. The final field in which to make an entry before saving the contact is the Referred by: field. The highlight is now in that field. Type Magazine AD and press Enter.

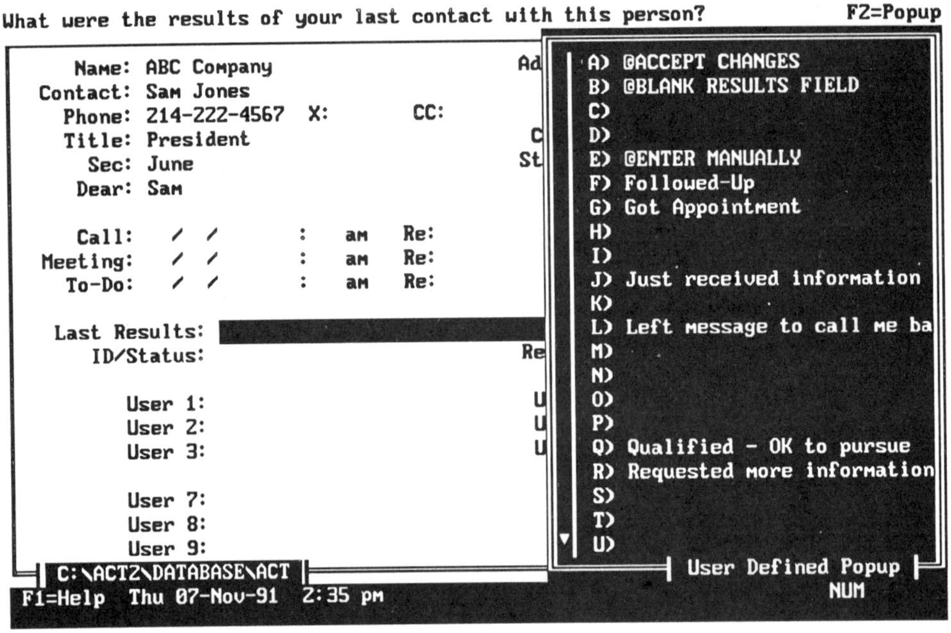

Fig. 1-9. The Last Results Popup window.

Saving a new Contact

Before making entries in the remaining fields, save the Contact that you just entered. Press the F10 key. ACT! saves the Contact. In the lower right side of the screen in the border, ACT! displays the database status in terms of how many Contacts are in the database. The display should read Name 1 of 1, indicating that the Contact you are looking at is the first one in the database and that a total of one Contact is entered.

ACT! sorts contacts in alphabetical order by the entry in the Name field, which normally holds the name of the company. If the contact has no company entry, as in the case of a list of friends, the contacts are sorted by the last name.

Entering information on the second side of the ACT! screen

Press the F6 function key. The second side of the ACT! contact screen displays (Fig. 1-10). To enter information, press the F2 key. ACT! has automatically inserted Sam Jones in the Contact field. The remaining fields in the top section of the screen can be used to enter an alternative address and phone for your contacts. The alternative can be a home address or a different business location. As you might expect, the Popup windows are accessible with the F2 function key for quick and consistent data entry.

The middle section of the screen is used to enter alternate contacts and their

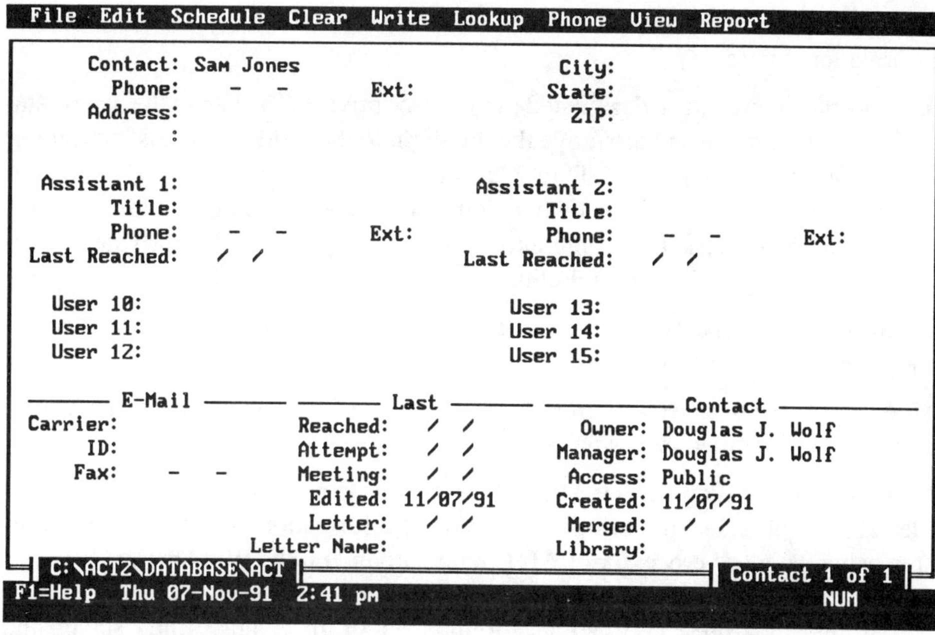

Fig. 1-10 Contact Screen 2.

phone numbers. When you access the phone menu from screen two, ACT! displays a list of all the contact's possible phone numbers, including the assistants.

The bottom third of the Contact screen is broken into three sections. On the left are fields for entering the information on the contact's fax number, E-Mail carrier and number. ACT! does not directly access E-Mail systems, but version 2.1 does directly access fax boards, and therefore other fax machines.

Enter the fax number of ABC as follows:

1. Press F2 to begin an edit.
2. Move the highlight to the Fax: field.
3. Type 214-222-4568
4. Press F10 to save the change.

The second section, Last, is a record-keeping area that ACT! updates for you (provided that you are entering your calls, as described later), or that you can enter manually. The most important field to be aware of at this point is the Edited field. When you begin entering information, you will want to know the last time that any changes were made to the record. ACT! will also automatically record any letters that were sent and the name of the letter, if you saved it as a file.

The third section, Contact, has the following fields:

Owner The entry in this field is completed by the entry you made in the Manager Information window.

Manager The entry in this field is completed by the entry in the Manager Information window.

Access Contacts can be designated as public or private. To change the access status, press F2 to begin an edit, move the highlight to the field, and press the right or left arrow key. In doing so, ACT! toggles the words Public or Private. The effect of making a contact private is that when you print a report of any kind, the contacts specified as private (such as your dentist) do not print. To include a private contact in a report, change this entry to Public.

Created ACT! inserts the date created as the first time the Contact was edited and saved.

Merged If the Contact was imported or transferred into the database, the date of that action is recorded in this field.

Library ACT! allows you to attach Library files to specific Contacts. A Library file can be a phone script, price list, or general information. A Library file is created using the word processor of ACT!, and is found on the Write menu.

At this point, press F6 to go back to the front of the Contact Entry screen and press F10 to save the Contact.

Editing the Contact information

Entering information into the Contact Entry form is as easy as typing. However, for many people, typing is not easy and mistakes are made. In this example, ACT! assumes that when you type a letter to Sam Jones, the salutation will be "Dear Sam." This is an informal salutation and might not be appropriate at the beginning stages of a business relationship.

ACT! makes extensive use of the function keys and one function key in particular, the F2 Edit key. Change the salutation using the F2 key.

1. Press F2. The highlight is on the field after the label Name:.
2. Use the down arrow key to move the highlight to the Dear: field.
3. The cursor is positioned at the beginning of the field. The default data-entry method for ACT! is the Insert mode. When characters are typed, they are inserted at the cursor location. When editing Contact information, it is sometimes easier to use the Overstrike mode, which overwrites characters at the cursor position. Your keyboard has a key labeled Insert or INS; pressing it when you are in the process of editing a Contact, acts as a toggle between the Insert or Overstrike modes. ACT! alerts you to the mode you are using with a screen message at the very bottom right side of the screen. If the letters INS are visible, the keyboard is in the Insert mode.
4. Press the Insert key until the letters INS are no longer visible.

5. In the Dear: field type Mr. Jones and press Enter.
6. Press F10 to save the new salutation.

Editing keys

ACT! uses several keys for editing; these keys are:

Right, Left Arrow Moves cursor within the field.
Up, Down Arrow Moves cursor from field to field.
Back Arrow Deletes character to the left of the cursor.
Home Moves cursor to beginning of field.
End Moves cursor to end of entry.
Del Deletes character at cursor location.
Enter Moves highlight from current field, either to next field below or across to next field.
F2 Opens Popup menu for the highlighted field.
F4 Displays calendar for date entries.
F5 Deletes entire entry from the cursor position to the end of field.
F6 Displays reverse side of the contact form.
F10 Saves changes to contact.
Esc Cancels editing session, no changes are saved.
TAB Moves the highlight from section to section in Contact Entry screen.

The most important Contact

ACT! demands that every activity you schedule is attached to a Contact. Obviously, some activities that require action do not merit you entering a contact. An example would be picking up dry cleaning. It is doubtful you would ever need to send a letter, make an important call, or attend a meeting with the dry-cleaning establishment. But, you might often have to drop off or pick up your clothes.

The simple solution is to create a Contact called ME, which is you. That way, you can schedule calls and tasks that do not merit a Contact record. Because ACT! allows you to make any Contact entry private, your dry-cleaning trips will not show up on a task report to your boss.

Exiting ACT!

After pressing F10 to save any changes you have made to a Contact, press the Escape key. ACT! responds by displaying a warning message (Fig. 1-11). Selecting Yes ends the session with ACT! and returns you to the DOS prompts.

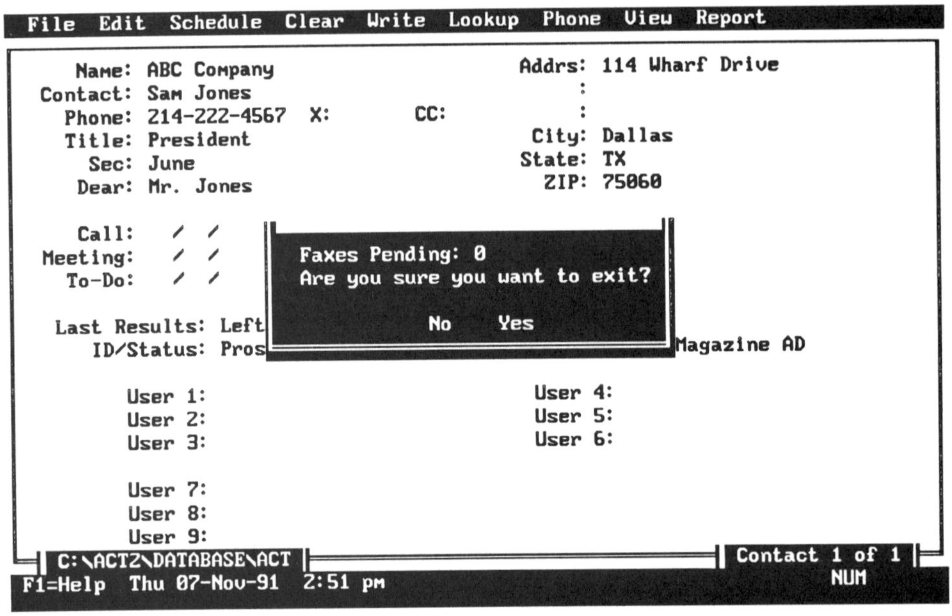

Fig. 1-11. The Exit Warning message.

Launching, not Exiting

ACT! provides a menu option that provides a gateway to other programs. It is found on the File menu and is listed as the Launch option. In order to launch another program, you must have created a DOS batch file to do so.

To launch a different program:

1. Open the File menu, either by pressing F or moving the highlight to the menu name and pressing Enter.
2. Select the Launch option by pressing L or by moving the highlight to the word Launch and pressing Enter.
3. ACT! opens the File Directory window, listing the subdirectories on your hard disk and any .BAT files it finds in the root directory.
4. Move the highlight with the up or down arrow keys to highlight the batch file desired. Press Enter.

   Note: the process for creating batch files to launch other programs is covered in chapter 5 on using the word processor.

ACT! starts the program for you. When you exit this program, you are returned to ACT! automatically.

Warning: never shut off your computer until you have exited ACT! properly. For example, if you have used the Launch item to start a different program, never turn off your computer before returning to ACT! and exiting. Failure to do so corrupts the ACT! index files and you will have to reindex before being allowed back into ACT!.

Editing a User-defined Popup window

In the process of entering a contact, you have seen the multitude of Popup windows that ACT! offers for entering information. There are several compelling reasons to use the Popups to enter information. First, using a Popup reduces the amount of typing that you have to do. ACT! was designed for nontypists by nontypists. Secondly, the powerful lookup capabilities of ACT! are greatly enhanced when field entries are uniform.

1. To edit a Popup, press F2 to enter the Edit mode.
2. Move the highlight to the field that has the Popup you wish to change and press F2. In Fig. 1-12, the Title Popup window is displayed.

   ACT! comes with some options already. The window includes all the letters of the alphabet, making 26 possible options.
3. Press the F2 edit key. The cursor is not visible in the field where the highlight had been. You can either change the field option at the cursor, or use the up or down arrow keys to move the highlight/cursor to a blank field.
4. Let's add an option. Move the highlight/cursor to the option designated as Z. Type Director of Purchasing.
5. Press F10. The new option is saved.

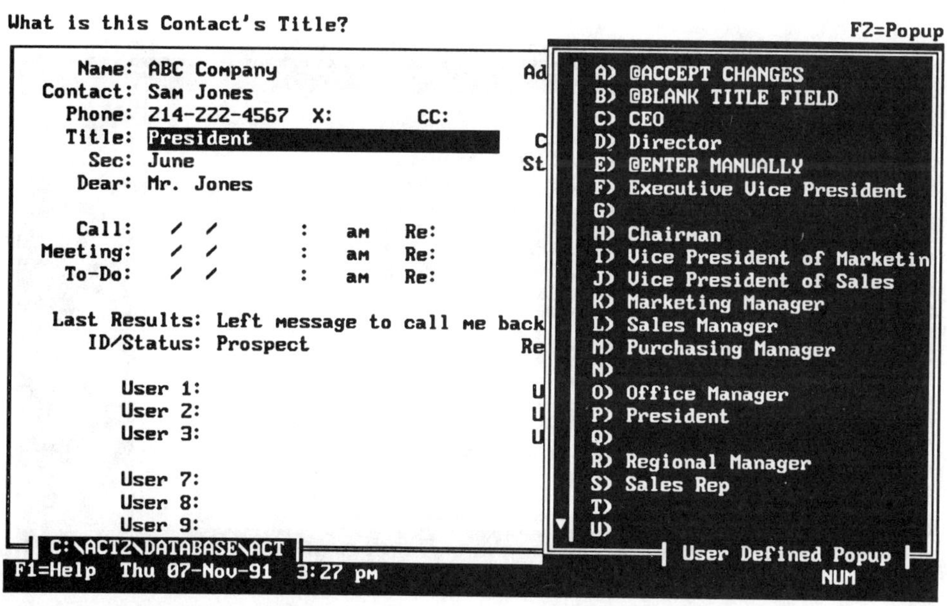

Fig. 1-12. The Title Popup window.

Notice that the color of the letter that designates the new option changes appearance.

Note: When editing a Popup menu option, all of the editing keys are available. If you want to discard changes made to the menu, press Escape before pressing the F10 key.

Making an entry in the Popup

You might have noticed that several of the Popup windows had an entry followed by a | symbol and a description of the entry. For instance, in the Area Code Popup, the number 214 is followed by the name of the city associated with that number, Dallas.

When you want to make an entry and add an associated piece of information, simply separate the entry from the other information with the | symbol. ACT! will insert only the entry to the left of the symbol.

Getting help

If at any point in ACT! you feel stuck or lost, you can access the Help system. For example, move the highlight so that the File menu name is highlighted:

1. Press F1. The Help screen for using the File menu options appears (Fig. 1-13). ACT! is "context-sensitive" in that it displays the Help screen appropriate to your place in the program.
2. Press the Home key. This key causes ACT! to display the Help Topics window (Fig. 1-14). At this point, you can move the highlight to any of the top-

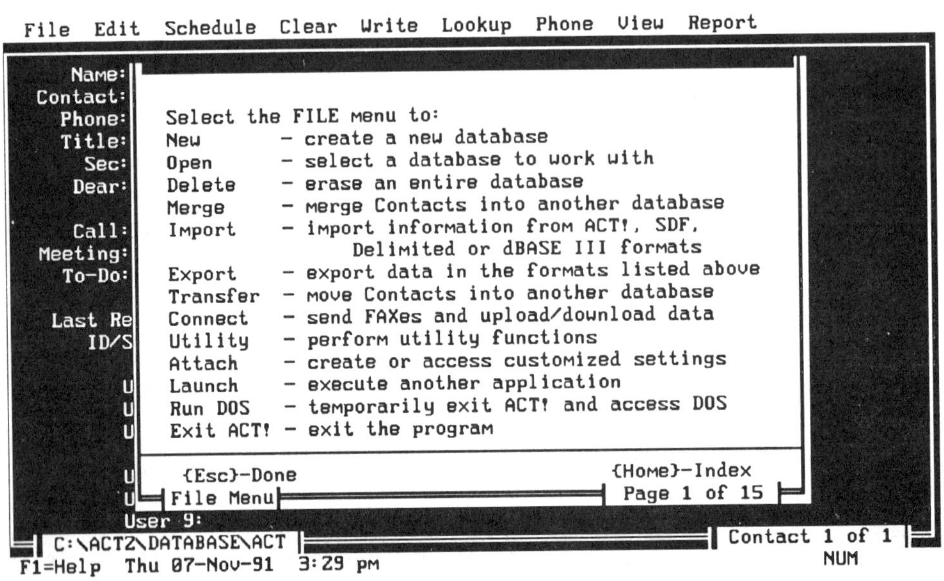

Fig. 1-13. The File menu help screen.

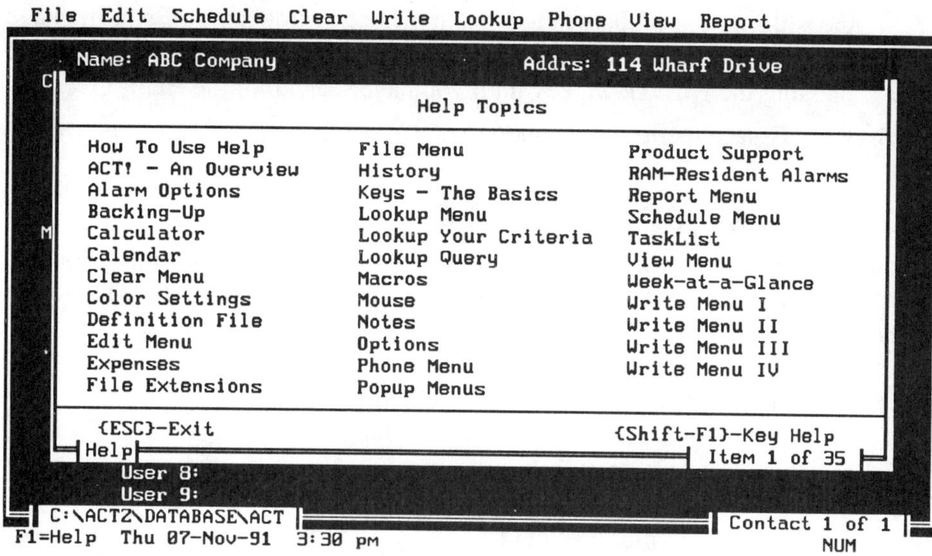

Fig. 1-14. The Help Topics window.

ics listed in the window and press Enter. The detail screen attached to the topic you selected will be displayed. If more than one screen is available, press the Page Down key to see the next screen.

3. Press Escape to exit Help.
4. Press and hold the Shift key, then press F1. The function keys windows appear (Fig. 1-15). The actions that can be executed with the function keys in normal mode and in conjunction with the Shift key are listed. Notice that at

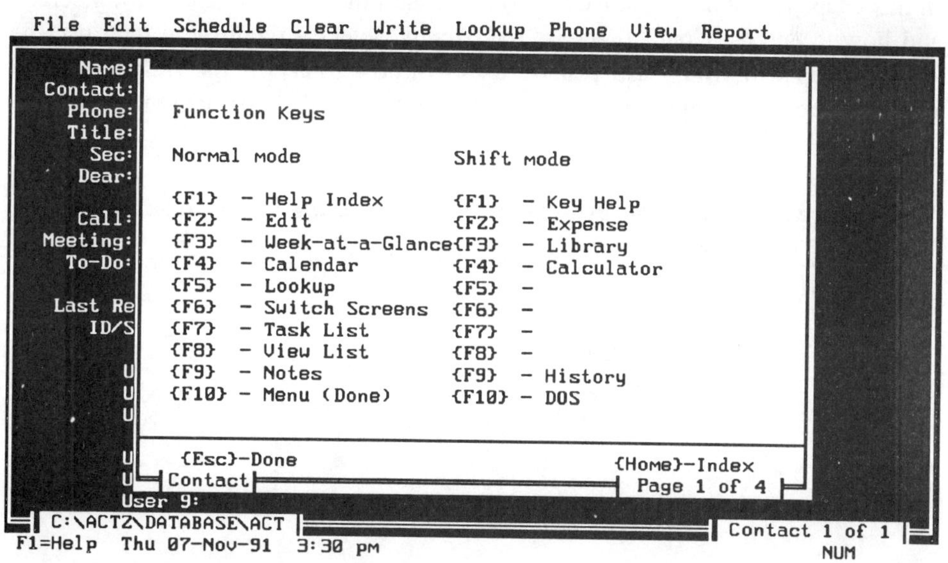

Fig. 1-15. The Function Keys Help window.

the bottom right of the window is the message Page 1 of 4. Press the Page Down key to see the next page of help on using the function keys. Continue pressing the Page Down key until you have seen all of the Help screens.

5. Press Escape to close the window.

Adding a second Contact

If you have just started with ACT!, and have only entered the Sam Jones Contact, add the following Contact to your database in order to perform exercises in the rest of the book:

1. Press the Insert key and select the Default item.

   Name: Kelly Computer Supplies
   Contact: Robert Kelly
   Phone: (900) 447-2929
   Title: President
   Sec: Rona
   Addrs: 1321 White Bear Ave.
   City: St. Paul
   State: MN
   Zip: 55106
   ID/Status: Inventor

2. Remember to press F10 to save the new Contact!

Summary

In this chapter, you have learned the basic parts of the ACT! database entry screen and how to enter a Contact, access the Menus, select a menu item, and use the ACT! Popup windows. Last, you were shown how to access the Help system in ACT!. In the next chapter, you will learn how to find the Contacts that you have entered.

"There is only one success—to be able to spend life in your own way."

CHRISTOPHER MORLEY

2
CHAPTER

Working with Contacts

"I have learned that success is to be measured not so much by the position one has reached in life as by the obstacles which he has overcome while trying to succeed."

BOOKER T. WASHINGTON

In the previous chapter, you entered two Contacts into the ACT! database. When you first start using ACT!, the initial database is created with the name ACT.CCD. It is also the default database. That is, whenever you start ACT!, that database will be automatically loaded into ACT!. However, you can set up any number of databases as you need them. Later in this chapter, an example of setting up and using multiple databases is covered. For now, we will work with the ACT.CCD database.

Starting ACT!

If you have not already started ACT!, do so now by typing ACT! at the DOS prompt. First, make sure you are in the ACT! subdirectory. ACT! will display the opening screen, and after you press any key, the ACT.CCD database will open. The first Contact appears (Fig. 2-1).

In the lower right-hand corner of the screen is the message Name 1 of 2. This tells you that this database contains a total of 2 Contacts; when you start ACT!, every Contact is considered.

Moving to another contact

Use the Page Down (PgDn) key to see the second contact in the database.

1. Press Page Down. The second Contact, Kelly Computer Supplies, is now visible on the screen. Notice that the indicator in the lower right-hand corner now reads Name 2 of 2.
2. Press the Page Up Key. The Sam Jones Contact now is back on the screen.

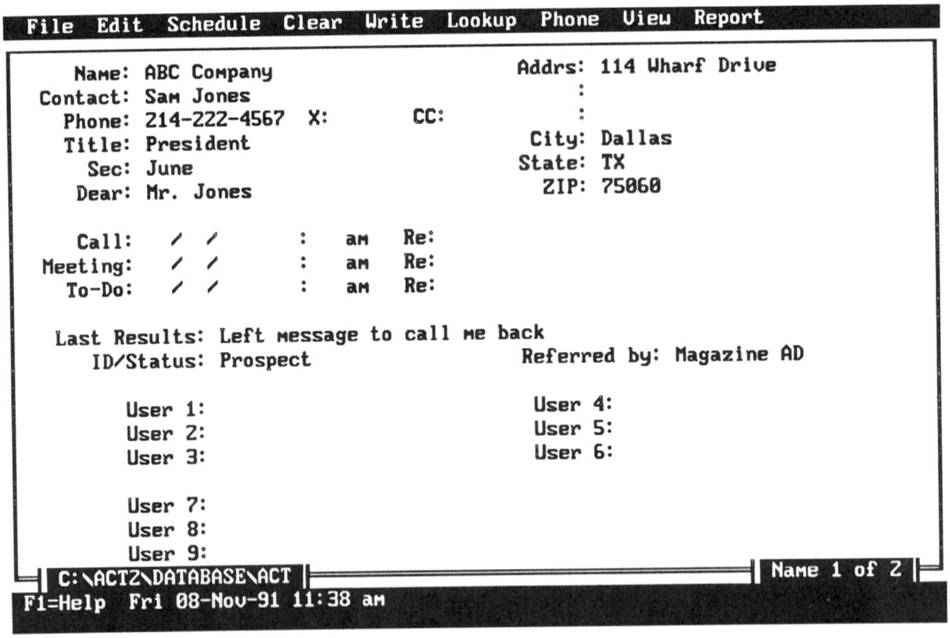

Fig. 2-1. The ACT! First Contact entry.

This system of pressing Page Up or Page Down allows you to flip through your Contacts one at a time. The ways of moving in the database are:

Page Up	Up one contact.
Page Down	Down one contact.
Home	To the first contact in the database.
End	To the last contact in the database.
Insert	To insert a new contact.
Del	To delete a contact.

Finding a Contact

With several hundred Contacts entered into ACT!, using the Page Down or Page Up keys to find a specific Contact, is terribly inefficient. Fortunately, ACT! has a multitude of ways to find contacts, with the Lookup menu.

Type L or move the highlight to the word Lookup with the arrow keys and press Enter. The Lookup menu appears (Fig. 2-2). The Lookup options are:

Name

The first way to look up a Contact is by the entry in the field that is used for entering the name of the company where the contact works. Suppose that the company name is Multiplexing Inc. and you forgot how to spell the name. ACT! allows you to enter only a partial name and it finds all of the contacts that use the letters you entered:

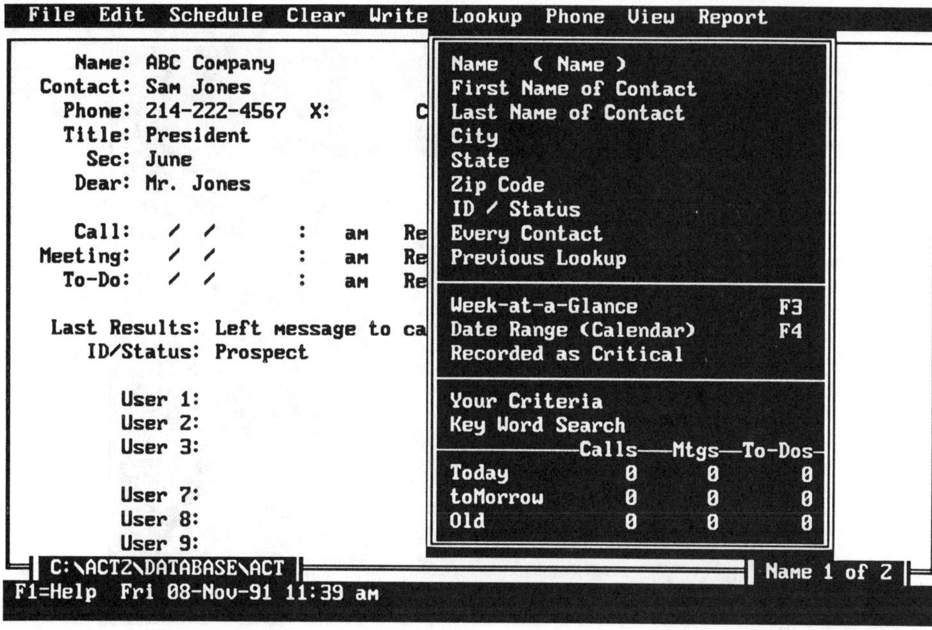

Fig. 2-2. The Lookup menu.

1. With the highlight positioned on the Name option, press Enter. The Name entry appears (Fig. 2-3).
2. Type MULT
3. Press Enter.

ACT! searches the database for all of the contacts that have a company name beginning with the letters MULT. In the lower right corner of the screen, the search indicator displays the number of contacts that match the search criteria. ACT! finds contacts with names such as:

Multiplexing Inc.
Multiple Systems
Multimation
Multiplying Inc.
Multisource

The key is that the four letters of the name were matched. The search indicator would read NAME 1 of 5, showing you that a total of five Contacts were found that matched the entry made.

Pressing Page Down scrolls through all five Contacts and then ACT! beeps at you, alerting you that you have viewed all five Contacts that match your search criteria. This point confuses many new users of ACT!. In the example, five Contacts were located. The entire database might consist of 500 Contacts. ACT! has seg-

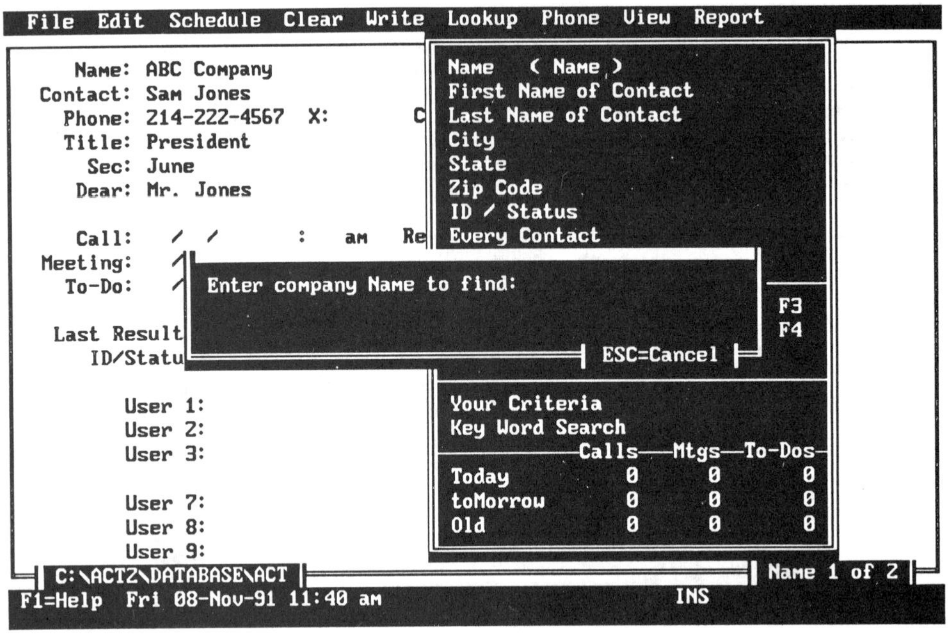

Fig. 2-3. The Company Name entry window.

mented a small portion of the Contacts in the database, allowing you to work with them only. There is a very good reason for this segmentation: If your next step was to send a form letter to all of the companies whose name began with Mult, you need no other steps to find just those companies.

Regrouping the database

After you perform a Lookup, only those Contacts that were found are accessible using the Page Up or Page Down keys. If you had 200 Contacts in the database, and used a Lookup that found 4, you can use the Lookup menu to Regroup the database so that every Contact is accessible using the Page Up and Page Down method.

Okay, so how do you now get the other 495 Contacts back?

1. Open the Lookup menu.
2. Move the highlight to the item "Every Contact."
3. Press Enter.

All of the Contacts are once again available for use. In the lower right corner of the screen, ACT! displays Name 1 of XXX, with XXX standing for the total number of Contacts in your database.

A second way to access the other Contacts after using Lookup is to enter another Lookup. In other words, if you have grouped the Contacts, you can use the Lookup menu find a second Contact group.

ACT! finds Contacts, using the Lookup menu items, based upon the entries in a single field. But what if you want to use two or more criteria, such as the State, and the Name of the company? ACT! can do that too, as explained in the section on Lookup, Your Criteria.

Suppose that after you find the five contacts with the company name beginning with Mult, you wanted to find all of the contacts that live in the great state of Texas.

1. Open the Lookup menu.
2. Highlight the "State" item.
3. Press Enter. The name-of-the-state-to-find window appears (Fig. 2-4).
4. Type TX
5. Press Enter.

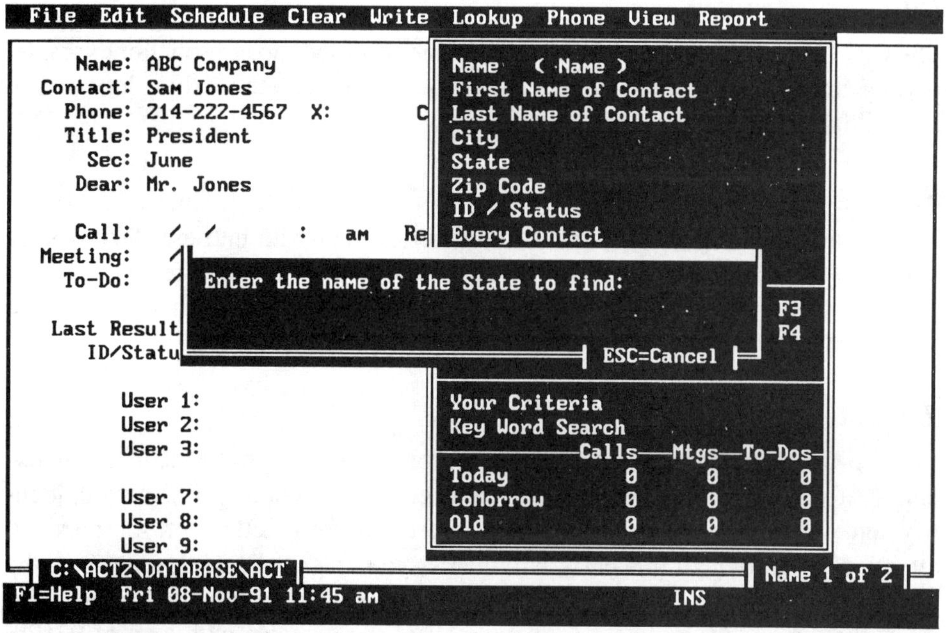

Fig. 2-4. The Name of the State to find.

First name of Contact

No matter how you enter a contact's name, ACT! determines which entry in the Contact field is the first name and which is the last name and finds it. For example, you could enter the same Contact name as:

Joe Smith
or
Smith, Joe

In either case, ACT! understands that Joe is the first name. The key to ACT! determining which name is first and which is the last, is by the comma. If you leave the comma out in the second instance, ACT! cannot discern which is the first or last name. As was true with the Company Name Lookup, you do not have to enter the entire name for ACT! to find a match.

Last name of Contact

This is a search criteria that is frequently used. As is true in using the First name to search for a Contact, ACT! understands which entry in the Contact field is the last name and which is the first. The same rules apply for entering the search criteria, too. For example, if you cannot remember whether a client"s name is spelled *Larsen* or *Larson*, entering "Lars" finds both spellings.

City

The City Lookup entry operates the same as the other lookup criteria. For example, if you enter San, ACT! finds all city entries that begin with those three letters: San Diego, San Francisco, San Antonio . . .

State

The State field is a good example of being consistent with entries. Decide early whether you are going to enter contacts from the Lone Star state (Texas) as TX or Texas. By being consistent, you can find every contact in a particular state with one search entry.

Zip code

The Zip Code Lookup is one of the more powerful options on the menu. As an example, if you have contacts in a particular region of the country, it is easy to identify and segment those contacts for purposes of form letters or for personal attention. Even though this entry is numeric, you enter the search criteria in the same way. For every contact in San Diego, you would enter only the first two digits of the zip code (i.e., 92). ACT! finds all of the contacts with zips of 92129, 92128, 92067, etc.

ID/Status

The ID/Status field is mainly used in one of two ways. First, it can be used to identify the level of a prospective client. Using a simple system (e.g., A, B, C, D) as levels of possible conversion to customers, you can quickly identify the Contacts in your database that merit your attention. Upon conversion from a prospect to a client, you change the ID/Status to Client. The second way to use this field, is to enter contacts by profession. If you are an executive search consultant (headhunter) you might categorize the contacts by job title in order to quickly locate potential placements.

Every Contact

After conducting a lookup, you might wish to Regroup the database so that all Contacts are available. Remember, you do not have to use this Lookup option after performing a lookup, before performing another lookup. Selecting this option reverts to the default Name Lookup option and sorts the database accordingly.

Previous lookup

If you performed a lookup and found the Contacts you wanted, then selected the Every Contact option, and subsequently decided that you wanted to work with the Contacts that you found in the initial lookup, this option repeats that lookup.

Week-at-a-Glance

The Week-at-a-Glance Lookup option is different from the other options, in that it does not retrieve Contacts, rather it causes ACT! to display your schedule for the week. Because this lookup is used frequently, the F3 key is assigned to displaying the Week-at-a-Glance Lookup. You do not have to open the Lookup menu to see the weekly calendar; simply press F3 and it appears. Figure 2-5 is an example of a weekly calendar.

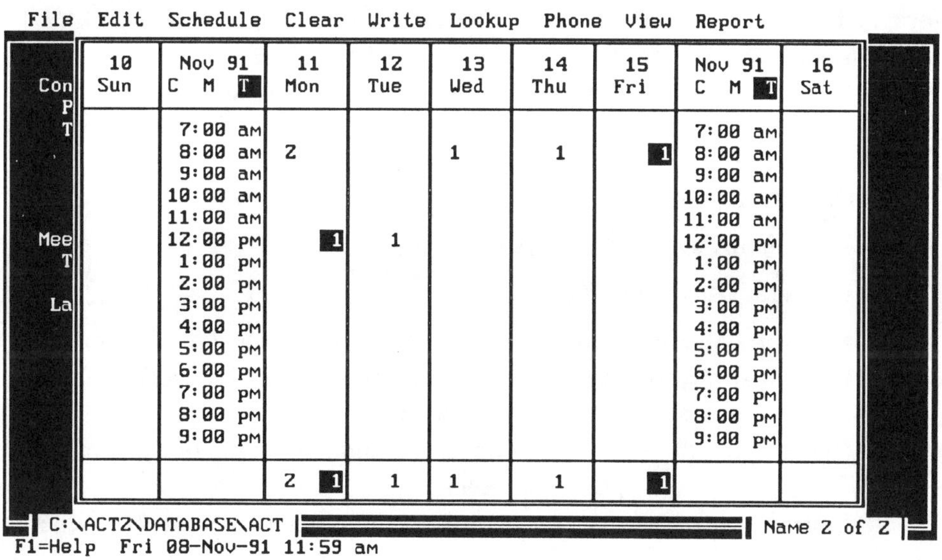

Fig. 2-5. An example Week-at-a-Glance.

Use the following keys in the calendar:

Right arrow, Left arrow Move the date highlight at the top of the calendar to a specific day. For example, if you move the highlight to Wednesday and press Enter, the Daily Task List is displayed. You may move ahead or back in time using these keys.

Up arrow, Down arrow The time notation can be scrolled using these keys. The notation is continuous covering a 24-hour day, but only 14 hours are visible at one time.

Page Up, Page Down Pressing Page Up displays the previous week's calendar, pressing Page Down displays the following week's. Repeatedly pressing either key continues to move the calendar in the desired time direction.

Escape Closes the calendar and returns you to the Contact screen.

At the top of the time notations are the letters C, M, and T, which represent Calls, Meetings, and To-Dos. In the calendar itself, the particular activity is represented by the corresponding letter, and the length of the activity is blocked. At the bottom of the calendar are the totals for each day's activities.

The Week-at-a-Glance Lookup is a terrific way to see what is pending when you are adding to your schedule.

Date range

The Date Range Lookup lists the activities that you have scheduled in the Task List format. This gives you the flexibility in deciding which days are included in the lists of scheduled activities.

To display a list of activities by a specific date range, using the Lookup menu:

1. Open the Lookup menu and select the Date Range option.
2. The monthly calendar appears (Fig. 2-6).

   Calendar Movement Keys:

Right or Left Arrow Keys	Moves the highlight one day at a time
Up or Down Arrow keys	Moves the highlight back a week or forward a week
Home	Moves the highlight to the first day of the month
End	Moves the highlight to the last day of the month

3. Move the highlight to the first date that you want to include in the display.
4. Press the . (period) key. The period anchors the highlight to the beginning date.
5. Using the keys described after step 2, move the highlight to the end date. The highlight is stretched over the dates, giving you a visual cue as to the dates included.

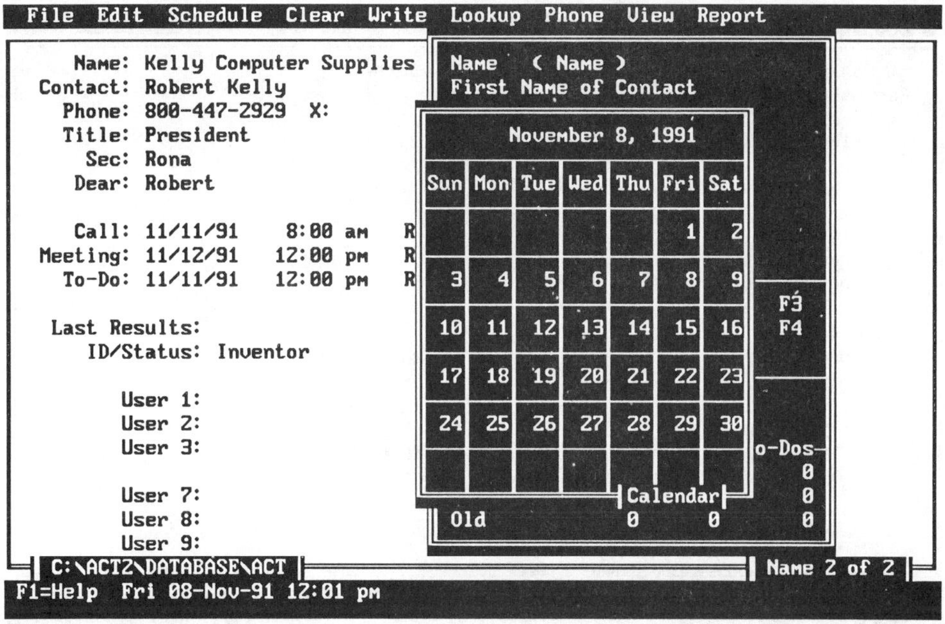

Fig. 2-6. The Monthly Calendar.

6. Press Enter. The activities for the selected date range are displayed in columnar fashion. See chapter 6 for more information on using the Columnar Activity report. You can also access this lookup method by pressing F4 to display the calendar, then selecting the dates, as previously described.

Recorded as critical

When you schedule an activity, if you include a lead time, ACT! records that particular activity as being critical. Selecting this option displays the Contact records with critical activities scheduled. All meetings, by default, are critical to ACT! because it includes a lead time. All of the alarm settings can be modified, as described in chapter 7.

Your Criteria

The Your Criteria Lookup item is used for those inquiries when a single field is not specific enough. Suppose that you want to find all of your A-level prospects (as categorized by the entry in the ID/Status field) in the city of San Diego. This procedure is called a *multiple criteria search*. Assuming that you have entered the prospect level in the ID/Status field. The task is straightforward. When you use this lookup, ACT! presents you with the Query Template, which includes a blank contact record and a new set of menu choices (Fig. 2-7).

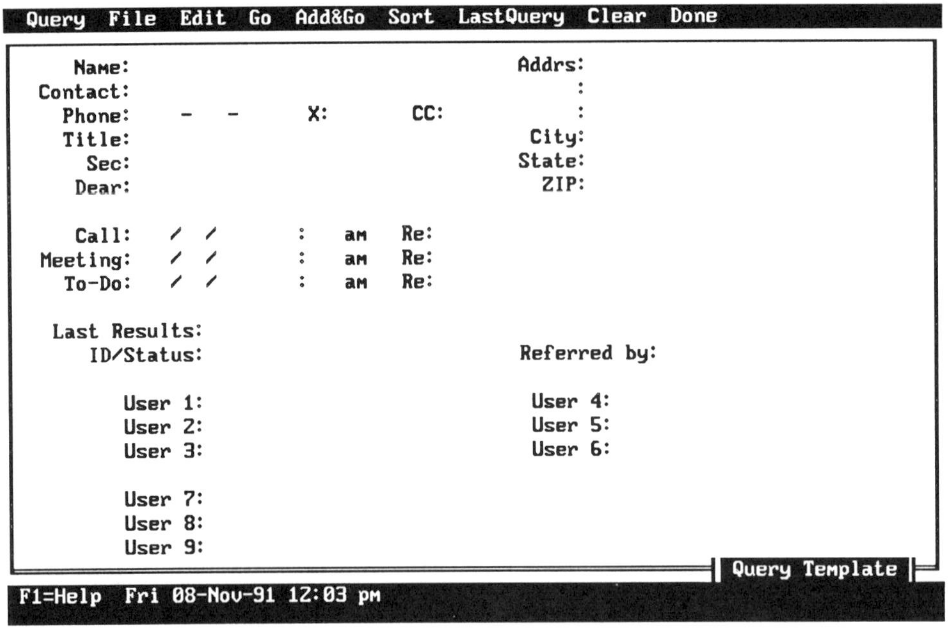

Fig. 2-7. The Query Template.

To perform a multiple criteria search:

1. Select Edit from the menu. The Name field is highlighted.
2. Use the down arrow key to move the highlight to the first field you want to use in the search. In this example, the first field is City.
3. Enter the search criteria. In this example, the city is San Diego.
4. Move the highlight to the next field that you want to use. In this example, the ID/Status field contains the prospect's level, A being the highest.
5. Enter the second search criteria, in this example the letter A. If you need to, you can enter search criteria in as many fields as you want. To use the fields on Contact Screen 2, press the F6 key and make the entry.
6. Press the F10 to go to the Query Template menu. Figure 2-8 shows the Query Template with the two entries; in the City field, San Diego and in the ID/Status field, the letter A. These entries can be in upper- or lowercase and they might only be the first few letters of the search criteria.
7. Select the Go menu choice.

ACT! finds the contacts that match the search criteria. In the lower right corner of the screen, the message reads CUSTOM 1 of XX (XX is the number of matching contacts). If the search works properly, you can go with your work. If not, you can edit the current search criteria or add more search criteria with the Add&Go menu choice in the Query Template.

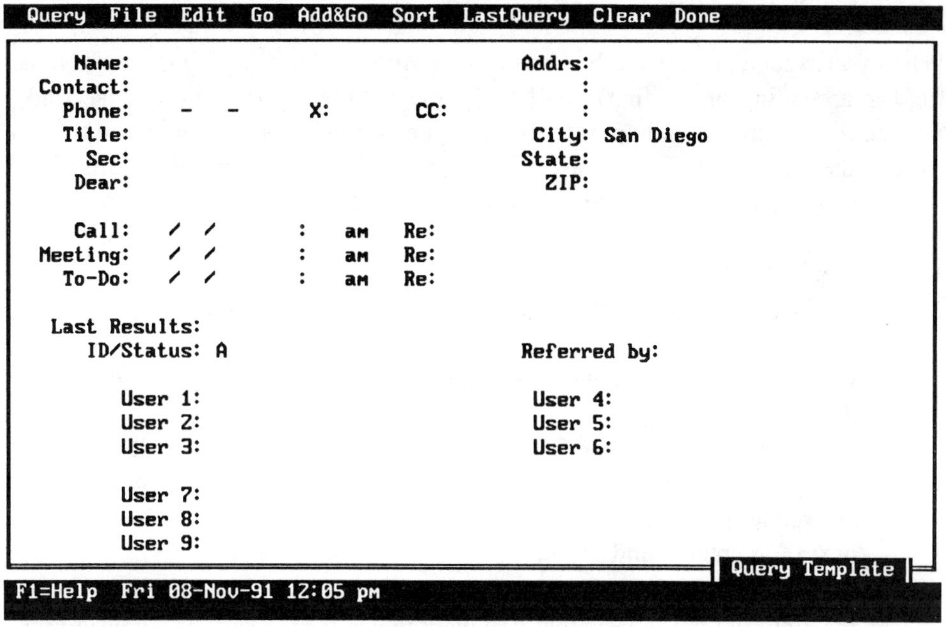

Fig. 2-8. The Query Template with two search criteria.

Saving a query as a file

If you use a particular query repeatedly, it is easy to save the query format so that you do not have to re-enter the search criteria.

After creating a query that works:

1. Open the Lookup menu, and select the Your Criteria option.
2. Open the File menu.
3. Select the Save item. ACT! displays the File Directory window.
4. Type a name for the query, using up to eight characters. ACT! automatically adds a QCD extension.
5. Press Enter.

Retrieving the query

To retrieve the query:

1. Open the Lookup menu.
2. Select the Your Criteria option.
3. Select the File menu. ACT! opens the File Directory window, move the highlight to the query file you want and press Enter. The search criteria are entered into the Query Template.
4. Select the Go option to execute the query.

Sorting queried Contacts

When you execute the query, the Contacts are sorted in the following order: Name field in ascending order (first), the Last Name field is ascending order (second), and the First Name ascending order (third). The entries are sorted based on the entries in the Name field first, A ascending to Z. If two identical entries are in the Name field, ACT! looks to the last name to determine which Contact comes next.

Changing the sort order

To change the order in which the queried Contacts appear, follow these steps:

1. From the Query Template menu, open the Sort menu. The Sort Order window appears (Fig. 2-9).
2. Move the highlight to the field that you want to modify. The order of precedence moves from left to right. That is, first field ACT! sorts on is the one entered at the far left of the screen. Then, it sorts the Contacts based on the next field entered and so on.
3. Press F2. ACT! displays the field list. Use the up or down arrow to move the highlight to the field that you want to use for the sort, and press Enter.
4. If you wish to change ascending or descending order, move the highlight to the Order field and press the right or left arrow. You can also press F2, highlight your choice, and press Enter. Remember to resave the query if you want to save the new sort order.

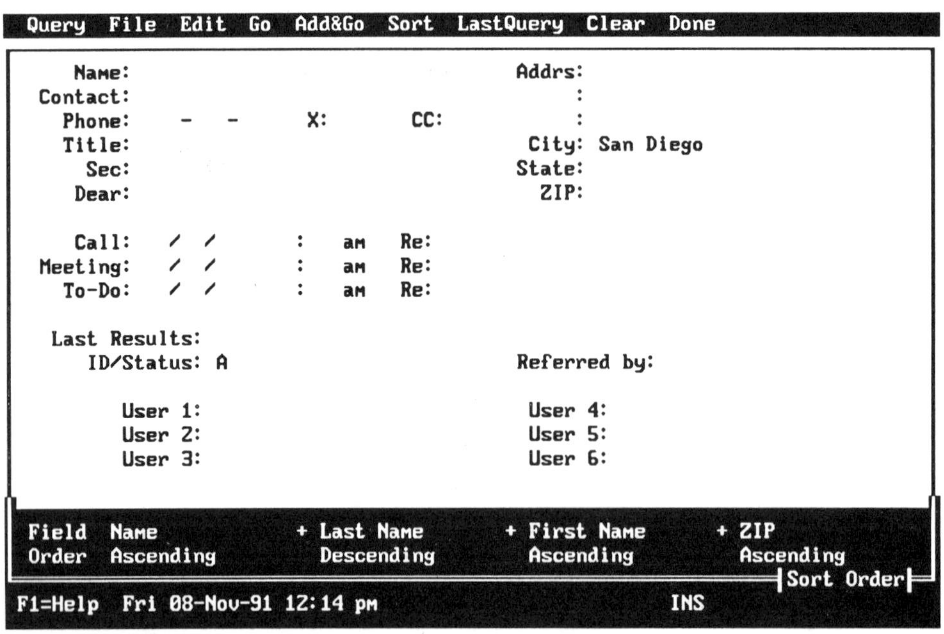

Fig. 2-9. The Sort Order Window.

Using Boolean logic to perform a search

Boolean logic is a method whereby you can add mathematical operators to the search criteria. For example, you can specify that the query find all Contacts with a zip code value equal to or greater than (=>) 920 and a name beginning with a letter less than (<) D.

To make a Boolean entry, follow these steps:

1. Open the Lookup menu and select the Your Criteria option.
2. Select the Query menu choice. The Boolean entry screen appears.
3. Press F2 to begin editing. The cursor is positioned in the Boolean field (Fig. 2-10). At this point no Boolean logical is needed.

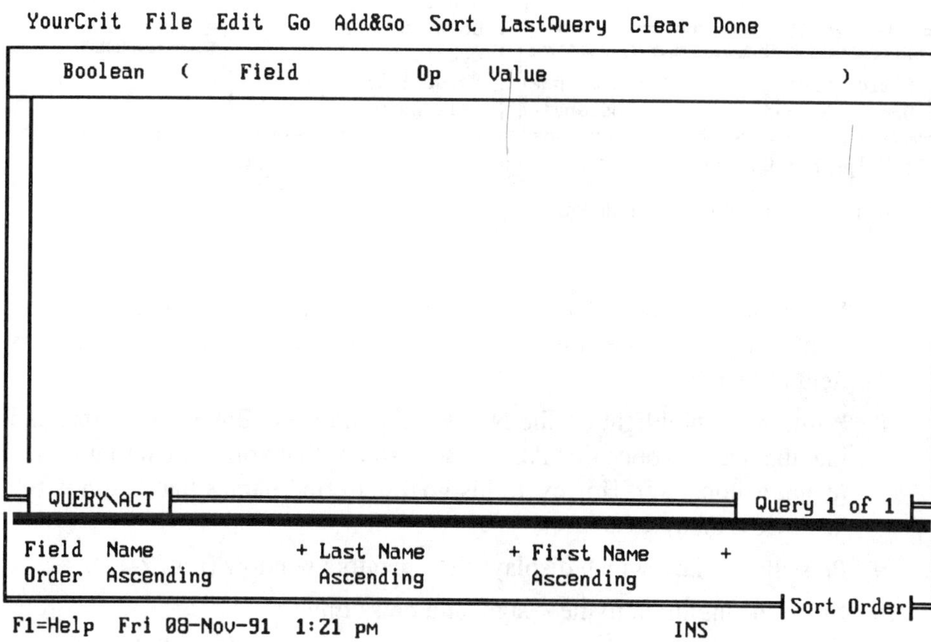

Fig. 2-10. The Boolean entry screen.

4. Press the TAB key to move the cursor to the open parentheses field.
5. Press the (right arrow) key. An open parentheses appears in the field.
6. Press TAB. The cursor is positioned in the column headed by the Name field. Now you can select the field in which you want ACT! to search.
7. Press F2. The alphabetical list of ACT! field names appears (Fig. 2-11).

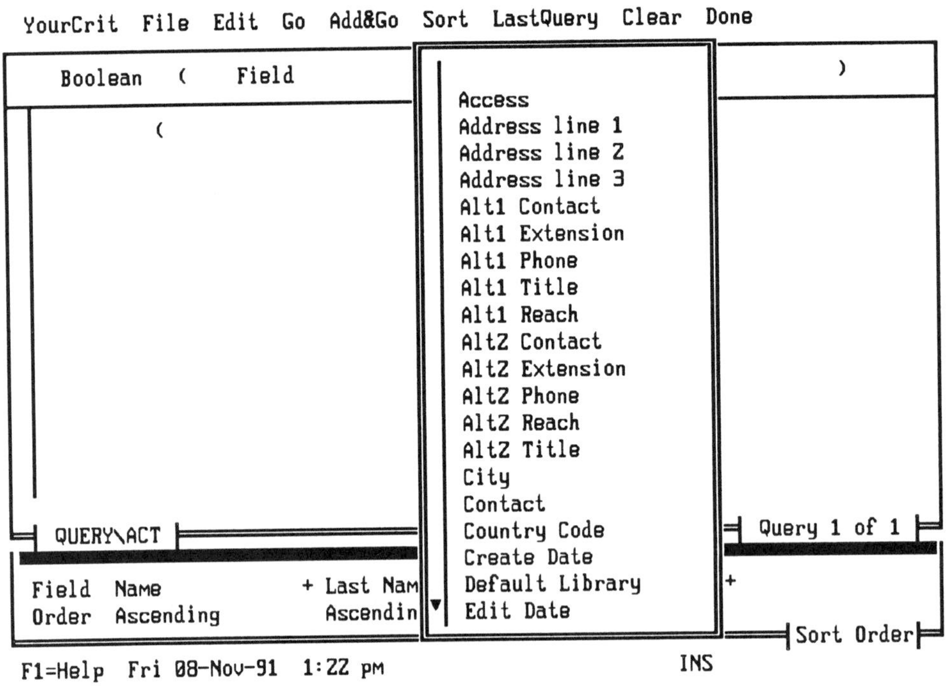

Fig. 2-11. The list of field names window.

Using the (up or down) arrows, scroll the screen to find the field name you want to use. In this example, you want to use the Name field as the first field to search.

8. Position the highlight on the Name field and press Enter. ACT! inserts it into the query. Notice that ACT! also assumes that you wanted to use the = (equal to) operator. However, this goal is to find names that begin with a letter (less than) < D.
9. Press the F2 key, which displays the operators window (Fig. 2-12).
10. Move the highlight to the < sign, and press Enter.
11. The cursor is positioned in the Value field. Type the letter D in either upper- or lowercase. Finish the entry by pressing Enter.
12. Insert) to close the first line of the query. Your screen should resemble Fig. 2-13.
13. Press F10 to save the query line.
14. Press Insert. A new query entry line appears and the line saved in the previous step appears below it.
15. Press TAB to move the cursor to the parentheses line. Enter ((open parentheses) to start the query and press Enter.

```
YourCrit  File  Edit  Go  Add&Go  Sort  LastQuery  Clear  Done

   Boolean   (     Field            Op    Value                         )
              (      Name            =   ┌────┐
                                         │ =  │
                                         │ >  │
                                         │ <  │
                                         │ <> │
                                         │ => │
                                         │ <= │
                                         └────┘

 QUERY\ACT                                                 Query 1 of 1
 Field  Name             + Last Name      + First Name      +
 Order  Ascending          Ascending        Ascending
                                                            Sort Order
F1=Help  Fri 08-Nov-91   1:23 pm                      INS
```

Fig. 2-12. The operators window.

```
YourCrit  File  Edit  Go  Add&Go  Sort  LastQuery  Clear  Done

   Boolean   (     Field            Op    Value                         )
              (      Name            <    D                            )

 QUERY\ACT                                                 Query 1 of 1
 Field  Name             + Last Name      + First Name      +
 Order  Ascending          Ascending        Ascending
                                                            Sort Order
F1=Help  Fri 08-Nov-91   1:24 pm                      INS
```

Fig. 2-13. The operators window.

16. Press F2. In the list of fields, move the highlight to Zip and press Enter. The cursor is positioned in the Op field.
17. Press F2. From the list of operators, select the => (greater than or equal to) symbol. The cursor moves to the Value field.

18. In this example, find those contacts with a zip code equal to or greater than 920. Enter 920 in the field, and press Enter.
19. Finish the query line by entering) (close parentheses).
20. Press F10 to save the new query line. Your screen should resemble Fig. 2-14.

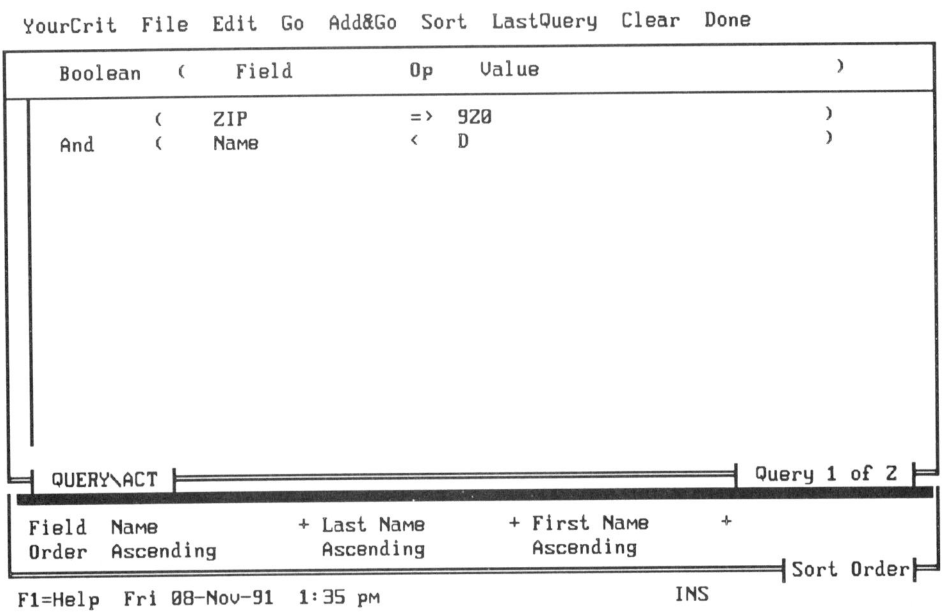

Fig. 2-14. The completed query.

ACT! completed an important entry for you. When you pressed F10, ACT! assumed that the connection between the two lines was the logical AND. So, it inserted it in the Boolean field of the second query line.

To execute the Boolean query, select Go from the menu. ACT! searches the Contacts that display a progress bar at the bottom of the screen. In the lower right corner of the screen, if a Contact or several Contacts meet the query criteria, the message is CUSTOM 1 of XX.

The logical operators

The logical operators that you can incorporate into your queries are:

= Equal to. The entry in the Contact record field must match the query value or character.

> Greater than. The entry in the Contact field must be of a higher value than the query value. For alpha characters, A is the least value, Z the highest.

< Less than. The entry in the Contact field must be of a lower value than the query value. For alpha characters, A is the least value, Z the highest.

<> Not equal to. The entry in the Contact field is not equal to the query value.

=> Equal to or greater than. The entry in the Contact field must be equal to or greater than the query value.

<= Less than or equal to. The value in the Contact field must be less than or equal to the query value.

Editing a Boolean query

After executing the search, you discover that the query lines need to be modified.

1. Open the Lookup menu and select Your Criteria. ACT! displays the query template with the field entries, but not the operators.
2. Select Query. The Boolean query screen appears.
3. Position the highlight on the YourCrit menu choice.
4. Use the (up or down arrow) keys to move the highlight to the query line you wish to edit.
5. Press F2. ACT! is in edit mode. If you wanted to change the relationship between the two query lines, you could position the highlight on the Boolean field, and press F2. The Boolean logicals are:

AND Find Contacts that meet the criteria in both lines 1 and 2. If you have more than two lines, the logic follows: find the Contacts that meet the criteria in lines 1 and 2 and 3 and 4 . . .

OR Find Contacts that meet the criteria in line 1 or that meet the criteria in line 2. If you have more than two lines, the logic follows; find the Contacts that meet the criteria in lines 1 or 2 or 3 or 4 . . .

AND NOT Find Contacts that meet the criteria in line 1 and do not contain the criteria in line 2. If you have more than two lines, the logic follows: find the Contacts that meet the criteria in line 1, and not in line 2, and not in line 3, and not in line 4 . . .

OR NOT Find Contacts that meet the criteria in line 1 or find the Contacts that do not have the criteria in line 2. If you have more than two lines, the logic follows: find the Contacts that meet the criteria in line 1, or do not contain the criteria in line 2, or not in line 3, or not in line 4 . . .

Using the logicals in combination with search criteria give you a powerful tool for a rifle shot approach to finding Contacts. In chapter 7, an example of entering birthdates into the user-definable fields is explained and using the Boolean logical to extract the exact Contacts.

Saving a Boolean query

After you are satisfied that the query is operating successfully, saving it for future use is as follows:

1. Open the Lookup menu and select Your Criteria.
2. Select File, and from the submenu, Save.
3. Enter a file name of up to eight characters and press F10 to save. ACT! adds the QCD file extension for you.

Erasing a query

To erase a query follow these steps:

1. Open the Lookup menu and select Your Criteria.
2. Select the File menu choice.
3. From the submenu, select Erase. The files window appears with a list of the saved queries.
4. Highlight the query you wish to erase and press Enter. ACT! verifies that you want to delete the file before executing the deletion.

Key Word Search

The Key Word Search is a frustration saver. Because ACT! includes a Notes capability, you might have entered a person's name, address, or the name of a seminar in the Notes section, but have forgotten which Contact contains the information you want. Or, you might have entered information into a User field and forgotten the entry.

Using the Key Word search, ACT! checks every word, no matter its location, in every Contact for a match. To use this lookup correctly, you must either enter the exact text you wish to find, or use wild cards to create a match.

The wildcard rules are identical to DOS rules:

* Finds a letter or series of letters. For example, if you enter W*D, ACT! matches words such as: wood, would, and word.

? Finds a single-letter match. For example, if you enter ?oor, ACT! matches words such as: poor, door, and moor.

To execute a Key Word search:

1. Open the Lookup menu and select Key Word search. ACT! opens the entry window.
2. Enter the exact text or partial text, including a wildcard.
3. Press F10 to execute.

A progress bar window appears, tracking the progress. When the search is complete, the message CUSTOM 1 of XX is displayed in the lower right corner. If no Contacts match the search, ACT! returns you to the Contact screen.

Today, displaying the Task List

The Lookup Today option displays your *Task List*, which is your schedule of calls, meetings, and to-dos in columnar fashion. This same Lookup option is directly accessible by pressing the F7 key at most points in the program. Figure 2-15 shows a typical Lookup Today screen.

As you can see in Fig. 2-15, the scheduled calls are in the first column, the meetings in the second column, and the to-dos are in the third. But this is not just a list of scheduled activities. Every one of the Contact records that is connected to the scheduled activity is directly accessible from this screen. For example, if you see on your screen that you have scheduled a meeting, you can move the highlight with the arrow keys to that meeting and press Enter. ACT! displays the Contact record, which replaces the Today Lookup screen.

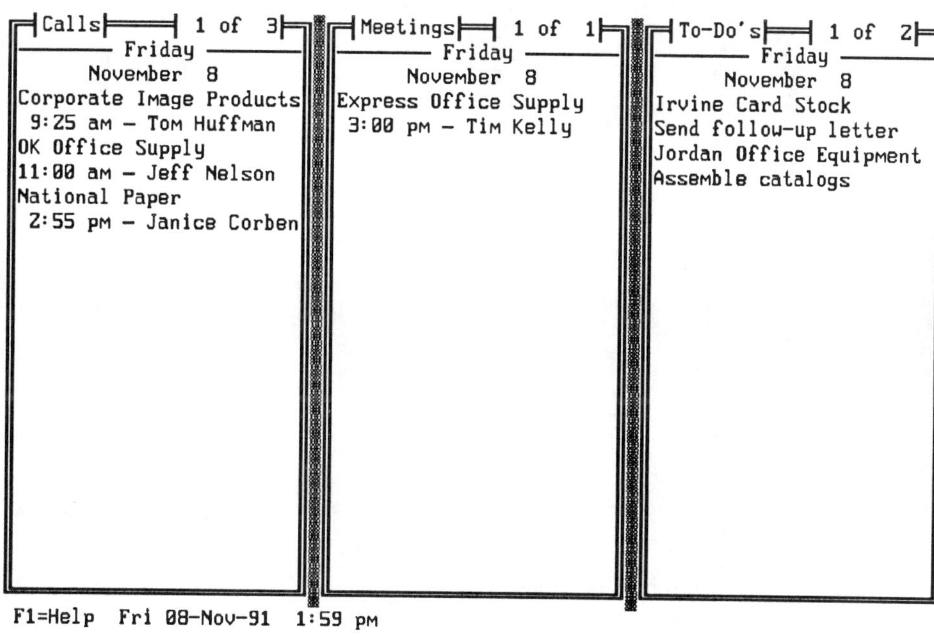

Fig. 2-15. The Lookup Today Task List screen.

Tomorrow lookup

This option does the same work as the Today Lookup, except that the activities that are displayed are for the next day. Using this item, you can quickly see what calls, meetings, and to-dos you have scheduled.

Lookup Old

When the Lookup Old option is selected, ACT! displays the Task List with all past activities that have not been cleared. You can select a past activity with the highlight and see the Contact record that is associated with the activity.

Summary

The Lookup menu makes it easy to find the contacts you need. ACT! can find Contacts in sophisticated ways, which can find a keyword no matter where it is in the Contact record.

> *"There is nothing more demoralizing than a small but adequate income."*
>
> EDMUND WILSON

3
CHAPTER

Getting scheduled

"The great end of life is not knowledge but action."

THOMAS HUXLEY

In the previous two chapters, you learned how to enter Contacts and how to find them. In this chapter, the activities that lead to successful completion of projects, sales campaigns, and fund raisers are discussed.

Three types of activities can be scheduled in ACT!: phone calls, meetings, and things to do. No matter what the activity, it must be connected to a Contact that is entered into the database (the reason for creating the ME Contact in chapter 1). The following steps illustrate the way to schedule a phone call to a contact.

Scheduling a call

1. Use the Lookup menu to find the contact you want.
2. Open the Schedule menu (Fig. 3-1).
3. Select the Call item. The schedule and call detail windows appear (Fig. 3-2).

These same detail windows appear for each of the three activities. Once you understand how they work for scheduling a call, the same steps apply for scheduling meetings and to-dos.

The window on the right is the Date/Time window. The highlight is positioned on the Five Minute option. If you want to call the current contact in five minutes, press Enter. ACT! checks the computer system time and adds five minutes. In Fig. 3-3, the Five Minute option has been selected. The date and time entries are made for you.

Adding date/time increments

Even though you selected the Five Minute option, ACT! does not close the Date/Time window. It assumes that you might wish to adjust the date/time that you have entered. Suppose that you wanted to add another five minutes to the call time.

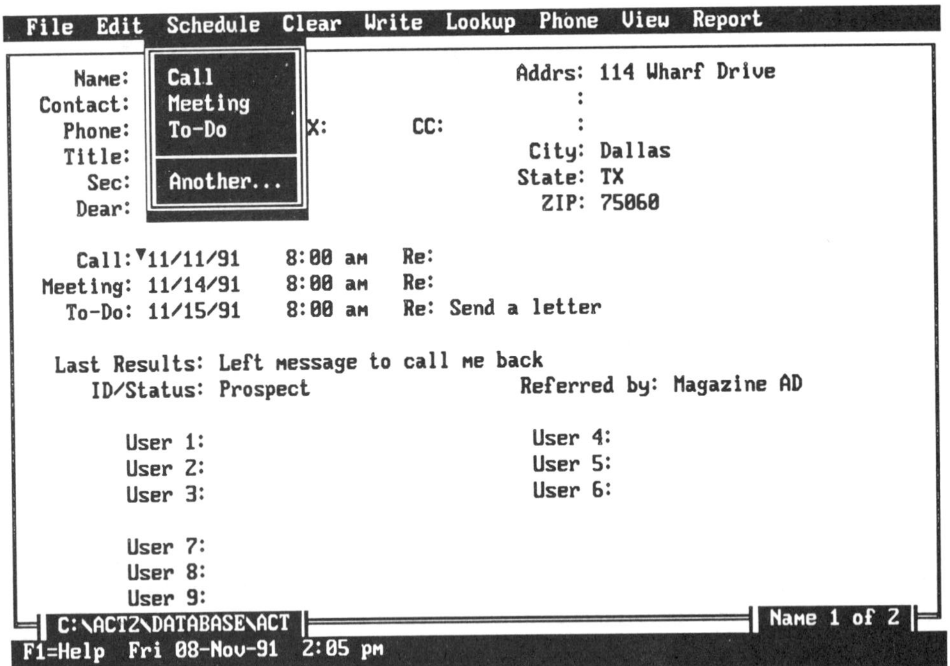

Fig. 3-1. The Schedule menu.

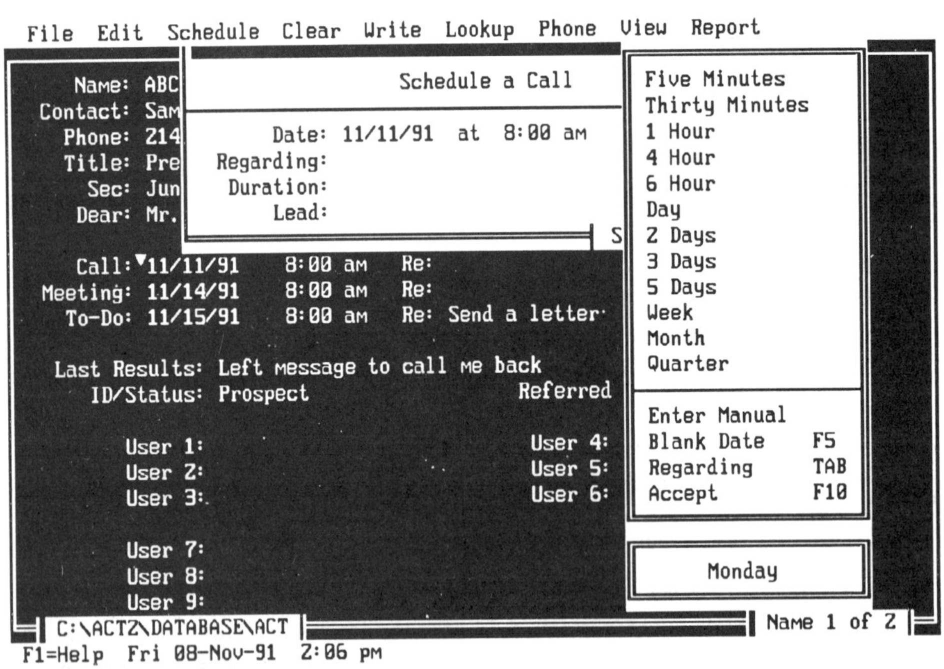

Fig. 3-2. The Schedule, Call windows.

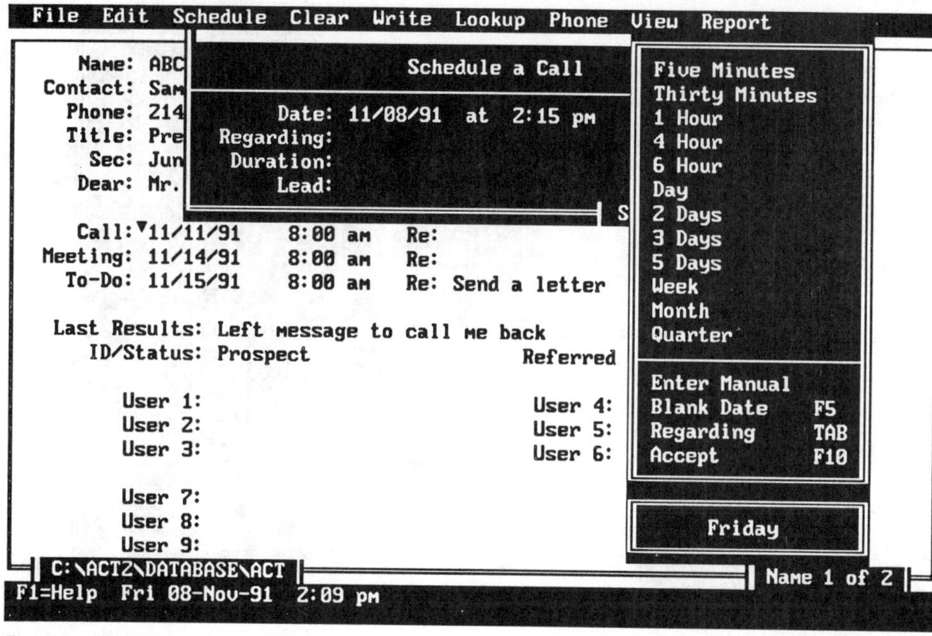

Fig. 3-3. The Date and Time entries.

Press Enter again with the highlight on the Five Minute option to increment the time by that amount. The same is true for every Date/Time option; repeatedly selecting the option increments the time or date.

Also, the + key can be used to increase the time quantity. Pressing the + key while the highlight is on the 1 Hour item increases the time by one hour.

Decrementing date/time

Just as pressing Enter on a particular Date/Time item causes the increment, moving the highlight to a particular item and pressing the – (minus key) decrements the date/time. For example, if you wished to decrease the scheduled time by five minutes, highlighting the Five Minutes entry and pressing the – key does so. Combining the incrementing and decrementing features allows you to specify a time within five minutes.

Using the Popup Calendar

If you are scheduling an activity far into the future and need to look at a calendar to determine the best date, ACT! provides an easy way to do so. After accessing the Schedule menu and selecting a call, meeting, or to-do, follow these steps to find the desired date for the activity.

1. Press the F4 key. The calendar appears (Fig. 3-4).

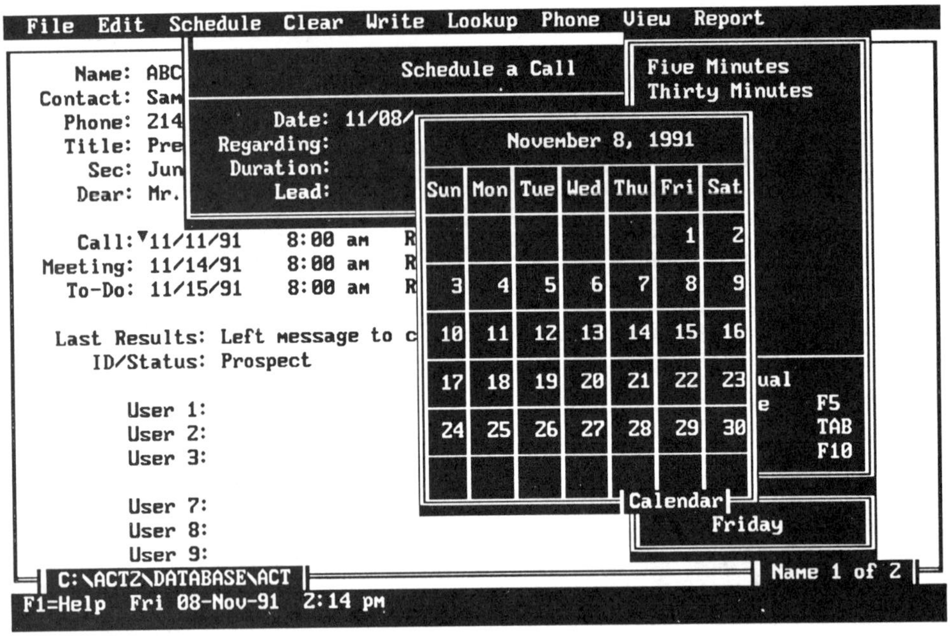

Fig. 3-4. The ACT! Calendar.

2. To insert a date into the Schedule window, move the highlight to the date desired and press Enter.

The ACT! calendar is accessible virtually anywhere in the program. The current date displays in a different color or in reverse video, depending on your screen. The following keys move the highlight in the calendar:

Right Arrow Moves the highlight to the next day
Left Arrow Moves the highlight to the previous day
Up Arrow Moves the highlight to the previous week
Down Arrow Moves the highlight to the next week
Page Down Moves the highlight to the next month, same date
Page Up Moves the highlight to the previous month, same date
Enter Inserts calendar date into schedule window
Esc Closes the calendar

When you use the calendar to enter a date, the default time that is entered is 8:00AM. Most ACT! users schedule all of their calls for that time, unless they have scheduled a specific time with the contact for the call. So by using ACT! as a scheduler, if you set a specific time to call, you will be reminded as you work to make the call.

After the date is entered, ACT! displays the day of the week that you have selected. If the day happens to be on a weekend, ACT! flashes the day name, alerting you that you have scheduled an activity during the weekend. If you accessed the Calendar for reference purposes only, pressing Escape closes the Calendar, but the scheduling windows remain open.

Manually entering the date/time

If you want to enter the date and time without using the Date/ Time window increments, select the Enter Manual item. ACT! closes the Date/ Time window and positions the cursor in the Time Entry field of the Schedule window. Enter the time you want. ACT! assumes that you will schedule in a normal business day. So, if you enter the number 2, ACT! adds the PM extension. You can edit the extension as needed. ACT! also assumes that you intend to make the call on the same day and it enters the date for you after you enter the time. Of course, you can enter a different date, if necessary.

Regarding entry

It is important that you make an entry in the Regarding field for every activity. Why? ACT! logs the activity and the reason for it in the History file. Later, when you want to look at the history of your activities with the contact, you not only have the date of the call, meeting, or to-do, but also the rationale.

After you enter the date/time, select the Regarding entry to open the Popup window. If you have used the Enter Manually option, the Regarding window (Fig. 3-5) opens immediately after you enter a time.

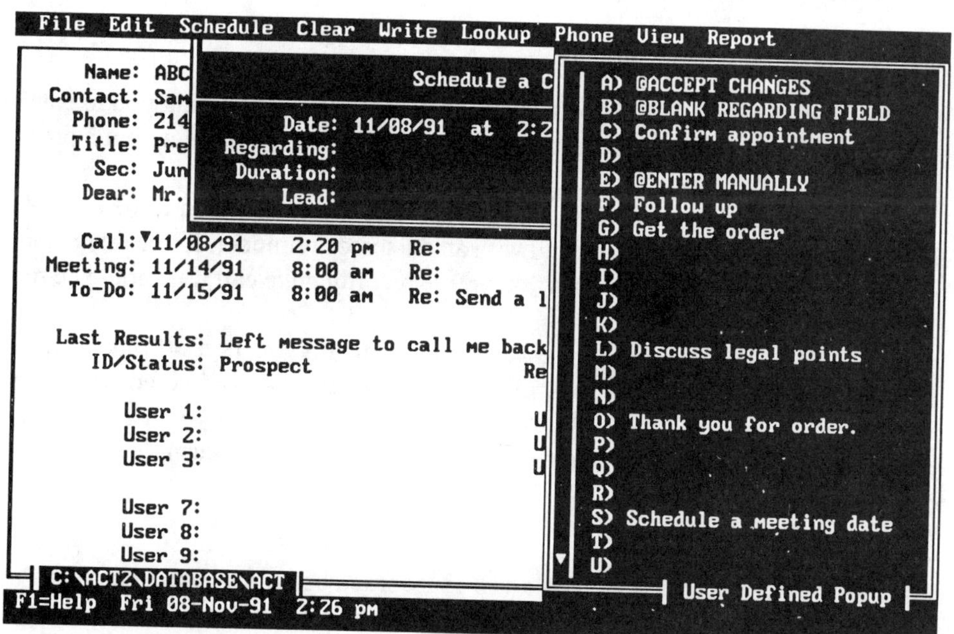

Fig. 3-5. The Regarding window.

Three of the entries on the Popup are different from the others. Selecting the Accept Changes entry closes both scheduling windows. Use this option when you have made an edit to the scheduled activity, such as a change in time for the activity.

The Blank Regarding Field is a shortcut for you to change the Regarding entry. Selecting it erases the current Regarding entry and leaves the Regarding window open.

The Enter Manually allows you to type an entry that is not included in the Popup. To make the Regarding entry, use the arrow keys to highlight the appropriate entry and press Enter. If you want to add a new Regarding entry to the Popup window, press F2, type the entry next to the letter you want and press F10 to save. A more detailed description of modifying Popups is found in chapter 1.

Entering a time duration

After you have selected a Regarding entry, ACT! moves the highlight to the Duration field. The duration entry is not absolute, but when you have a busy schedule, you will want to block off definite amounts of time for each activity. The time duration can be entered in several ways. For example, if you are scheduling a conference that results in your being gone for a week, you can enter that time block. Then, when you press F3 to check your weekly agenda, the block of time is allotted.

You can choose not to enter a duration by pressing the TAB key, or to erase the duration by pressing F5. When you schedule a meeting, ACT! inserts a default time of 1 hour for the meeting.

Entering a lead time

ACT! attempts to keep you on top of your daily schedule by allowing you to enter a lead time for your activities. After you decide the duration of the activity, press the TAB key to continue to the Lead entry.

When you schedule a lead time for a call, that call is assumed to be critical. ACT! then alerts you to make the call with an on-screen reminder. If you do not enter a lead time for a call, ACT! asks you before recording the call if it should be recorded as critical.

When you schedule a meeting, ACT! automatically enters a 30-minute lead time, thereby making the meeting critical. Meetings and to-dos entered without a lead time are considered by ACT! to not be critical, therefore no on-screen alarm appears. At the end of this chapter, the process for editing ACT! alarms is discussed.

Reminder alarms

When a lead time is established or a call is recorded as critical, ACT! displays a Popup window alarm over the ACT! screen. Depending on what you are working on at the time and what type of activity it is, several options are presented:

SNOOZE Resets the alarm to the time period you specify, five minutes up to four hours.

ALL SNOOZE Resets the alarms for all critical activities from 5 minutes up to 4 hours.

FORGET IT Cancels the alarm.

GO to IT Takes you to the Contact screen, for which the alarm was set. If you are on that contact when the alarm is triggered, this item does not appear.

Figure 3-6 is a Call alarm. If the alarm had displayed when you were working in any Contact screen, the Go to It item would have been included as an item.

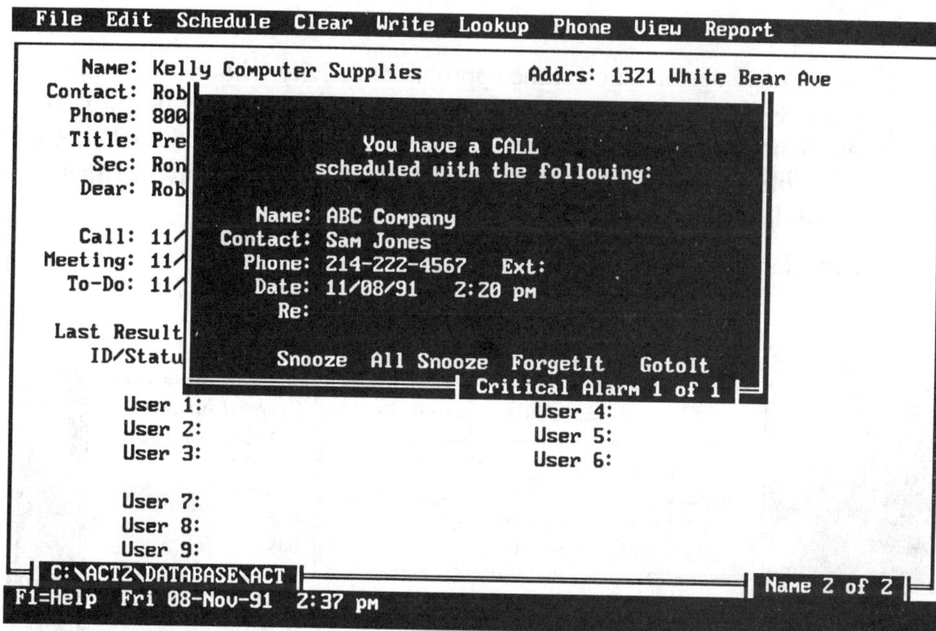

Fig. 3-6. The Call Alarm.

Accepting the activity

After entering the date and time of an activity, you can immediately save the activity by pressing F10. At any point after entering the date and time, you can press F10. The Regarding, Duration, and Lead entries are optional for ACT! to record the scheduled activity.

Aborting the activity entry

If you decide not to schedule the activity, press Escape. The windows close and the activity is not scheduled.

Checking your schedule

In chapter 2, you used the Lookup menu to open the Task List. As you are making entries, you can check the day's schedule by pressing F7; or you can check the entire week by pressing F3.

Adding another call, meeting, or to-do to a contact

Many times you are going to encounter a situation where you have several calls, meetings, or to-dos with the same contact. ACT! allows you to schedule as many activities as you need with the Another option on the Schedule menu.

To schedule multiple activities:

1. Open the Schedule menu and select Another.
2. A submenu appears. Select the appropriate activity with the highlight and press Enter. The Date/Time and Schedule window appear plus the Activities Scheduled window, as seen in Fig. 3-7. The addition of the Activities Scheduled window gives you a visual display of all activities that are scheduled for the contact.
3. Enter the new activity as discussed previously.

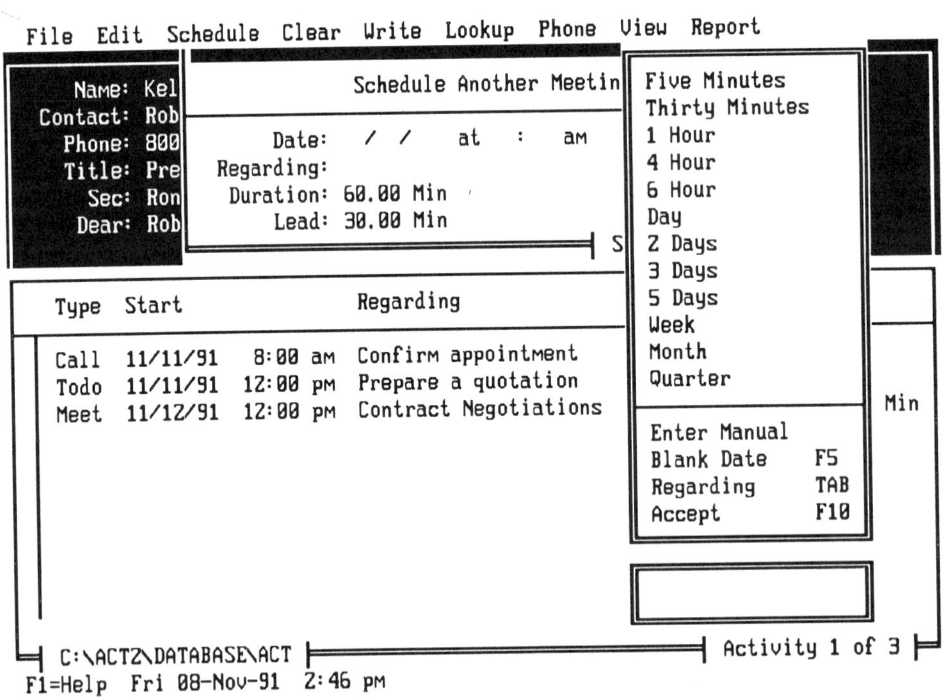

Fig. 3-7. The Activities Scheduled window.

Scheduling conflicts

If you enter an activity for a contact that ACT! detects to be at the same time as another previously scheduled activity, a message window appears to warn you of the conflict. At that point, you can either accept the conflict or reschedule the current activity.

Note: Conflicts are recognized only if you have not changed the default setting of Yes in the Default Scheduling Information window to No. Modifying the default settings is discussed at the end of this chapter, under *Editing alarm defaults*.

Editing scheduled activities

Scheduled activities can be edited in two ways. The first is to locate the Contact and press F2, which puts ACT! in the Edit mode. Move the highlight to the Call, Meeting, or To-Do field; make the change and save it by pressing F10. The second way is to access the Activities Scheduled window and make the changes there:

1. Open the Edit menu and select the Activities option.
2. The Activities Scheduled window appears. Use the arrow keys to move to the parameter you want to edit. For example, if you want to change the date of a meeting, move to the data entry.
3. Press F2. ACT! is now in edit mode.
   - In the Type field, press the right or left arrow to scroll the three types of activities. Press Enter to insert the new activity.
   - In the Start, Time, Duration, or Lead fields, press F2 to open the Date/Time window and highlight the entry you want. Then, press Enter to insert.
   - In the Time field, you can use the Calendar, F4, to insert a different date.
   - In the Regarding field, press F2 to make an entry from the Popup window.
4. Press F10 to save the edited activity or Escape to cancel the edit.

Using the Calendar to look up activities

Pressing F7 displays the current day's Task List. Using the Calendar, you can display a Task List for a range of specific dates. Suppose that you wanted to see the Task List for the next three days:

1. Press F4, the Calendar displays.
2. Press the right arrow key once. The highlight moves to the next day.
3. Press the period key. This key anchors the date highlight.
4. Press the right arrow key three times. The day highlight extends to cover three days (Fig. 3-8).
5. Press Enter. ACT! displays the Task List for all three days (Fig. 3-9).

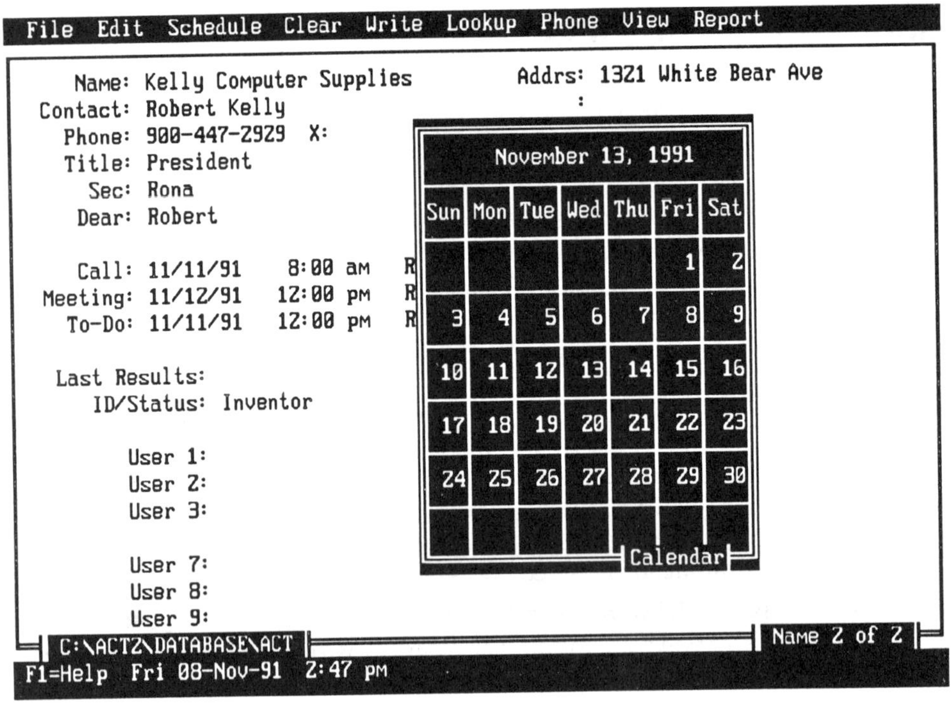

Fig. 3-8. The Day highlight extended to cover three days.

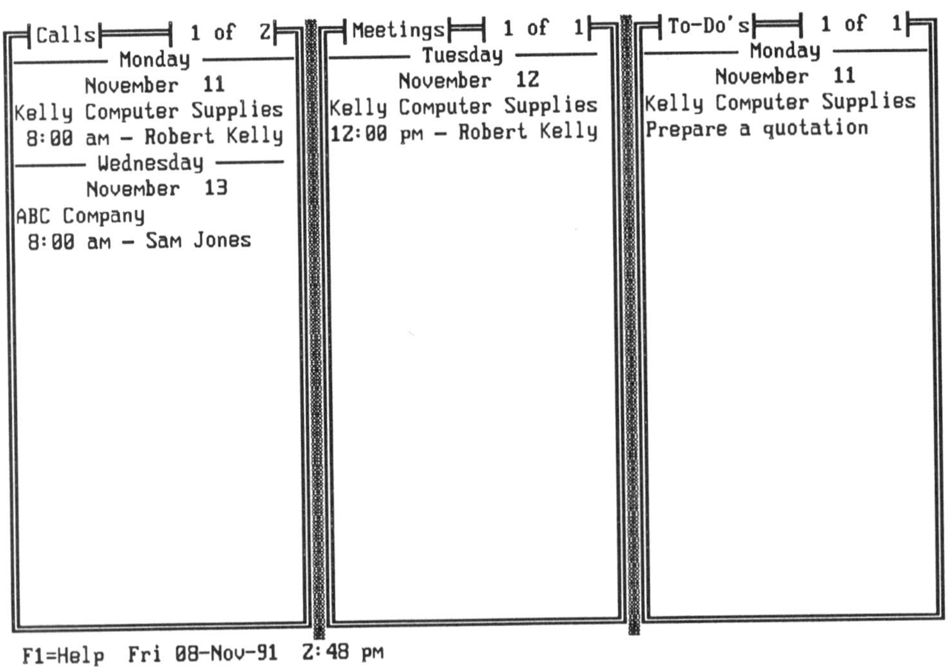

Fig. 3-9. Three day Task List.

Editing alarms defaults

As was discussed earlier, the key to ACT! determining if an activity is crucial (and thereby displaying a screen prompt) depends on whether or not a lead time is included. You might want to have all of your activities considered crucial, or only those where you entered the lead time manually.

To edit the default lead times:

1. Open the Edit menu and select Options.
2. From the submenu, select Alarm Settings. The Default Scheduling Information window appears (Fig. 3-10).

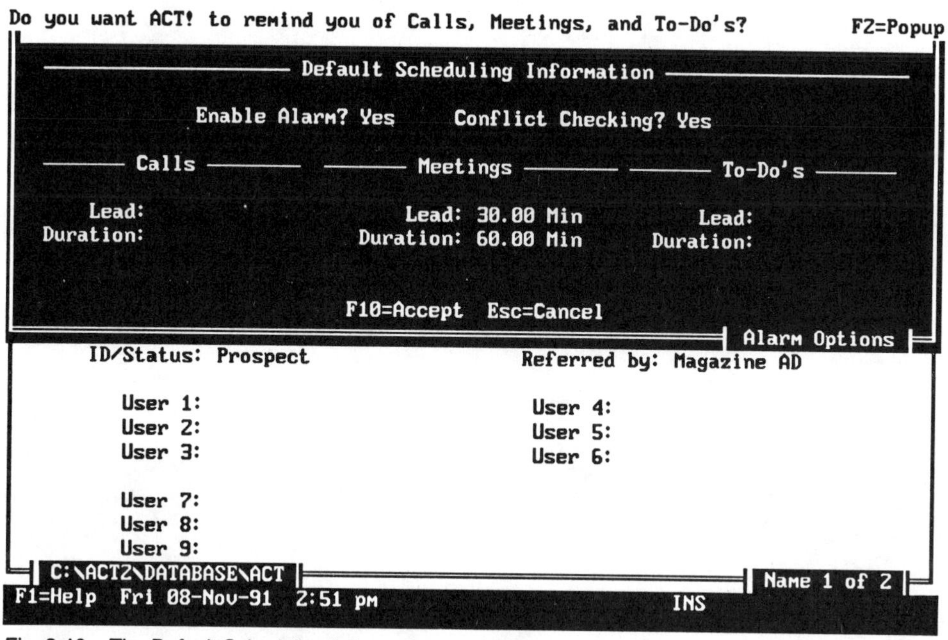

Fig. 3-10. The Default Scheduling Information window.

If you want to shut off all alarms, Enter No in the Enable Alarm field.

1. Move the cursor to the field in which you want to make a modification.
2. Press F2 to display the Time menu.
3. Move the highlight to the time increment desired and press Enter. If you want to erase a time setting, select the Blank item.
4. After making all the modifications you want, press F10 to save.

Summary

After entering Contacts, you can begin scheduling activities. To print a schedule of your activities, see the chapter on reports.

"However brilliant an action, it should not be esteemed great unless the result of a great motive."

FRANCOIS DE LA ROCHEFOUCAULD

4

CHAPTER

Tackling activities

"Intellect annuls fate. So far as a man thinks, he is free."

RALPH WALDO EMERSON

Now that you have scheduled activities with your contacts, it is time to execute the schedule. The first step of the day is to press F7 to open the Task List. When you do, the list of calls, meetings, and to-dos is presented (Fig. 4-1). Assume that you want to start by making your scheduled phone calls.

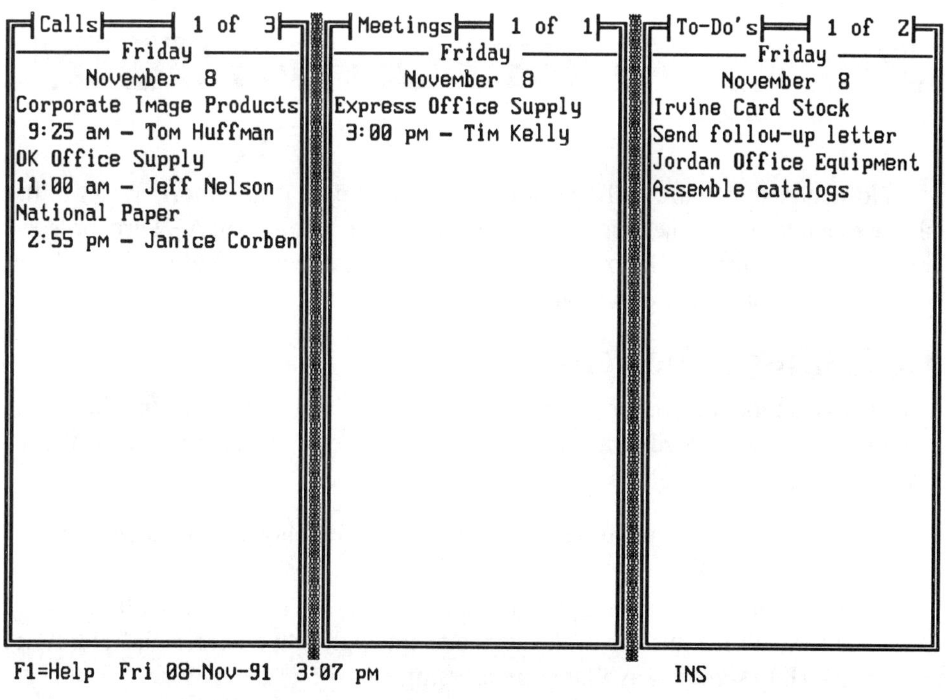

Fig. 4-1. The Day's Task List.

1. Press F7 to open the Task List. The highlight is positioned on the first call scheduled for the day.
2. Press Enter. The Contact record for that first call is displayed.
3. Open the Phone menu. It is displayed in Fig. 4-2.

You can follow two paths here. If you have a modem, you can use it to dial the phone for you. If not, you can dial the phone yourself. If you do not have a modem, skip to "Using the phone menu without a modem."

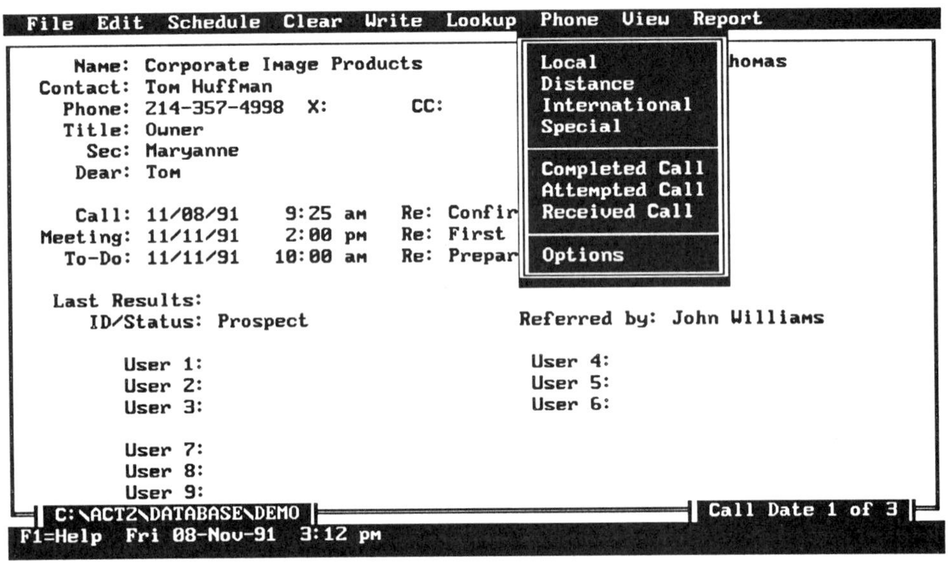

Fig. 4-2. The Phone Menu.

No matter if you are calling out or receiving a call, it is important to use the phone menu to record the disposition of every call. By doing so, ACT! records every call in the contact's History file. Over time, it becomes second nature and you will find the benefits are enormous.

Installing a modem

If you have a modem, you must install it before ACT! can access it. In addition, if you also have a fax board or a combination fax /modem you need to follow the installation steps. To install the modem:

1. From the Phone menu, select Options. The Telephone options window appears (Fig. 4-3).
2. Make the entries appropriate to your system. ACT! provides a line of help information at the top of the screen as the highlight enters each field. Also, the Help screen is available by pressing F1.
3. Press F10 to save the modem settings.

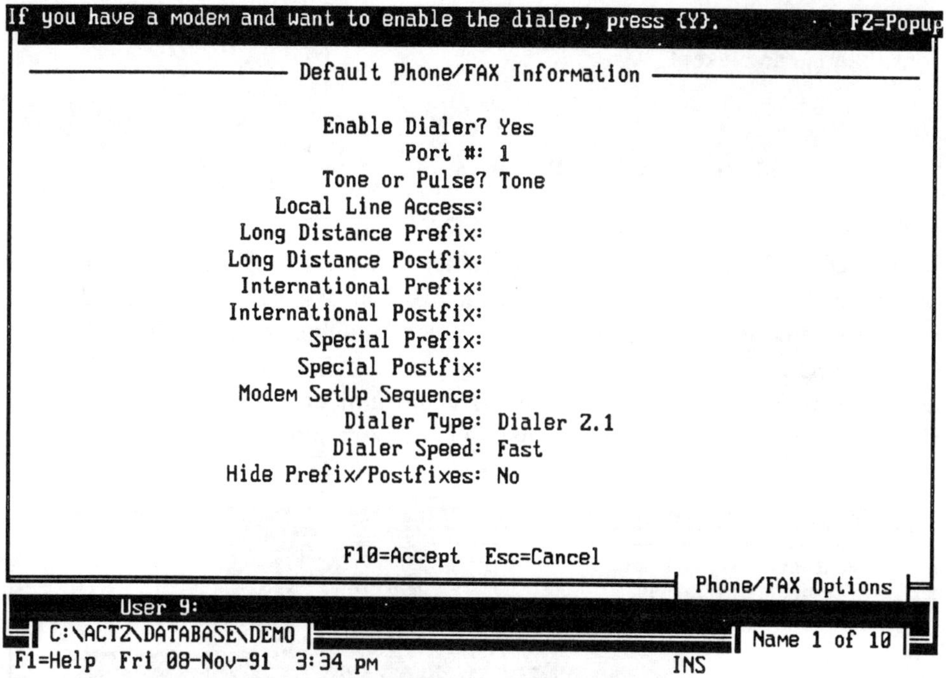

Fig. 4-3. The Telephone Modem options window.

Dialing with a modem

Dialing a call, whether local, long distance, or international is straightforward. After opening the Phone menu, highlight the appropriate option and press Enter. ACT! displays a screen window with a message that details the number it is dialing. When dialing is completed, this message is displayed: Dialing completed, lift handset and press SPACE.

ACT! then displays another message window that asks if you reached the person you were calling. Selecting Yes or No records that fact in the History file for the contact.

Using the timer

Along with recording whether the contact was reached, you have the option of timing the call. Selecting Timer, starts the timer and opens the Reason for Timing window. The Timer window can be edited the same as other popups. After entering the Reason entry, the timer runs until you press the Control and F4 keys together. A window at the bottom of the screen appears displaying the elapsed time. When you stop the timer, the elapsed time is recorded with the call in the History file.

Even if you look up a different contact while talking and shut off the timer there, ACT! records the call to the correct contact. The Timer is an ideal tool for people who bill clients based on time. A complete and accurate record of every consultation can be kept.

Redial

Selecting Redial causes ACT! to Redial the same number.

Dialing from Contact Screen 2

If you access the Phone menu from Contact Screen 2, ACT! displays all of the phone numbers it finds in the Contact record. The first number displayed is the number entered in Contact Screen 1. The second number is the number entered in Contact Screen 2, as the alternative phone. Next are the numbers entered for both assistants (if any). Use the highlight to select the number you wish to dial and press Enter. An example of the Screen 2 dialing window is shown in Fig. 4-4.

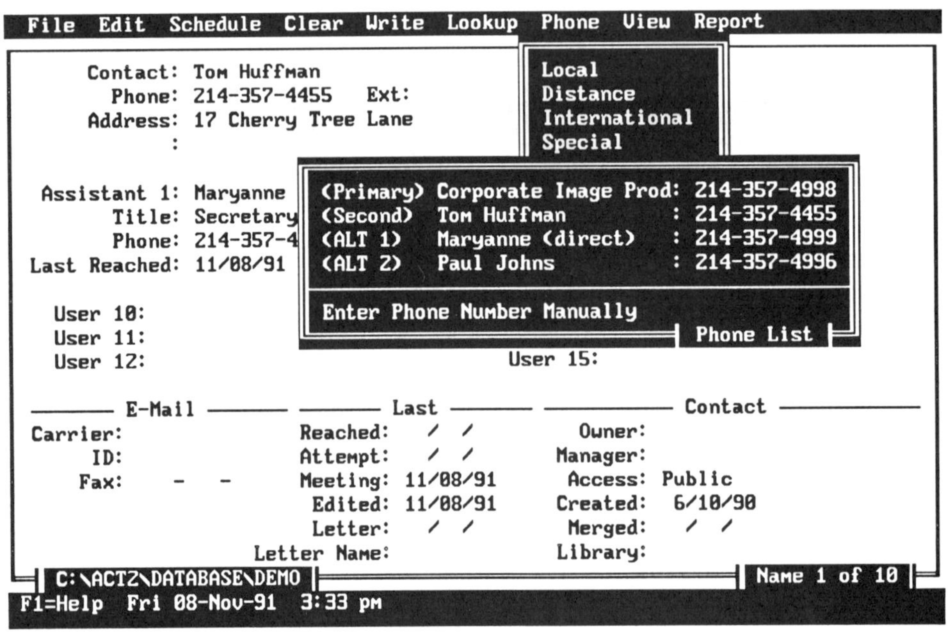

Fig. 4-4. The Contact Screen 2 dialing window.

Using the Phone menu without a modem

Even if you do not have a modem, it is important that you use the Phone menu every time you dial out and every time you receive a call. If you don't, you cannot get the full benefit of ACT!.

As you can see in Fig. 4-2, three options are presented regarding the status of the phone call. Highlight the status that is appropriate to the call and press Enter. The time of the call and the status are recorded in the History file.

Using the timer

Along with recording whether the contact was researched, you have the option of timing the call. Selecting Timer starts the timer and opens the Reason for Timing window. The Timer window can be edited the same as other popups. After making the Reason entry, the timer runs until you press the Control and F4 keys together. A window at the bottom of the screen displays the elapsed time. When you stop the timer, the elapsed time is recorded with the call in the History file.

Even if you look up a different contact while talking and shut off the timer there, ACT! records the call to the correct contact. The timer is an ideal tool for people who bill clients based on time. A complete and accurate record of every consultation can be kept.

Clearing an activity

After you have completed an activity, clear it from the daily activity schedule. This accomplishes two purposes. First, it removes the activity from the Task List. Second, it stores the result of the scheduled activity in the History file.

To clear an activity:

1. Look up the contact that has the scheduled activity. Remember, you can press F7 to see the Task List, and then move the highlight to the scheduled activity and press Enter.
2. Open the Clear menu.
3. Highlight the activity you wish to Clear, and press Enter.

Clearing a call

If you clear a call, a submenu appears (Fig. 4-5). If you select the Erase option, ACT! treats the scheduled call as if it never existed. The other three options are recorded in the History file, along with the time and date. So, if you had scheduled a call and the contact called you first, you can clear the call and record it as having been received. Again, the salient point is to remember to record every phone conversation, whether incoming or outgoing.

Clearing a meeting

When you clear a meeting, ACT! prompts you as to whether or not the meeting was held. Answering yes records that result in the History file. A No answer is not recorded.

Clearing a to-do

When you clear a to-do, ACT! prompts you as to whether or not the to-do was done. Either answer is recorded in the History file.

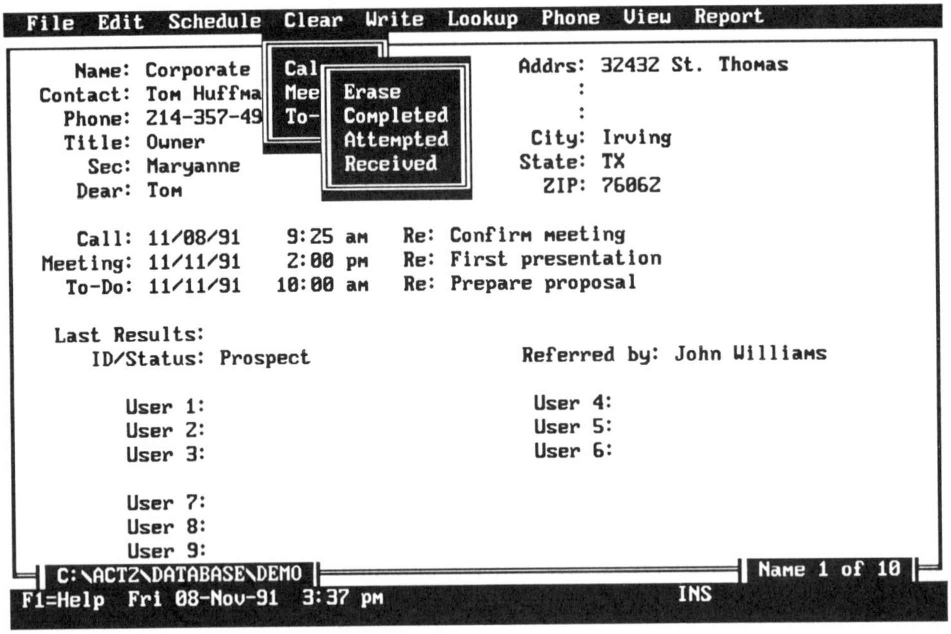

Fig. 4-5. The Clear, Call submenu.

Aborting a clear

Before you answer the screen prompt on the disposition of the scheduled activity, you can abort the clearing procedure by pressing Escape until the Clear menu is closed. The scheduled activity then remains valid.

History file, Shift/F9

The Contact History file is created when you enter a contact into ACT!. The History is unique to each contact. Some of the entries in the History file are entered for you automatically as you use entries in the Contact record. Others, such as the disposition of scheduled calls, meetings, and to-dos, are recorded based on your responses to screen prompts. For example, in the previous section, the instructions for clearing a call, meeting, or to-do were explained. When you clear a previously scheduled activity, a History entry results (unless you used the Erase item for a scheduled call or meeting).

The History file is invaluable when tracking the number of calls, meetings, and to-dos you have undertaken. ACT! provides two report types that use History entries. The first is the History Summary that compiles the number of calls, meetings, and to-dos for the contacts that you designate. The second is the Contact Report that prints the entire Contact record, including the History. The different ways to use ACT! reports are covered in chapter 6.

To see the History file of a contact:

1. Use the Lookup menu to find the contact.
2. Press and hold the Shift key, then press the F9 key. In Fig. 4-6, an example of a History file is shown.

The History file contains the record of the activities that have been undertaken with this contact and several other types of entries. For example, if you change the entry in the Last Results file, it is recorded by date in the History. Most ACT! users use the Last Results field as a means of qualifying where they are in terms of their working relationship with a contact. A change in the ID/Status, Referred By, or Access fields also generates a History entry.

```
File  Edit  Schedule  Clear  Write  Lookup  Phone  View  Report

    Name: Corporate Image Products          Addrs: 32432 St. Thomas
 Contact: Tom Huffman                            :
   Phone: 214-357-4998  X:         CC:           :
   Title: Owner                              City: Irving
     Sec: Maryanne                          State: TX
    Dear: Tom                                 ZIP: 76062

 Date      Type          Event

 11/08/91  TO-DO         Prepare proposal * DONE *
 11/08/91  MEETING       First presentation
 11/08/91  TO-DO         Send proposal * DONE *
 11/08/91  CALL          Cmplt  9:25 am Confirm meeting
  5/09/91  MEETING       new business!
  5/05/91  ID/Status     Prospect
  5/05/91  TO-DO         order new catalog from National Paper * DONE *

 C:\ACT2\DATABASE\DEMO                               History 3 of 7
F1=Help  Fri 08-Nov-91  3:54 pm                   INS
```

Fig. 4-6. An example History file.

Deleting a History entry

When the people at Contact Software created ACT!, they looked at the History file as being inviolate. After all, what good was a history unless it was recorded without the editing of the users. However, users of the product (ACT1) demanded the ability to rewrite history, so to speak. So, in ACT2, you can open the History file and delete unwanted entries. Also, when you have made a mistaken keyboard input, such as recording a call as completed when it was actually attempted, you will want the history of the call to be correct.

To delete a history entry:

1. Use the Lookup menu to find the contact.
2. Press the Shift and F9 keys together.

3. Use the up or down arrow keys to highlight the Date of History entry you wish to delete.
4. Press Delete. ACT! responds with a screen message that asks you if you are sure that you want to delete the entry.
5. Type Y for Yes to delete the entry or N to keep the entry.

You can print the history for a contact, a group of contacts, or for all contacts. See chapter 6 for details.

Totaling your activities

ACT! compiles the number of activities that you have undertaken with each client. Chapter 6 details the creation of a summary report of activities for all your contacts. You can also see a quick total of activities for a single contact with one of the function keys.

To see the activity totals for a particular contact:

1. Use the Lookup menu to find the contact.
2. Press and hold the CTRL key, then press F9. The total window appears (Fig. 4-7).

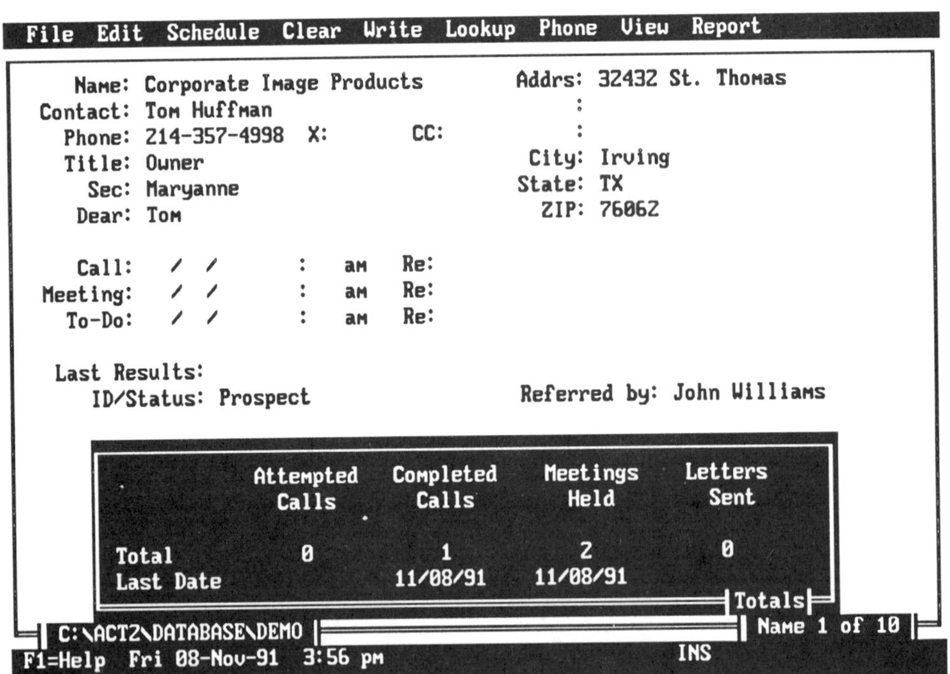

Fig. 4-7. The Activities total window.

Printing your daily schedule

If you do not have a portable computer and are away from your office frequently, you might want a printed schedule of your activities. You must have already installed a printer in order to print a Task List.

To print a Task List:

1. Open the Report menu.
2. Use the highlight to select the Task List item.
3. Press Enter.
4. ACT! displays the Print To window (Fig. 4-8).

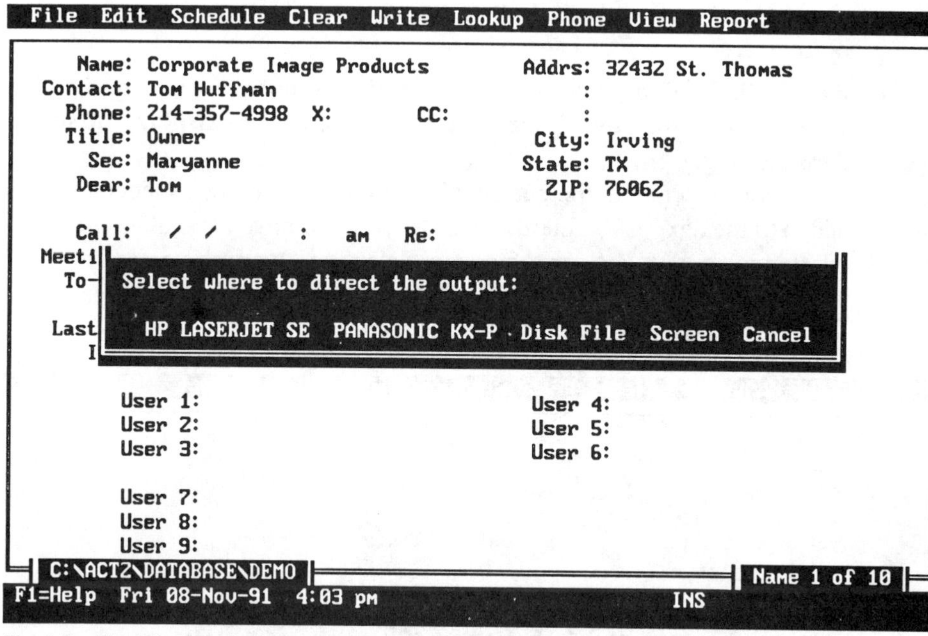

Fig. 4-8. The Print To window.

5. Select where you want the Task List to be printed by highlighting the choice you want and pressing Enter.

If you want to see the Task List before it prints, select Screen as the destination.

Editing the tasks not done today

When you have a full schedule, chances are that you cannot complete one or several of the calls or to-dos. At the end of the working day, you can move all of the uncompleted calls and to-dos to the next day very simply.

1. Open the Lookup menu and select Today. ACT! displays the Task List for the current date. You can see which activities have not been finished.

   Note: activities still appear on the Task List (even if completed), if you failed to use the Clear menu to record their disposition.
2. Press Escape.
3. Open the Edit menu and select the Group item. ACT! displays a blank Contact screen.
4. Move the highlight to the Call field.
5. Press F4 to display the calendar.
6. Move the highlight to the next day (or the day on which you want to reschedule the Calls) and press Enter. ACT! inserts the date and moves the highlight to the Time field. Enter a time and a note in the Regarding field, if necessary.
7. Press F10. ACT! prompts you as to whether or not you are sure that you want to update the group. Select the Yes answer. ACT! displays the screen message (Fig. 4-9).

   If you select Add, the current Call remains on today's schedule and is added to the next day's. In other words, you will have two calls scheduled, one for today and one for tomorrow. Selecting Overwrite erases the Call scheduled for today with the new Call for tomorrow. Most ACT! users select the Overwrite option.

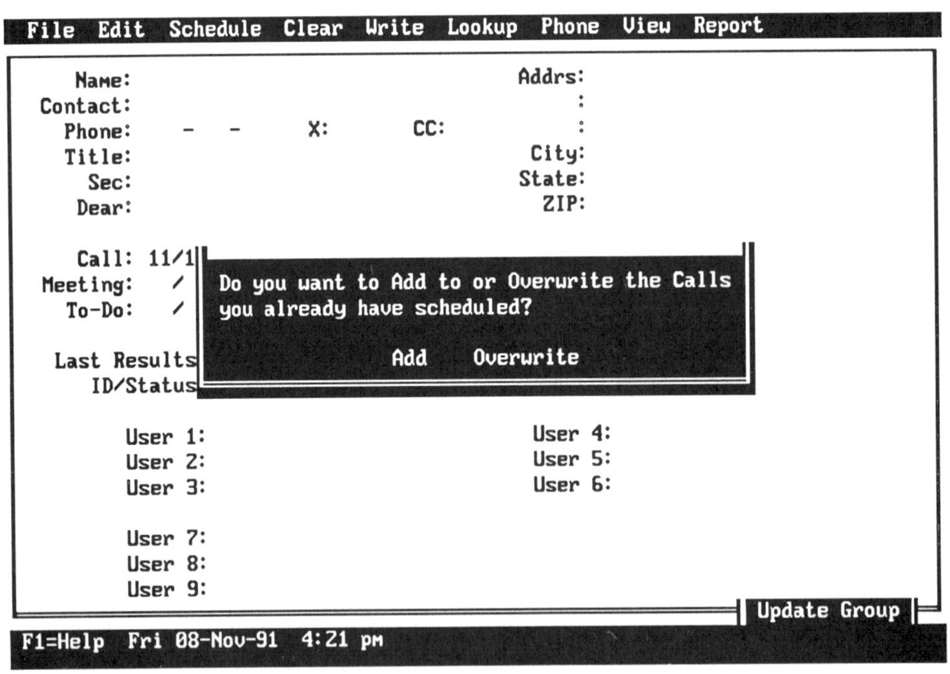

Fig. 4-9. The Add to or Overwrite window.

8. ACT! begins updating the contacts that had a scheduled Call. If you have not included a lead time in default alarm settings, ACT! checks to determine if the Call is Critical.

   To move the to-dos, follow the same steps as for Calls, except enter the new date in the To-Do field. You can also move meetings, but doing so becomes problematical. It is better to move meetings on a contact-by-contact basis.

Taking notes, F9

When you talk to a contact via phone, or schedule a meeting or a to-do, normally you will want to record some things that do not fit into a Contact field. For example, if you want to record the gist of a conversation or the possible ideas that were generated, you need a free-form space in which to do it. That is what the Notes do for you. The Notes can work in conjunction with the Last Results field. After recording notes, many ACT! users make an entry in the Last Results field, such as "See Notes." That way, when you access the Contact record, you remind yourself that important information is contained in the Notes section.

The note-taking facility of ACT! is a word processor that creates notes that are then stored as part of the Contact file.

To access the Notes portion of ACT!:

1. Use the Lookup menu to find the contact.
2. Press F9. It is easy to remember this as the Notes key by thinking "F9 for notes."

   The Notes window opens over half of the Contact screen (Fig. 4-10).

   As you can see, ACT! has already entered the current date for you. In version 2.1, ACT! also inserts your user ID so that anyone accessing the Notes can identify the entry by the person who made the entry. This feature is very critical for Network users of ACT!, in that many different people can add Notes to a Contact record. At the very top of the screen is the message, "Press Alt-F to activate the Notes menu . . .", you do not have to access the Notes menu to enter a note.

   The default typing mode is Insert. When you type, the characters are inserted to the right of cursor location; any characters to the right of the cursor are pushed ahead. If you press the INS key, the typing mode switches to Overstrike; the characters are inserted at the cursor location, but any characters to the right of the cursor are overwritten by the new characters. Generally speaking, the Overstrike mode is used mainly for editing fields or text.
3. Type the note you want to record.

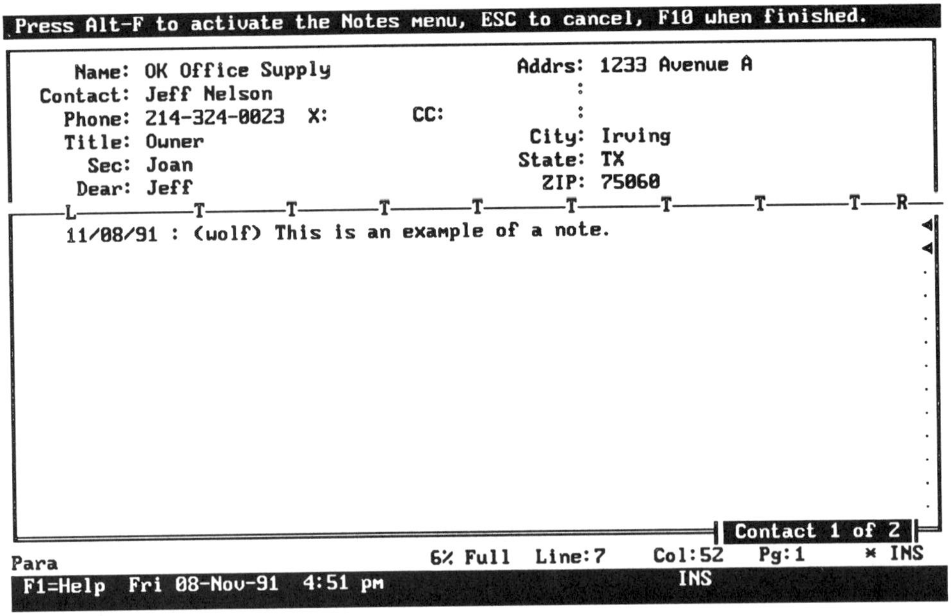

Fig. 4-10. The Notes window.

4. Press F10 to save the note. After you have recorded notes for a Contact, ACT! alerts you to the fact that notes are attached to the Contact by adding a musical note symbol to the Lookup indicator in the lower right corner of the Contact screen.

Using the Notes menu

After opening the Notes window, you can use more of its word processing capability via the Notes menu.

File The three items are: Combine, eXtract, and Export.

Combine The Combine item allows you to insert a previously saved document (not necessarily an ACT! document) into the Notes. After selecting Combine, ACT! prompts you to position the cursor where you want the file to be inserted. Next, ACT! opens the File window, allowing you to use the highlight to select a file. When you highlight the file name and press Enter, it is inserted into the Notes, including the file format.

eXtract The eXtract item allows you to select a portion of the Notes and save that portion in a distinct file. When you select the eXtract item, ACT! prompts you to "Select block to save." So, you must position the cursor at the beginning point of the text that you want to extract before selecting the item. Then, use the arrow keys to extend the highlight over the text that you want to extract and press

Enter. The File window appears. You can replace an existing file with the new text or create a new file. Creating a new file is discussed in chapter 5 on using the word processor.

Export The Export item moves the entire document to an ASCII format file. You can export the Notes to an existing file or create a new file at the File Window.

Edit Selecting the Edit menu puts you in the Editing Notes mode.

Print This menu has two options. The first prints the entire Notes file to the destination of your choice. The second is concerned with setting up your printer(s) and the layout for envelopes, mailing labels, and Rolodex-type cards. Printing setups are covered in chapter 5 on word processing.

Block The Block menu includes several tools for rearranging and modifying text. A *block* is a portion of text that consists of a single character, a single word, or an entire document. Selecting any of the options on the Block menu puts the cursor in extend mode. So the cursor is anchored at the point where it was when you selected the block item; it will highlight text as you press the arrow keys. For example, if the cursor is at the beginning of a sentence when you select the Block Cut option and then you press the down arrow key once, the entire sentence would be highlighted.

Copy The Copy item selects a block of text and duplicates it in another place in the Notes.

Cut The Cut item deletes a block of text.

Move The Move item removes a block of text from one area of Notes to another.

Paste The Paste item is used to repeatedly insert copied or moved text. When you select a block to be copied or moved, even after you have executed the copy or move, the text remains on the Notes clipboard. Selecting Paste inserts the text from the clipboard to the cursor position.

Typestyle The Typestyle option changes the selected block to a new typestyle.

Typestyle The Typestyle menu includes seven typestyle options, including Normal. You can modify the typestyle in a document with 2 methods. You can either select the typestyle you want by opening this menu prior to beginning the note and selecting a typestyle, or by selecting a block of text after the notes have been entered and selecting a new typestyle.

Check The Check menu is the spellchecker. When this menu is opened, you have three options: checking the entire document, checking the words from the cursor position forward to the end of the document or just the word itself. For more details on the spellchecker, see chapter 5 on word processing.

Search If you have copious notes on a contact, you might need to search through them to find a specific reference or a specific date. Select the Search menu and ACT! opens the Search Entry window. Enter the text or date you want (For the uninitiated, this entry is called a *search string*). You cannot use wildcards such as * or ? in the search pattern. ACT! prompts for a Forward or Backward search from the cursor position. Select the direction. ACT! finds the first occurrence and prompts you as to whether to go to the next occurrence or to replace the search string with a new entry.

Done Saves changes and closes the Notes window.

Fast menu-access keys

While you are working in the Notes window, you can instantly open the Notes menu by pressing the ALT key and the access letter together. For example, to open the Block menu, pressing ALT and B at the same time opens the menu.

Remember, if you entered an important piece of information into a note and cannot recall the Contact to which it is attached, the Lookup menu Keyword option searches Contacts and their Notes to find your keyword.

The Notes editing keys are:

Right Arrow Cursor right one character.

Left Arrow Cursor left one character.

Up Arrow Cursor up one line.

CTRL /Up Arrow Cursor to the beginning of the Notes.

CTRL /Down Arrow Cursor to the end of Notes.

Down Arrow Cursor down one line.

Enter Starts new line of text.

BackArrow Deletes character to the left of cursor.

Delete Deletes character at the cursor position.

Escape Closes Notes window; edits not saved.

TAB Cursor to the next tab stop right.

Home Cursor to the beginning of the current line.

End Cursor to the End of the current line.

F2 Displays list of field names. With the highlight, you can select a field name and press Enter. The information entered in the Contact Record field is then inserted at the cursor position. For example, if you wanted to insert the contact's fax number in your notes, you would highlight the fax Phone entry from the list and press Enter.

Shift/F2 Displays a list of time stamps that can be inserted, such as the Formal Date, the designated manager of the contact, and other information.

F3 Displays the Week-at-a-Glance window.

F4 Displays the calendar. Press Enter to insert the highlighted date.

Shift/ F4 Displays the calculator. Enter a calculation and press the Insert key to insert the result in the Notes.

F5 Deletes text from the cursor position to the end of the current line.

Shift/ F5 Inserts the words "I said" at the beginning of a line. Used to record a conversation.

F6 Deletes word at the cursor position.

Shift/ F6 Inserts the words "They said" at the beginning of a line. Used to record a conversation.

F7 Centers the current line of text.

Shift/ F7 Inserts the current time at the cursor position.

F10 Closes Notes window and saves edits.

Shift/ F10 Temporarily exits ACT! to DOS. The DOS prompt appears and you can execute any DOS command at this point. When finished with DOS, typing EXIT returns you to the exact spot in ACT! that you left.

Summary

ACT! makes it easy to schedule the activities that lead to successful execution of the day. By adding Notes to a Contact, you keep key information literally at your fingertips. The History of your activities with a contact engenders a sense of perspective and aids accountability.

"Anybody can make history, only a great man can write it."

OSCAR WILDE

5
CHAPTER

Letters, labels, and more

"Words without action are the assassins of idealism."

HERBERT HOOVER

No matter what type of business you are in, written forms of communication are necessary. Not long ago, experts were predicting the era of the "paperless" office, assuming that computers and E-Mail would transmit documents without a need for printed copies. Experts are often wrong and the widespread use of computers has increased the amount of paper being generated by businesses. ACT! makes the process of creating written communications mercifully easy.

ACT! generates letters, personalized form letters, memos, and fax cover letters. It prints concomitant mailing labels or envelopes. In short, it becomes a mass-mailing machine that one person can easily operate. This chapter covers the operation of the ACT! word processor and the enhancements that make it easy to send 50 or 500 letters out in a hurry.

For those of you using ACT! 2.1, a software program called *Books, Cards, and Labels (BC&L)* is seamlessly integrated into ACT!. BC&L extends the viability of your ACT! database by creating specialized labels, printing records in formats (such as Pocket Daytimer or FiloFax) and prints calendars in several formats. Some of the capabilities of BC&L are discussed in this chapter. Others are covered in the next chapter on ACT! reports.

Creating a letter

When you want to create a letter, ACT! automatically inserts the current date, the inside address of the current contact, and the salutation and closing for you. When you save an ACT! letter, it is saved without the inside address, salutation and closing, for a very good reason. The design philosophy behind ACT! is that every letter you create is a variation of something you have already created. For example, if you are a good salesperson, you routinely send letters confirming your sales appointments, then a thank you after the fact. The wording of routine communication varies little, but the fact that you take the time to generate a letter sets you apart.

With ACT!, when a letter is saved, the inside address, which is specific to a contact, is left out. When you open the letter, the inside address of the contact that you were working on when you accessed the word processor is inserted. This might sound a little confusing, but an example makes it clear.

To create a letter:

1. Use the Lookup menu to find the contact to which you want to address the letter.
2. Open the Write menu (Fig. 5-1).

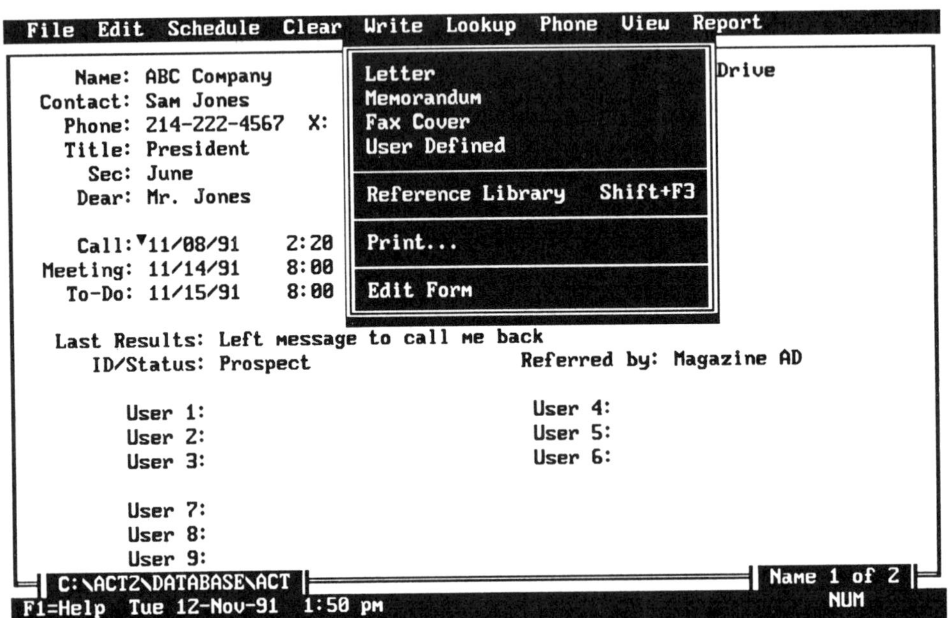

Fig. 5-1. The Write menu.

3. Highlight the Letter option, and press Enter. The ACT! word processing screen appears (Fig. 5-2).

As you can see, a new set of menu names appear at the top of the screen. The first line below the menu bar is the Ruler line, which indicates the left margin (L), the tab stops (T), and the right margin (R). The next line down is the Salutation Begin line. Because ACT! separates the inside address from the body of the letter,

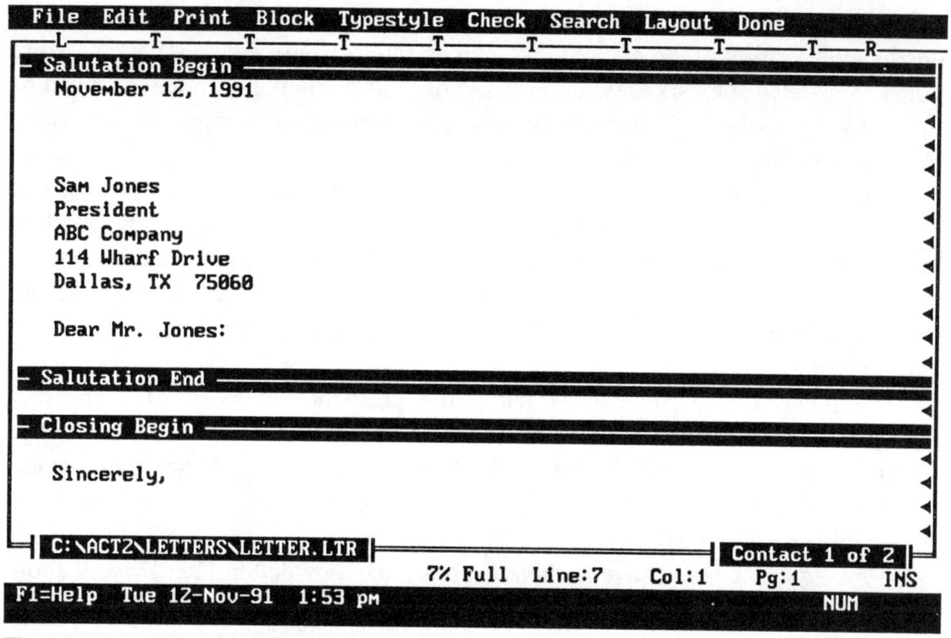

Fig. 5-2. The ACT! word processing screen.

a visual line indicates where the salutation begins and ends. In ACT! parlance, the salutation includes the current date, the inside address, and the formal salutation.

Further down the page is another horizontal line that demarks the beginning of the closing of the letter. The space between the end of the salutation and the beginning of the closing is where the body of the letter is typed.

At the bottom of the screen is a DOS path statement, which indicates the drive, directory, subdirectory, and the name of the letter. At this point, the letter is named LETTER.LTR, the default name ACT! uses before you save the letter with its own name. The second line up from the bottom is the status line. The amount of space left in memory for the letter is indicated by the percent Full (% Full). The Line indicator shows you what line on the page the cursor is on and the Col indicator shows the vertical column position of the cursor. The Pg indicator shows what page of the letter you are on and the INS shows the keyboard status. INS indicates that you are operating in Insert mode, so when you type a character, it is inserted to the right of the cursor and any letters further to the right are pushed ahead.

In the very bottom line is the F1=Help message, which alerts you that the Help screens are a keystroke away. Last, the current date and time are displayed (if your computer automatically turns the NUM LOCK key on, the word NUM is visible, too).

Entering text

Typing in ACT! is identical to typing on a typewriter. You simply type the characters you want. The blinking underline is called the *cursor*. When you type a character, the cursor moves to the right and the character appears at the cursor's previous location. Think of the computer screen as an electronic piece of paper. Before you save a letter, it exists only in the RAM of your computer and therefore can be infinitely manipulated. You can move words, sentences, and paragraphs anywhere in the letter with utmost ease.

Thc only mechanical difference between a typewriter and the computer is that you do not have to decide when to end a line of text, ACT! does it for you. This feature is called *word-wrap*. The way it works is that ACT! calculates the amount of space available on each line as you type. When you type a word that is longer than the remaining space, it moves the word down to the next line and creates a soft carriage return.

When you want to create a new paragraph, press the Enter key; ACT! inserts a hard carriage return and moves the cursor down to a new line. At the far right edge of the screen is a triangular symbol, which is the line marker. When a new paragraph is created, the triangle disappears. I prefer two carriage returns between paragraphs in my letters.

Type a sample letter, save it, then insert it into a new letter. Don't worry about spelling errors, the spellchecker will correct them.

1. Press F2, which moves the cursor into the body of the letter. The cursor should be positioned between the Salutation End and the Closing Begin lines, at the far left of the line. When you come to the end of a paragraph, press the Enter key twice.

Type the following text:

Thank you for taking the time to meet with me today. As you requested, I will be sending you a sample of my product, prior to our next meeting. You should recieve them shortly.

I would like to invite you to visit our booth at the Consumer Electronics Show. It is booth #333, and we will be exhibiting all of our new products. I have enclosed a guest pass for your use.

I hope your dog is feeling better!

2. Press F10. The menu bar is activated, and your letter should resemble the one in Fig. 5-3.

Saving a letter

After creating a letter, and before adding enhancements and spellchecking, it is a good idea to save the letter. That way, if by accident you exited out of the word processor (to take a phone call, for example), you would not lose your work. Plus, after making edits, you might find that the original draft was better and you would rather use it instead.

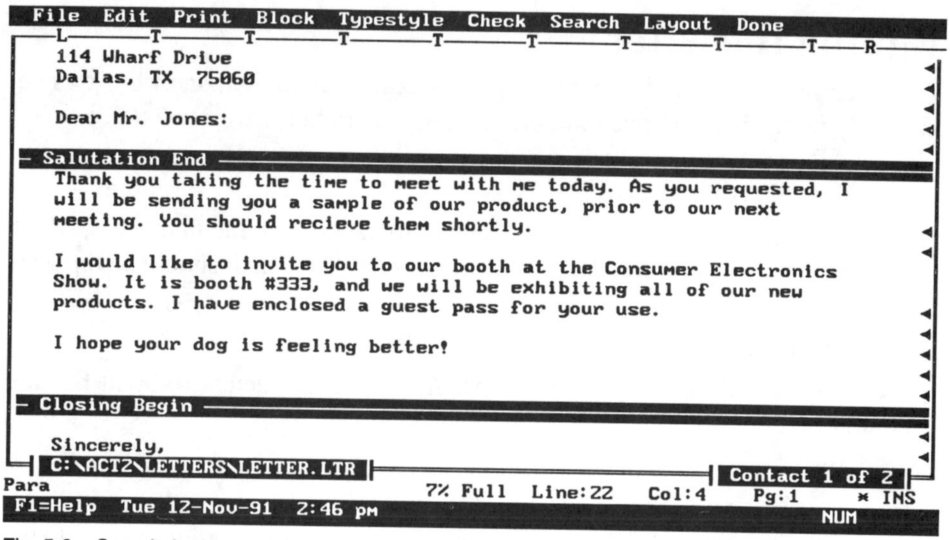

Fig. 5-3. Sample Letter.

To save the letter:

1. Open the File menu, and select the Save option. The File Directory window opens (Fig. 5-4).
2. Type TEST
3. Press Enter. The File Directory window closes. Notice at the bottom left of the screen that the name of the letter has changed from LETTER.LTR to TEST.LTR.

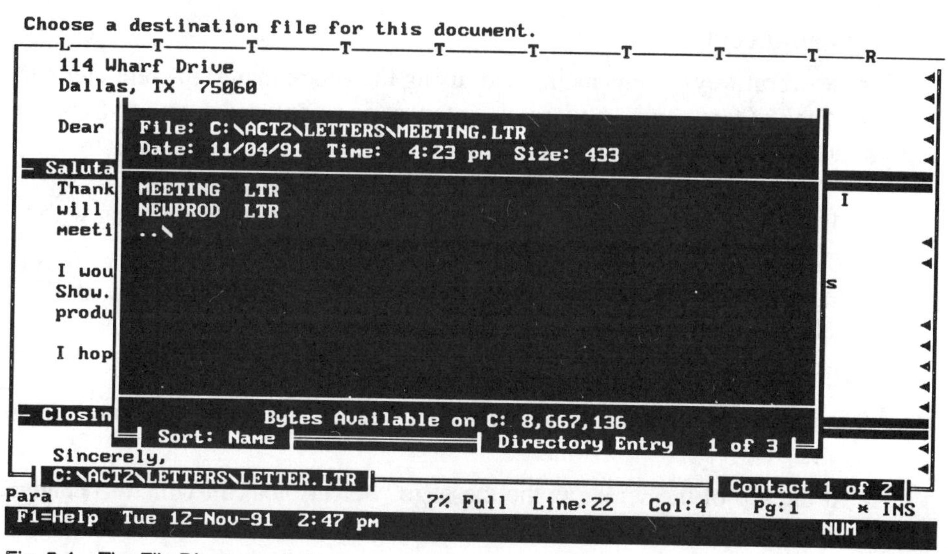

Fig. 5-4. The File Directory window.

Editing the letter

This letter needs editing. If you have typed it exactly as shown, one word was deliberately misspelled and one sentence has passive, rather than active voice.

1. To begin editing, press F2.
2. Use the arrow keys to move the cursor to the second line in the text, which begins with the words *I will be*. *Will be* is passive, and it should be replaced with the active *am*.
3. Position the cursor on the letter *w* in *will*.
4. Press the Delete key seven times. All of the characters in "will be" are erased.
5. Type AM
6. Notice that the word *meeting* is in the third line of the letter. Press the down arrow key once. ACT! adjusts the text and moves the word *meeting* into the second line. This happens because ACT! formats the letter so that every line of the letter has the maximum number of characters.

Erasing an entire line

The last line of the letter regarding the health of the dog should be completely erased.

1. Move the cursor to the beginning of the sentence.
2. Press F5. ACT! erases the entire line.

Adding enhancements

ACT! has several ways of enhancing text, using the Block menu. In computer parlance, a *Block* of text can be a word, a sentence, or an entire document. Suppose that you want to make the invitation to your booth at the show stand out.

1. Move the cursor to the second paragraph at the sentence beginning with "I would like."
2. Press and hold the ALT key, then press B. The Block menu opens (Fig. 5-5).
3. Highlight the Typestyle option and press Enter.
4. From the submenu, highlight the Continuous underline item and press Enter.
5. At the top of the screen is the message "Select block in which to change typestyle." ACT! needs to know which letters, words, sentences or paragraphs that you want to block.

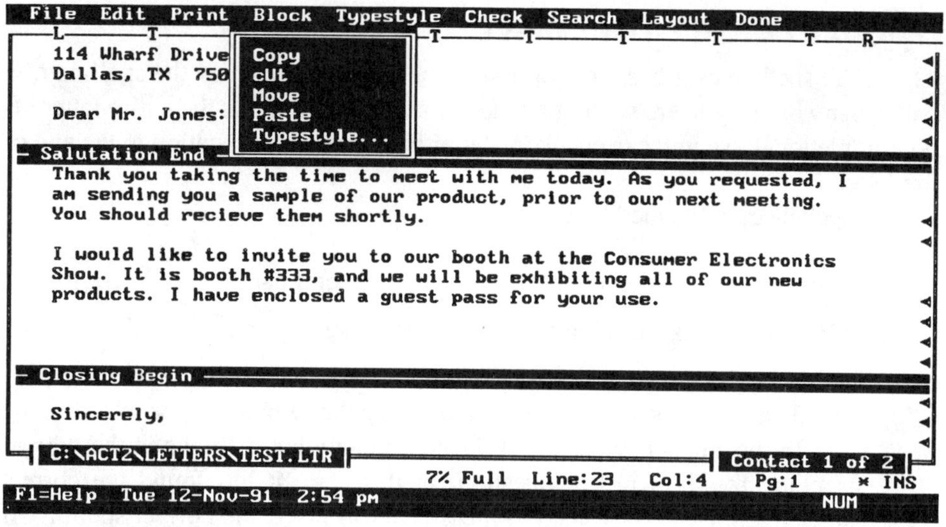

Fig. 5-5. The Block menu.

6. Press the right arrow key to extend the cursor over the entire sentence (Fig. 5-6).
7. Press Enter.

On a color screen, the enhanced sentence appears in a different color. On a black and white screen, the sentence displays in a different intensity. Notice that the second line up from the bottom left of the screen is the message "Font-Cont. Underline." ACT! identifies the type of formatting used, as determined by the position of the cursor.

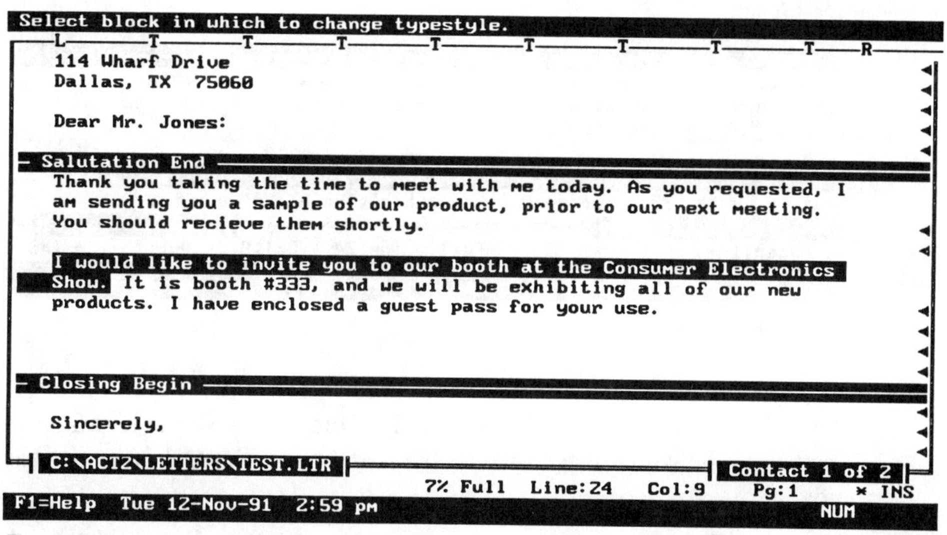

Fig. 5-6. The sentence blocked.

Spellchecking the letter

The ACT! spellchecker has three options. One option is to verify the spelling of a particular word as you are writing a letter. A second is to check the entire letter after completion. Last, you can check the letter from the cursor location to the end of the letter.

To spellcheck a finished letter:

1. Press F10 to exit the letter and activate the menu bar.
2. Open the Check menu and select the Document option.
3. ACT! begins to verify the spelling of each word. In Fig. 5-7, a misspelled word has been located (recieve) and the Speller window appears.

   In the Speller window, ACT! highlights what it thinks is the correct spelling for the word in question. In this case, it has found the correct spelling and you only need to press Enter to insert the correct spelling. If ACT! cannot find a substitute spelling, no list of suggested words appears.

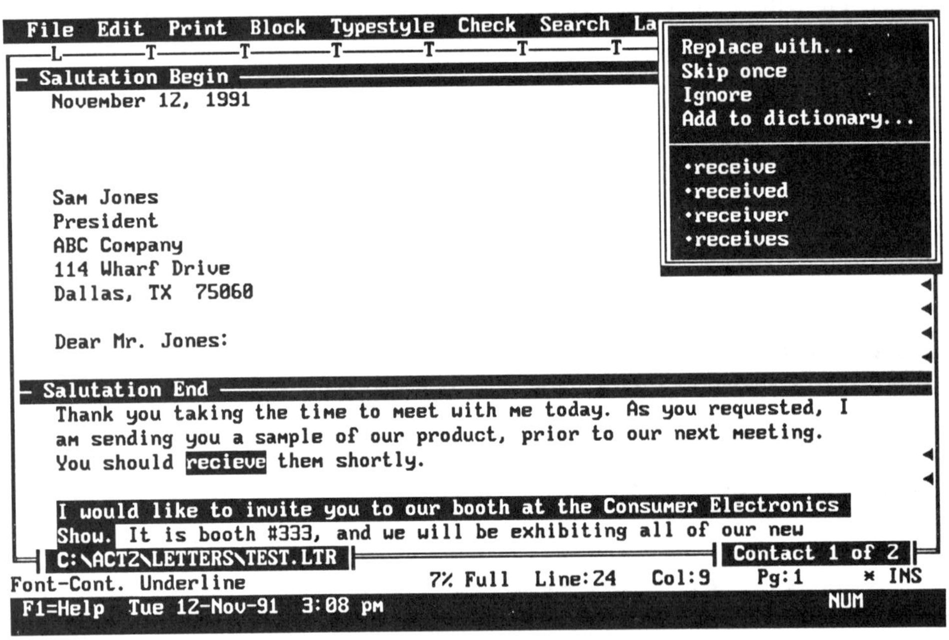

Fig. 5-7. The speller window.

4. Press Enter to accept ACT!'s suggested spelling or move the highlight to another of the words listed as possible corrections. Several other options are:

   Replace with Select this item to type in the correct spelling of the word.

Skip once ACT! ignores this particular misspelling, but stops if it finds it again.

Ignore The misspelled word is ignored throughout the entire letter.

Add to dictionary Select this item to add words that ACT! is not familiar with the spellchecker dictionary. When prompted to enter the word, make it precise, and include upper or lowercase.

5. Press Enter to finish the spellcheck. When completed, ACT! displays a window alerting you to the number of words checked. This feature is handy if you need to know the word length of your documents.

   A quirk of all spellcheckers is that they do not perform well with people's names and addresses. So, many ACT! users position the cursor in the first line of the letter, and select the All Remaining option, thereby ignoring the inside address and salutation.

Resaving a letter

After making changes to a letter, you can save it under the save file name or you can create a new one. By creating a new name, you can create a draft, revise the letter and save it again so that both versions are available. Normally, the user will save a letter, make changes, and then resave it.

1. Press F10.
2. Open the File menu and select Save. The File Directory window opens and ACT! inserts the name of the letter in the File field. The highlight is positioned on the file name. If you press an arrow key and highlight a different file, ACT! displays its attributes, such as the date and time it was created and the size of the file in bytes.
3. Press Enter. ACT! displays a message, asking you if you want to replace the existing file.
4. Answer Yes and the edited file replaces the previously saved file. If you answer No, you can create a new file name by typing it.

Saving a letter to a different drive or directory

When ACT! is installed, it automatically creates several subdirectories, one of which is used to store your letters. DOS uses the term *path* to describe how it saves files in specific locations. For example, if your hard disk is designated as drive C, the DOS path for letters is C:\ACT\LETTERS\.

Suppose that you want to save a letter named NEW.LTR to a floppy disk and that disk is in drive A. Follow these steps:

1. Press F10 to activate the menu bar.
2. Open the File menu and select the Save option. The File Directory window opens and the default path is displayed in the File field.

3. Press Escape several times until ACT! erases the current path completely.
4. Type A:NEW
5. Press Enter. The letter is saved to drive A. ACT! uses its own word processing file format, so you cannot access the letter unless you are using ACT!. However, if you need to save a letter that can be used by any word processor, the File menu Export item can do so.

Exporting an ACT! letter

If you want to use a letter created in ACT! in a different word processor, you can do so using the Export item on the File menu.

1. Press F10 to activate the menu bar.
2. Open the File menu, and select Export.
3. In the File Directory window, enter the path and the name of the file. For example, ACT! expects that you are going to export the current document to an existing file. Normally, you are not going to do that, but instead are saving the file either on a floppy disk or in a different directory on your hard disk. If the floppy disk is drive A:, press Escape until the path is erased and type A: and the name of the file. ACT! automatically adds a TXT extension. The letter is stored in ASCII format, which any word processor can import.

Printing an ACT! letter

Before you can print a letter, you must first install your printer. Because ACT! automatically assumes that you want to print an envelope after you print a letter, you should follow the steps to setup envelope printing at the same time. When you installed ACT!, you were prompted to install two printers. If you want to make a change, or did not install any printers, follow these directions:

1. From the word processing screen, open the Print menu and select Options. Or, from the Contact record screen, open the Write menu, select Print, and Options.
2. From the Options submenu, select Printer 1. The Printer 1 Options screen appears (Fig. 5-8). Fortunately, you do not have to type in the myriad of control codes that your printer needs, ACT! does it for you.
3. The highlight should be in the Printer Name field. Press F2. ACT! displays a list of printer models in alphabetical order. Use the up or down arrow keys to scroll the list and find your printer, or type the first letter of the printer name.
4. With the highlight on the printer name, press Enter. ACT! inserts the name and the attendant printer codes in the printer window.

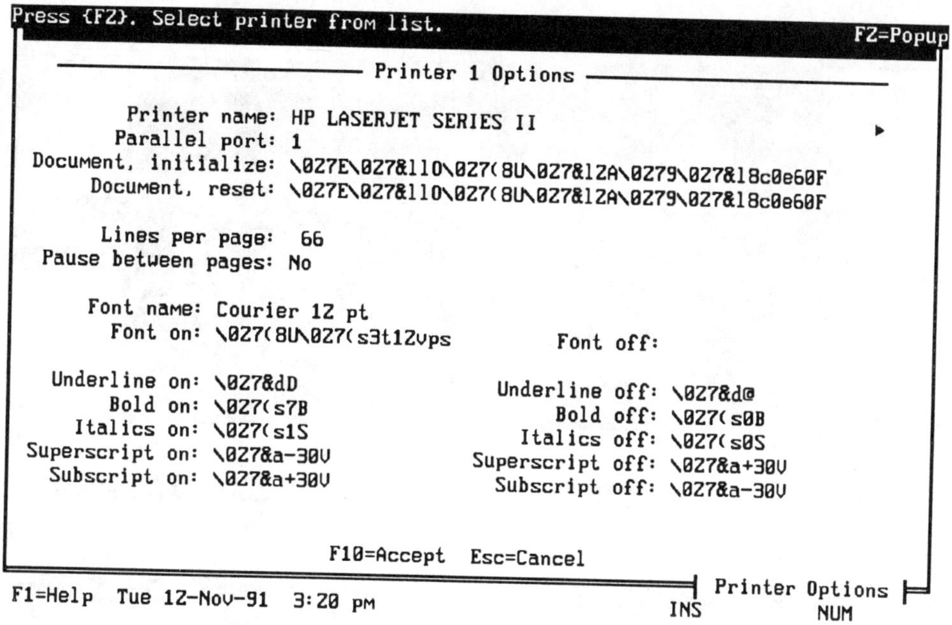

Fig. 5-8. The Printer 1 menu.

5. The Parallel port must be indicated. Normally, the setting is 1.
6. In the Pause Between Pages Field, enter Yes if your printer can print only a single page at a time.
7. Press F10 to save the settings.

If you have a second printer, select the Printer 2 item and follow the same steps. By installing two printers, you can use one for documents and one for envelopes or labels.

Installing the envelope defaults

The default settings that ACT! uses usually work, but if you are using a laser printer, you will have to install the setup codes to print envelopes.

1. From the word processing screen, open the Print menu and select Options. Or, from the Contact record screen, open the Write menu, select Print, and Options.
2. From the submenu, select Envelopes. The Default Envelope Settings displays (Fig. 5-9).
3. Enter the size of your envelope. If it is a standard #10, the default settings work. If you are using a laser printer, move the highlight to the Printer Setup field and press F2. With any luck, the printer you have is listed in the

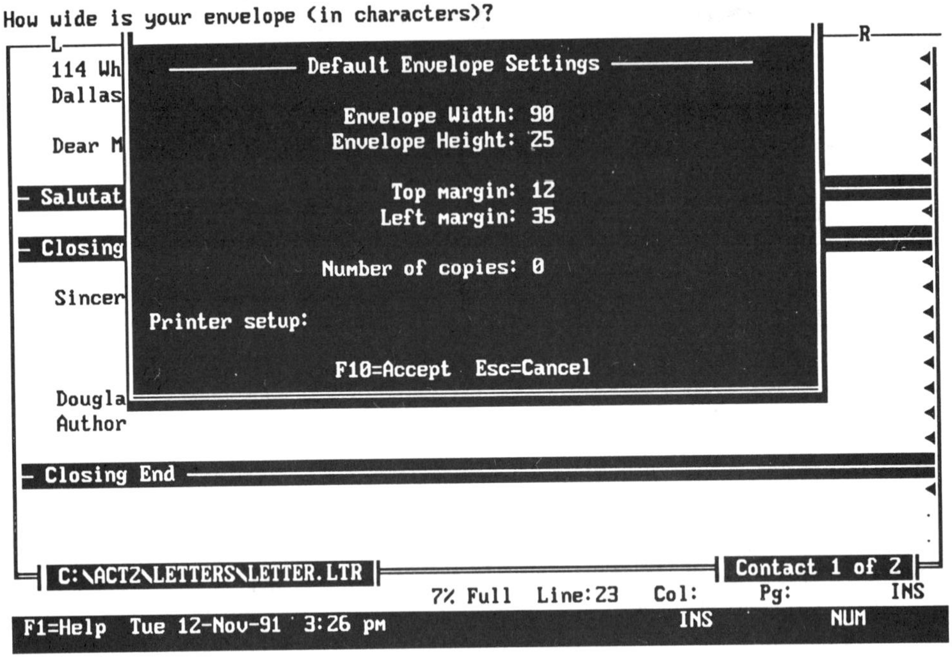

Fig. 5-9. The Default Envelope Settings.

Popup. Otherwise, you will have to locate the printer codes yourself. If you are using a laser printer, such as the HP IIP, you must also enter new margins. The settings for the HP IIP are:

Width: 95	Top: 10
Height: 19	Left: 45

In the Printer Setup field, press F2. From the Popup window, select the item that corresponds to your printer. As a result of the length of the printer setup codes, the name of the printer is followed by the codes in the field below the name.

4. Press F10. With the printer type installed, and the envelope settings you can now print the letter.

Printing after installation

1. Open the Print menu and select document. ACT! opens the Print To window.
2. Select the printer you have installed and press Enter. ACT! displays the Print Control window (Fig. 5-10). To change the print options, select Edit. The following options are available.

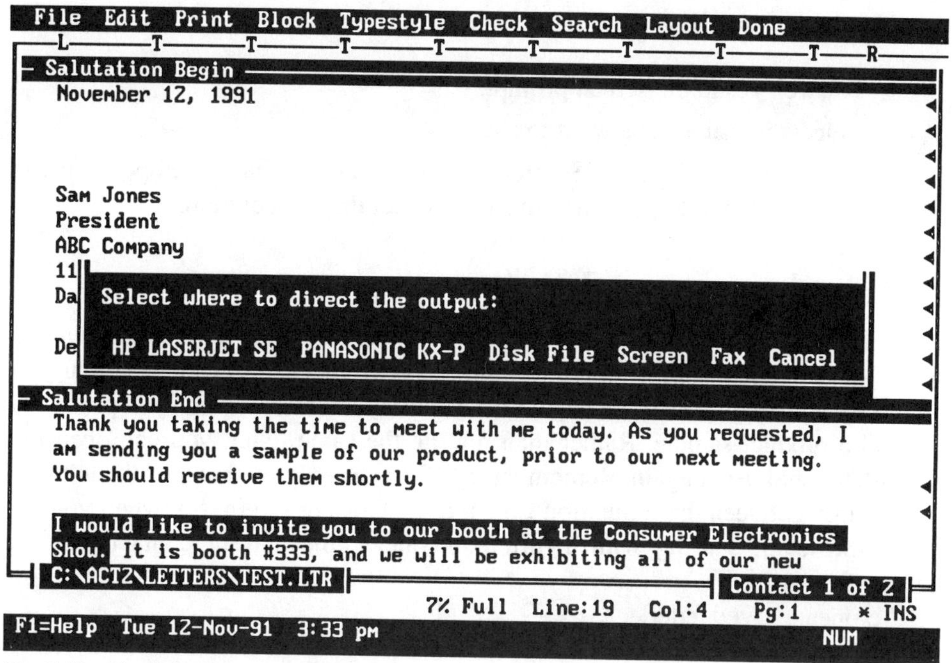

Fig. 5-10. The Print Control window.

Start page Select this option to start printing on a page other than the first page. For example, if your letter was four pages long and you wanted to print only the last page, you would enter 4.

End page Select this option to determine the last page printed. For example, if your letter was four pages long and you wanted to print only pages one and two, enter 2 here. The default of 999 prints from the Start page setting to the end of the document.

Pause between pages Select this option to override the installation setting. For example, if you have a laser printer and want the first page of the letter to be printed on a different type of paper from the rest of the letter, use this option to stop printing after the first page. ACT! prompts you to restart printing when ready.

3. Select Ok. After the file is sent to the printer, ACT! displays the message Is this a finished document that will be sent out? If you answer Yes, the letter is recorded as being sent in the History file and in Contact Screen 2.

   Proofread the letter before you answer the prompt. If you answer Yes and the letter needs to be reprinted, you can inadvertently record two letters as having been sent instead of one.

4. If you answered Yes to the previous prompt, ACT! will then prompt you as to whether you want to print an envelope.

To print the envelope:

1. Answer Yes to the screen prompt.
2. Select the printer you want to use.
3. Press Enter at the Print Session Options window. The envelope prints. If you decide not to print the envelope, select the Cancel item.

Retrieving a saved letter

The TEST.LTR letter file that you created could be used with some modifications for all of the contacts you wanted to invite to visit your booth. Suppose that you had a second meeting the same day with a different contact, in which you promised to send a product sample. Rather than rewrite the same letter, you can open the saved letter and use it again. Remember, ACT! saves only the body of the letter—that portion between the Salutation End and the Closing Begin. So, when you retrieve the letter, starting with a different contact, the current contact's inside address is used.

To open a saved letter:

1. Use the Lookup menu to find the contact to which you want to address the letter.
2. Open the Write menu and select Letter. The word processing screen appears. The current contact's inside address is inserted.
3. Open the File menu and select Open. The File Directory window opens.
4. Position the highlight on the name of the letter you want to open. To verify it as the correct letter, check the information line at the top of the window, which displays the date the letter was created.
5. Press Enter. The body of the letter is retrieved. Exiting from the File Directory window without retrieving or saving a file requires that you press Escape several times. A faster way to exit is to press and hold the Shift key and then press Escape.

Creating a form letter

If you have ever tried to create a form letter with a word processor and database program, you know that you have to be a computer programmer to figure it out. Creating a form letter in ACT! is no different than creating any other letter. The difference is what you do before you access the word processor.

The first step in creating an ACT! form letter is to use the Lookup menu to find a group of contacts. For example, if you have been identifying your Contacts by inserting the word Prospect in the ID/Status field, simply look up the Contacts by that classification and you have the group. If you have a more complex lookup to perform, such as all the contacts in a certain zip code, and have entered "Prospect" in the ID/Status field, use the Lookup menu and the Your Criteria item to group the Contacts, as explained in chapter 2.

The designers of ACT! wanted to make it as easy as possible to create form letters. So, you can successfully create form letters in two ways. The first is to group the Contact records before opening the word processor, then opening a previously saved letter. It is used for the body of the letter or to create a new letter from scratch.

When you access the Form Letter item from the Print menu, ACT! inserts the contact information as always. However, when ACT! is directed to print the document, it creates and prints form letters for every Contact record that was a part of the group when you opened the word processor.

Secondly, you can create a file that is a form and is saved in a different subdirectory from the letters. The creation of a customized form letter is discussed later in this chapter. Then, when you access the Write menu from the Contact record screen, and select Print and then Form letter, ACT! assumes that you want to use a file that was created specifically as a form.

To print a form letter using a letter:

1. Use the Lookup menu to select a group of contacts.
2. Open the Write menu and select Letter.
3. Create a new letter or retrieve a saved letter.
4. Open the Print menu and select Form Letter. ACT! displays the Print To window. To check if the letter is going to the correct group of contacts, you can print the letters to the screen first. If you are satisfied with the group, open the Print menu and select Form Letter, sending the output to your printer.

Printing envelopes or labels to match the form letters

If you want to print envelopes or mailing labels for the form letters, follow these steps:

1. Open the Print menu and select either the Mailing Labels or the Bulk Envelopes item.
2. ACT! displays the Print To window. Select the printer or print them to the screen to verify the addresses. ACT! prints the labels or envelopes.

If your mailing labels did not print correctly, use the following steps to modify the settings:

1. Open the Print menu and select Options.
2. From the submenu, select Mailing Labels. The Default Mailing Label Settings window opens.

3. If you know the label type, press F2 and select from the list presented. If you do not know the type, select the Continuous Form Labels item and enter values as to height, width, margins, etc. You might have to experiment with these settings in order to print the labels properly. Before it begins printing, ACT! asks if you wish to align the printer. This is the opportunity to test print a few labels.
4. Press F10 to save the new envelopes settings.

Suppose that you got interrupted after printing the letters and forgot to print the labels or envelopes. You can print them at a later time by exercising the following steps.

1. Use the Lookup menu to find the same group of Contacts that you used to create the form letters.
2. Open the Write menu and select Print.
3. From the submenu, select the Print item. Another submenu opens. Select the Envelopes item. The Print To window opens; choose where you want the output to print. ACT! also offers the opportunity to print a label just for the current Contact, the current group (the correct choice for a form letter), or for all Contacts.

Looking at forms

ACT! uses prebuilt forms to insert information into letters, memos, and fax cover sheets. When you access the form, it looks for the information in the current Contact and inserts the information where directed. All of ACT!'s forms can be modified to fit your needs. Take a moment to look at the structure of the LETTER.FRM to understand how it can be modified.

1. Open the Write menu and select the Edit Form item. Or, from the word processing screen open the Layout menu, select the Form item and from the submenu, select Open. The File Directory window opens with a list of all the ACT! forms.
2. Position the highlight on the LETTER.FRM and press Enter. The form appears (Fig. 5-11), and the word processing menu appears at the top of the screen, even if you have accessed the form from the Contact record screen. As you can see, the form is a template. Each piece of information that is inserted into the Contact record has its own unique identifier. For example, to have ACT! insert the entry from the Name field, the form has a [#NAME] as its identifier. You can insert the contact information to see how the form works.
3. Open the Layout menu and select the Form item.

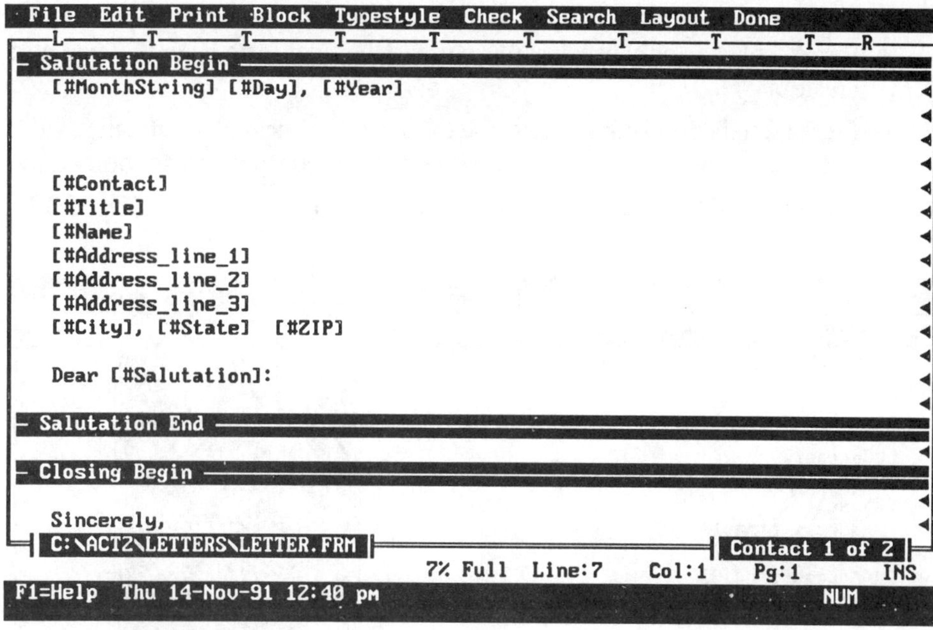

Fig. 5-11. The LETTER.FRM.

4. From the submenu, select the Fill-in item. ACT! inserts the information from the current Contact into the form.

Get the idea? Now you can modify one of the prebuilt forms to create the customized Confirm form.

Creating a customized form letter

Creating a customized form letter is easy to do, so open one of the forms that is provided with ACT!, modify it, and save it under a different name. Using this method, the result is that you have two forms, one that is used as a template, and one that you have customized. Earlier in this chapter, the method for creating a form letter was discussed using a saved letter or by typing a new letter. Now, you are going to create a specialized file that is saved as a FORM. When you saved a new form, ACT! adds the three letter extension .FRM to the name. This is the second method for creating form letters, as was mentioned before.

1. Assuming that you are still in the word processor, press F10 to access the menus. If you are in a Contact record, open the Write menu and select Edit Form, then go to step 4.
2. Open the Layout menu and select Form.
3. Select Open. ACT! prompts as to whether or not to discard the current file. Answer Yes and the File Directory window appears.

4. Position the highlight on the AMERICAN.FRM and press Enter (This form is selected only because it is close to the final form letter that you will create).
5. Press F2 to begin editing. Move the cursor to the line under Salutation End. Type the following text: Just a note to confirm our meeting scheduled for
6. Press F2. ACT! displays the list of Contact record field names (Fig. 5-12).

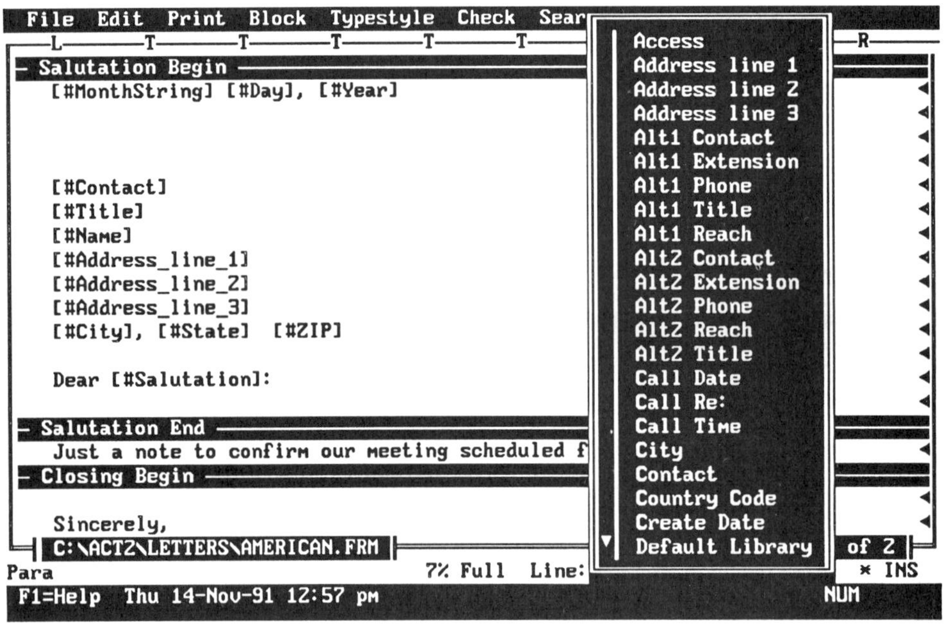

Fig. 5-12. The Contact record field names list.

7. Use the down arrow to scroll the list so that the highlight is positioned on the Meet Date field name.
8. Press Enter. The [#Meet_Date] identifier is entered into the letter.
9. Now add the time of the meeting, too. Press the space bar once. Press F2 to open the field name list. Scroll the list until the highlight is positioned on the Meet Time field name.
10. Press Enter. The Meet Time identifier [#Meet_Time] is inserted in the text. Type a period to end the sentence and press Enter to create a new paragraph.
11. Type the following text: I look forward to meeting with you. If you need to reach me prior to our meeting, please call me at
12. Press and hold the Shift key, then press F2. ACT! displays a different list. Part of the list is of date and time variables and the rest are manager identifiers.

13. Scroll the list until the highlight is positioned on the ManagerPhone field name. Press Enter to insert the field name in the letter. Finish the sentence with a period. The CONFIRM form is complete, now you need to save it for later use. Your form should appear as the one in Fig. 5-13.
14. Press F10 to activate the menu bar and open the Layout menu. Select the Form item and from the submenu Save. The File Directory opens and ACT! assumes that you are resaving the AMERICAN form, because that was the form on which you were working. ACT! also inserts the file name in the File field at the top of the directory window.
15. Type CONFIRM. The file name AMERICAN is erased and replaced by the new name, CONFIRM.

The new form is saved as CONFIRM.FRM. Because you gave it a new name, the AMERICAN.FRM is still available for use. The CONFIRM form remains on the screen.

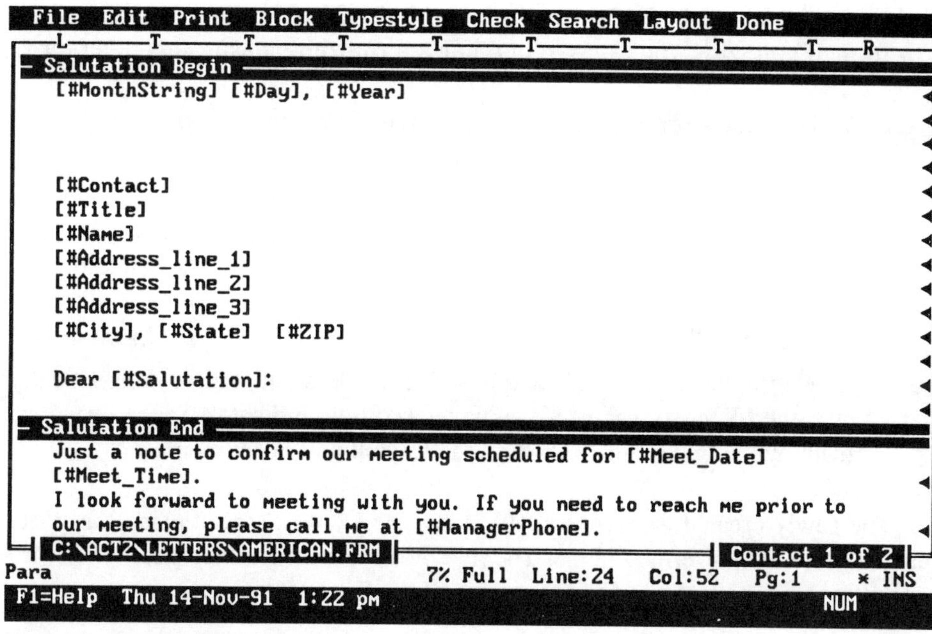

Fig. 5-13. The completed CONFIRM form.

Testing the new form

To test the Confirm form, you need to schedule a meeting with a contact. Any contact will work, as you can later erase the meeting after the test.

1. With the contact that has a meeting scheduled on screen, open the Write menu and select the User-Defined item.

2. The File Directory list of forms appears. Position the highlight on the CONFIRM.FRM form and press Enter. ACT! inserts information from the Contact into the letter, including the date and time of the meeting. Notice too that ACT! switches automatically to the word processing screen.

   Think about the possibilities this opens to you for automating your correspondence! Those routine letters, that you always intended to send but never got around to doing, are completed with the correct information in seconds. You can create a limitless number of user-defined forms and field identifiers that you can include in the form.

   Note: ACT! 2.1 also includes a macro capability. With a macro, you can automate the process even further by creating a macro to open the form letter, print the letter, and return to the Contact record with a pair of keystrokes!

More on forms

In the previous example, a form that came with ACT! was used as the basis for a new form. If you wish, you can start building a form without using any other form.

1. While in the word processor, open the Layout menu.
2. Select the Form option from the submenu, New. ACT! displays the word processing screen, including the lines for the salutation and closing. If you wish, you can delete either set of lines by positioning the cursor on one of the lines and pressing Delete. If you decide to reinsert the Salutation or Closing lines, use the Layout menu and the Form option and select Salutation or Closing; ACT! inserts your choice at the cursor location.
3. Create the new form, and save it with the File menu. ACT! automatically adds the FRM extension. If you have used field indicators in the form, test them by using the Fill-In item on the Layout and Form menu.

The newly created form is available from the Contact screen using the Write menu and the User-Defined items. The new form is also available from the word processing screen using the Layout menu and the Form, Retrieve items.

Changing the letter margins

ACT! assumes that you are printing on standard 8.5-x-11 inch paper. If you use nonstandard-size paper, you need to adjust the margins.

To change the page margins:

1. Open the Write menu and select Letter.
2. Open the Layout menu and select Page. The Page Layout Options window displays. Select Edit and enter the new margins.

3. Press F10 to save the new margins. Select Cancel or press Escape if you do not want to save the changed margins.

Adding a rule

Besides changing the font style to add emphasis to text, you can insert a second rule in the letter with margins or tab stops that are different from the default settings. One common use of this feature is when you wish to set off a column of numbers or a long quotation.

To insert a second rule:

1. Move the cursor in the text to the position where you want the new rule.
2. Press F10 to activate the menu bar and open the Layout menu.
3. Select the Rule option and press Enter. The new rule is inserted and you can edit the left and right margins and the tab stops. For example, to change a margin setting, move the cursor to the column you want and type the letter that corresponds to the margin, an L for Left and an R for Right. To add a tab stop, move the cursor to the column and type a T. To erase a tab stop, position the cursor on the T, which represents the tab stop and press Delete.
4. To begin typing, press the down arrow key so that the cursor is off of the rule and proceed. If you are using different margins to indicate a quotation, when you have finished typing the quotation, use the Layout menu to insert another rule. Text typed after that rule is formatted to the default margins.

Inserting a hard page break

In letters or other documents, you might wish to insert a hard page break before the place where ACT! automatically ends a page. When you print the letter, ACT! stops printing at the break and continues printing on the following page.

1. Position the cursor at the point in the letter where you want the page to break.
2. Press F10 to activate the menu bar.
3. Open the Layout menu and select the Page Break option.

ACT! inserts a large horizontal bar on-screen at the page break, as seen in Fig. 5-14. Use the up or down arrow keys to move the cursor from one page to another.

Deleting a hard page break

1. Position the cursor on the line that includes the words "hard page break."
2. Press the Delete key.

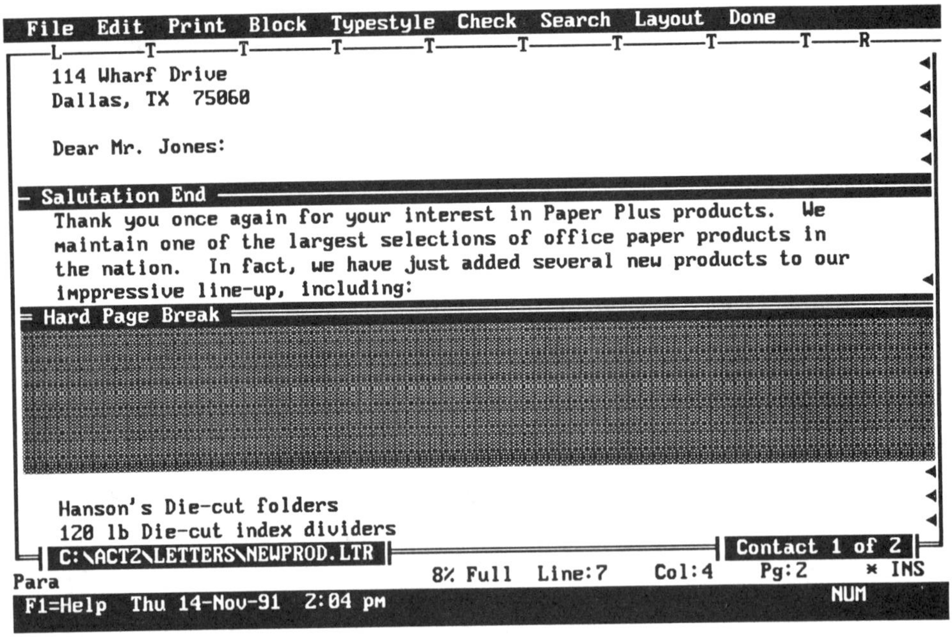

Fig. 5-14. The Hard page break maker.

Hiding and displaying the rules and form lines

You can hide the display of the lines that indicate the Salutation and Closing, and any secondary rule that you have inserted.

1. Press F10 to activate the menu bar.
2. Open the Layout menu and select Hide.

The lines are removed from the screen, but are still active.
To redisplay the lines and any rules:

1. Press F10.
2. Open the Layout menu and select the Display item.

The Lines and inserted rules are redisplayed.

Extracting and combining word-processed files

In the course of creating letters, you might use paragraphs or tables of information frequently. Rather than retrieving an entire letter, some of which might not pertain to the current letter, you can extract those frequently used paragraphs and save each in a unique file. Then, when you want to use the information again, you can combine them into the current letter.

To extract a portion of a file:

1. With the document on screen that has the text you want to extract, move the cursor to the beginning position in the text and press F10.
2. Open the File menu, and select eXtract.
3. ACT! prompts you to select a block of text. Use the arrow keys to extend the highlight over the text you want to extract.
4. Press Enter. ACT! displays the File Directory window, listing all of the subdirectories of ACT!.
5. Type in a file name for the text. If you want to save the new file in the Letters subdirectory, include that as part of the name. For example, press Escape to delete the current entry in the File field at the top of the window and type LETTERS\NEW.LTR and press Enter. In this particular instance, you must add the extension (the three letters after the period) you want.

Combining the extracted file with a current letter

1. Position the cursor in the letter where you want the text to be inserted.
2. Press F10 and open the File menu.
3. Select the Combine option. ACT! displays the File Directory window, including all letters, memos, and forms that you have created.
4. Position the cursor on the file name that you want to insert into the current letter and press Enter.

Importing a file

At times, you might want to access a file from a word processor other than ACT! or from the 1.0 version of ACT!. In either case, the Import option allows you to do so. If the file is from another word processor, it must be saved as an ASCII file before it can be imported. All word processors are capable of saving files to disk in ASCII format.

1. With the letter on screen into which you want to import another letter, position the cursor where you want the text to be inserted.
2. Press F10 and open the File menu.
3. Select the Import option. ACT! displays the File Directory window, but lists the subdirectories of ACT!, not the files.
4. Press Escape several times to erase the entry in the File field and type in the path and name of the file you wish to import. For example, if the file you want to import is stored in the directory Word on the C drive and is named INTER.DOC, you would type C:\WORD\INTER.DOC.

5. After entering the name of the file, press Enter. The file is imported, but special formatting is removed.

Exporting to an ASCII file

As is true with all word processors, ACT! can export a file to a standard ASCII format. After you have created a file in ACT! and saved it, follow these steps to export the file:

1. With the letter on screen that you want to export, press F10 and open the File menu.
2. Select the Export item. ACT! opens the File Directory window and lists any files with a .TXT extension. The TXT extension is ACT!'s (and most word processor's) way of identifying ASCII files.
3. Press Escape until the File field is erased. Enter a path and file name. For example, if you wanted to save the file to a disk in the A drive, you would type A:GONE.TXT.
4. Press Enter. The file is saved to disk and the File Directory window closes.

Creating a new file

After you create a letter to a contact and have saved and printed it, you might want to create a second letter. Rather than trying to erase all of the current letter, the New option on the File menu erases the letter entirely:

1. Press F10 and open the File menu.
2. Select the New option. ACT! prompts you as to whether you want to erase the template, which is the inside address, salutation, and closing lines. Answering No erases only the body of text. Answering Yes erases the entire screen.

Creating memos

ACT! has prebuilt formats for memos and fax covers. To create a memo with the prebuilt form, follow these steps:

1. From the Contact screen, open the Write menu and select Memorandum.
2. The Memorandum form appears with the current date and the contact's name inserted. ACT! uses the almost same format as for letters in terms of what portion of the memo is saved. That is, the portion after the end of the salutation is saved. So, you can use the memo repeatedly with different contacts.

3. Edit the memo and press F10 to activate the menu bar. You can print it directly or save it before printing.

   After you print the memo, ACT! does not ask if you wish to print an envelope. If you want an envelope, open the Print menu and select the Envelope item.

Creating a fax cover

The fax cover includes the fax number of the contact if you have entered it into the Contact screen. A prescient touch that obviates the need to track down the number after you get in line at the fax machine.

To print a fax cover sheet:

1. From the Contact screen, select the Write menu.
2. Select the fax option. ACT! displays the fax cover with the receiver's fax number if you have recorded it.
3. Edit the fax cover as needed and press F10 to activate the menu bar.
4. Open the Print menu and select Document. Select the print destination.

Deleting a file

From the word processing screen:

1. Press F10 and open the File menu.
2. Select the Delete item. ACT! opens the File Directory window and displays all of the letter files you have created. If you want to delete a different sort of file, such as a memo or a form, press Escape twice and type *.MMO (for forms, type *.FRM). All of the files with those extensions are displayed.
3. Position the highlight on the file you want to delete and press Enter. ACT! verifies that you want to delete the file. Select Yes.

Printing rotary index cards

Long before computers there were Rolodex cards. In fact, most every business in the world has at least one set somewhere in the office. Before you can print the cards, you need to purchase continuous-feed cards from your stationery store. Avery makes rotary index cards in sheet form; these are helpful if you have a laser printer.

To print Rolodex cards:

1. Open the Write menu and select Print.
2. From the submenu, select the Rotary Index Cards item. The Print To

Window opens, so select the destination. After you select the printer to use, ACT! prompts you as to whether or not you want to print only the current Contact, the currently selected group, or all Contacts in the database.

Updating the Rolodex card file

After you have printed the cards, you will need to update them as you enter new Contacts. ACT!'s powerful lookup capability makes it easy to determine which of the Contacts does not have a card.

In chapter 1, it was suggested that you enter a Contact called Me, for those activities that did not fit neatly into other Contacts. When you print the cards, make a note in your personal Contact record of the date that the Rolodex cards were printed. That way, you have a date to work with for updating. The next step is to create a Boolean search for those Contacts that were created after the card print date.

To update the Rolodex cards:

1. After determining the date of the previous printing of cards, open the Lookup menu and select the Your Criteria item.
2. From the new menu, select Query.
3. Press F2 to begin editing.
4. Move the cursor to the Field column.
5. Press F2. ACT! displays the list of field names.
6. Position the highlight on the Create Date field name and press Enter. The field name is inserted and the cursor moves to the Op (operator) field.
7. Because you want a date later than your last print date, enter the greater than sign (>) in the operator field. The cursor moves to the Value field.
8. In the Value field, enter the prior print date.
9. Press F10 to save the Query.
10. Select GO from the menu bar. ACT! performs the search and returns the number of Contacts found that were entered into the database after the last time you printed rotary index cards.
11. Open the Write menu and select Print. You are prompted for the number of pages to print. Select OK. ACT! asks if you wish to align the printer, which is a good idea to make sure the cards print properly. After the test, ACT! asks if you want to print This Contact, the Group, or All. Select Group.

ACT! prints the cards for your newer entries. Of course, if you were really efficient you should print a card immediately upon entering the new contact in the database.

Sending a fax from ACT!

You must have version 2.1 of ACT! to send a fax document directly from ACT!, and have installed either an Intel SatisFAXion or a Hayes JT fax board, and the corresponding fax software before you can follow the ACT! install steps. In chapter 4, the instructions for installing a modem were given. You must follow those same steps to get your fax board to work (even if you do not have a modem).

To install your fax board in ACT!, do the following:

1. From the Contact record screen, open the File menu.
2. Select the Connect item.
3. From the submenu, select Options.
4. From the submenu, select fax options. ACT! displays the fax board setup window.
5. With the highlight in the fax board field, press F2. The two fax board options are shown in Fig. 5-15.
6. Highlight the type of fax board you have in your computer and press Enter.
7. Enter your area code and your country code. The international country code for the United States is 001. Some of the other international codes are listed in Table 5-1.
8. Press F10 to save the settings.

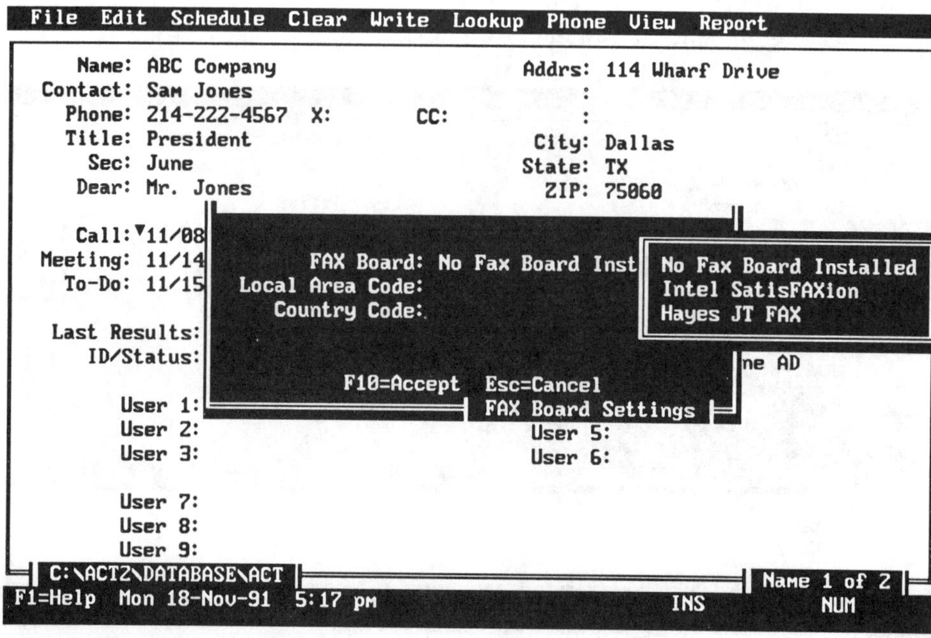

Fig. 5-15. The Fax board options.

Table 5-1 International Country Codes.

Australia	61	Ireland	353
Austria	43	Italy	39
Belgium	32	Japan	81
Canada	1	Mexico	52
France	33	Spain	34
Germany	49	Switzerland	41
Greece	30	United Kingdom	44
Hong Kong	853	United States	001

From the word processor, after you open the Print menu and select Document, ACT! lists the possible outputs for the document. One of the choices is fax. Selecting fax, causes ACT! to display a window asking if the fax (or faxes) should be sent immediately or at a later time. If you select Now, ACT! sends the document to the fax board and the software that comes with the board takes control.

If you decide to send the fax or faxes later, ACT! saves the document in a special file. The file is called the fax *spool* and is akin to a spool of wire. Later, when you are ready to send the fax, you can do so by following these steps:

1. From the Contact record screen, open the File menu.
2. Select the Connect item.
3. From the submenu, select fax. Two choices are presented, Send all Now, which directs ACT! to start sending the fax spool to the fax software. The Review Pending item opens a window (Fig. 5-16) if you have a fax or faxes pending. If none are pending, ACT! displays a message alerting you.

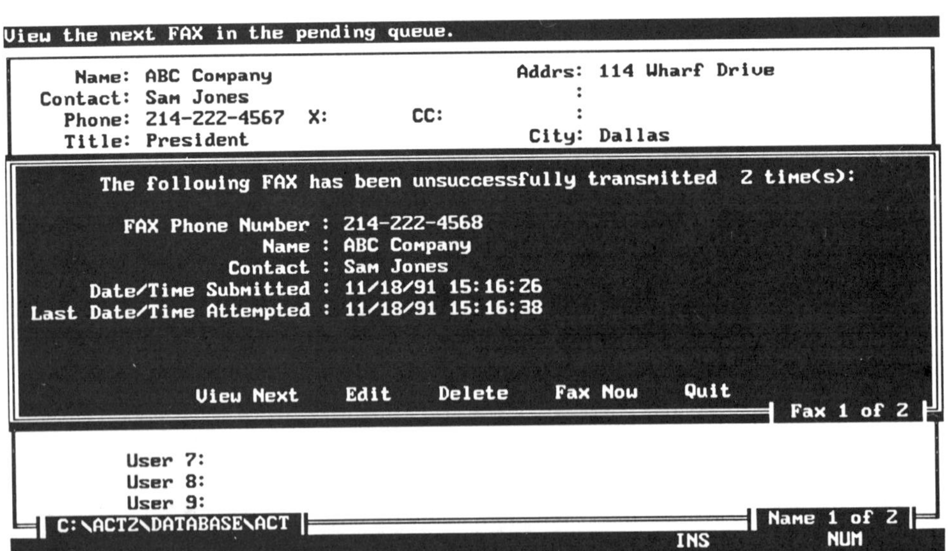

Fig. 5-16. The Fax, Review Pending window.

In Fig. 5-16, ACT! informs you that the fax has not been sent. The window also informs you of the time the fax was sent to the spool and the time of the transmission.

In the case of an unsuccessful transmission caused by an errant phone number, you can select the Edit item to re-enter the number. If more faxes are spooled, you can look at each with the View Next item. To send the fax number review, select the Fax Now item.

Creating a reference library

ACT! reference libraries are sources of information that you can attach to Contacts. A reference library is most useful in phone situations where you need to check a price, part number, or some other specification. Another frequent use of the reference library is as a script for telemarketing.
To create a Reference Library file:

1. Open the Write menu and select Reference Library.
2. The default reference library file appears (Fig. 5-17). Notice that the word processing menu bar has appeared in place of the Contact record menu bar.

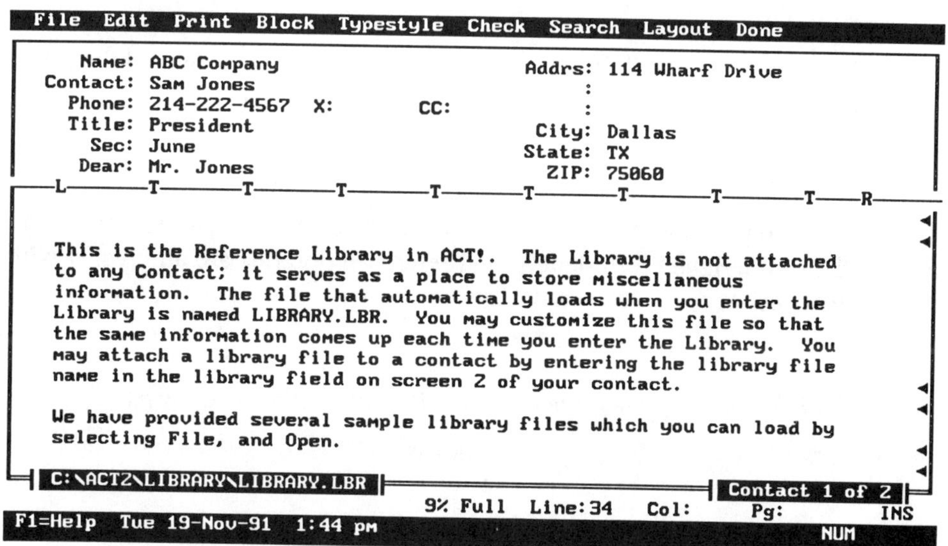

Fig. 5-17. The default reference library.

3. Open the File menu and select New. The library screen is blanked. You can now begin typing the text for the library file. All of the features of the word processor are available, so if you have price sheet stored in a word processing file other than ACT!, you can use the Import item to bring it in to the library, rather than retyping it.

4. After you have finished editing, press F10.
5. Open the File menu and select Save. The File Directory window opens with a list of library files. Library files all have the extension, LBR. ACT! includes several files for your perusal.
6. Type a name for the file, such as PRICE, QUOTE, or whatever is appropriate for the file contents, and press Enter.

Now the file has been created. The next step is to attach it to a Contact.

Attaching a library file

1. Use the Lookup to find the Contact to which you want to attach the library file.
2. Press F6 to go to Contact Screen 2.
3. Press F2. ACT! is now in edit mode.
4. Move the highlight to the Library field.
5. Type the name of the file you have just created, including the extension. For example, type PRICE.LBR.
6. Press F10 to save the entry.
7. Press and hold the Shift key, then press F3. If you have entered the reference library name correctly, it should appear on screen.

Summary

The ACT! word processor works with many aspects of ACT!. Letters, memos, fax covers, custom-designed form letters, and reference libraries are all created with the word processor.

"Without knowing the force of words, it is impossible to know men."

CONFUCIUS

6
CHAPTER

Working with the ACT! reports

"There will never be a system invented that does away with the necessity for work."

HENRY FORD

After scheduling activities, sending letters, and completing to-dos, the natural next step is to compile reports. Anticipating that need, ACT! includes nine prebuilt reports that cover most of the situations that you are likely to encounter. If one of these nine reports does not meet your requirements, you can use the User-defined reports option to custom build a report.

Figure 6-1 is the Report menu. Each of the following report types is summarized, followed by a more detailed discussion.

Activities completed This report provides you with a report that includes the name, contact, title, city, phone number, Status/ID, referral source, the date created any notes you might have entered, and the history. The report can include the current contact, the current group of contacts, or all contacts. ACT! includes a header on the initial page on every report, which includes the manager name and address, the date the report was created, and the time period covered.

History summary This report provides you with a report that includes a compilation of the attempted calls, the completed calls, the number of meetings held, and the number of letters sent, by contact. The report can include the current contact, the current group of contacts, or all contacts. Each contact is listed on the left side of the report and four columns headed by the type of activity complete the report. At the end of the report are the totals for each activity.

Future activity This report considers all contacts and reports whether or not activities are scheduled for that contact. The report is condensed in that only the

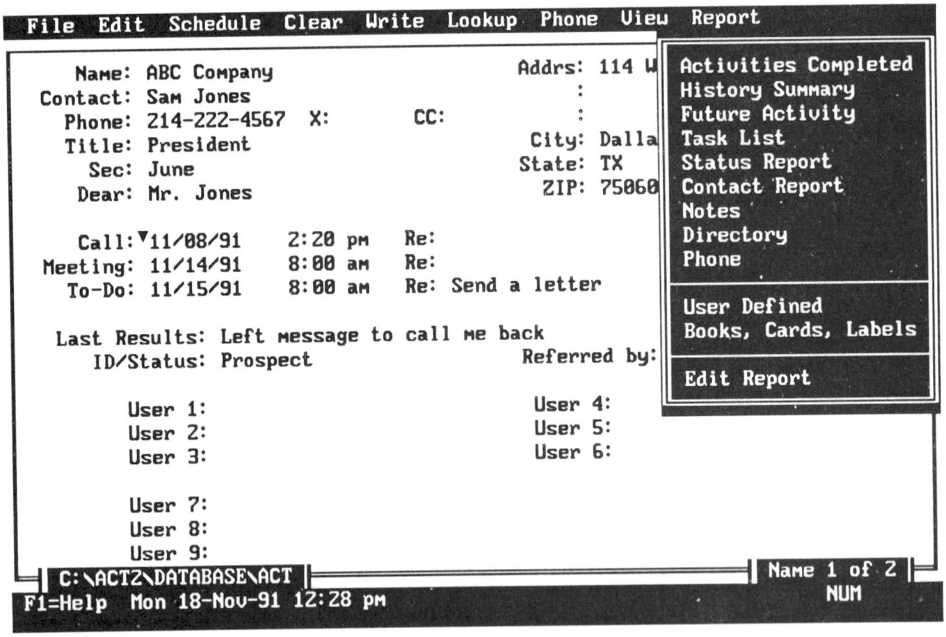

Fig. 6-1. The Report menu.

name, contact, and phone number are listed, plus the activities and their respective dates.

Task List This report is identical in format to the daily task list, except that you define a range of dates to be included. So, this report is used to print your list of calls, meetings, and to-dos for the coming week, month, or any future time period that you select.

Status report This report details the name, contact, and phone number of the contact, plus the current ID/Status, the last results, and the most recent unfinished to-do that you have scheduled.

Contact report The Contact report includes the entire contact record, including Screen 2. All user fields, the history, the notes, and a list of activities are included.

Notes report The Notes report includes the name, contact, title, city, phone, ID/Status, referred by, and the date that the contact was entered, followed by the date-stamped note entries.

Directory The Directory report gives you the primary and secondary name, address, and phone number of the contact.

Phone The Phone report lists each contact by name, and includes the contact and primary phone number.

User-defined reports

The User-defined reports are partially built templates for reports that you can use to design your own reports. The reports listed on the Report menu described previously, cannot be modified. ACT! includes several reports under the User-defined item. They are:

ADDR2 This report compiles the primary address of the contacts in an across-the-page format.

CALL This report includes the name, contact, state, phone, and recall time for each contact.

CUSTOMER This report includes the name, contact, Status/ID, city, state, and the phone number of the currently selected group of contacts.

MEETING This report lists the meeting date, the name, contact, state, phone, and meeting time for each contact that has a meeting scheduled.

MINIPHONE The Miniphone report is the same as the phone report, except that the entry in the EXT and CC are not included.

MINIPROF The Miniprof report is a smaller version of the Contact report. In this report, only Contact Screen 1 fields are included.

MINITASK The Minitask is a condensed list of the calls, meetings, and to-dos Task List.

TODO This report lists the name, contact, and the to-dos for each contact and the expected completion date of each task.

TOTALEXP This report compiles a list of expenses, based on the date range you select.

WP This report creates a file of the name, contact, and the complete address of the contacts for use in a WordPerfect mail merge file.

BOOKS, CARDS, LABELS This menu accesses the software program Books, Cards and Labels (BC&L) that has been integrated into ACT!. BC&L is a program that prints information from your database in many different formats. For example, if you presently use a Pocket Day-Timer and would like to continue doing so, BC&L can print your Contact records in a format that can be inserted into your Day-Timer. Likewise, it can print FiloFax, Lefax, Running Mate or Day Runner formats. That is not all! BC&L prints daily, weekly, and monthly calendars, based on the activities entered into your ACT! database.

Creating a report

The method for extracting a report varies with the report. For example, the Task List report only works if you have defined a range of dates before accessing the report. In the ACT! manual's appendix, the report template and a printed report are shown.

To exclude certain contacts from your reports (e.g., your dentist) you can do so. In the Access field on Contact Screen 2, enter Private. ACT! then disregards that Contact in creating reports.

Creating an Activities Completed, History, Future Activity, or Notes report

1. Open the Report menu and select the report you want. ACT! displays the Print To window. Select where you want the report to print. The Print Pages window is displayed; to print all pages of the report, select OK. ACT! then displays the Calendar.
2. Press Enter to create a report for the current date. To select a specific date range, press the period key and extend the highlight with the arrow keys over the days (or months) for which you want the report compiled. To see all activities on file, press the F7 key. To see all activities prior to the current date, type] . To see all activities after the current date, type [.

   After marking the calendar, ACT! displays a prompt to determine which contacts to include. The current contact, the current group of contacts, or all contacts in the database.
3. Select the contact(s) that you want to include in the report. When you do, ACT! begins to print the report.

Creating a Task List report

1. Press F4 to access the Calendar.
2. Pressing Enter creates a report for the current date. To select a specific date range, press the period key, and extend the highlight with the arrow keys over the days (or months) for which you want the report compiled. To see all activities on file, press the F7 key. To see all activities prior to the current date, type] . To see all activities after the current date, type [. ACT! displays the Task List in three column format.
3. Press F10 to close the Task List.
4. Open the Report menu and select the Task List item.
5. Select where you want the report to print. The Print Pages window is displayed; to print all pages of the report, select OK.

Creating a Status, Contact Report, Directory, Phone report

1. Open the Report menu and select the report you want. ACT! displays the Print To window. Select where you want the report to print. The Print Pages window is displayed; to print all pages of the report, select OK.

2. ACT! displays a prompt to determine which contacts to include: the current contact, the current group of contacts, or all contacts in the database. When you make your selection, the report begins to print.

Creating User-defined reports

Although ACT! includes a multitude of prebuilt report formats, you might want to change the information presented. For example, if you want the fax phone number on a report, you can do so.

Reports consist of two files, the Report Definition file and the Report file. The Definition file is the one that you modify. ACT! compiles the Definition file and creates a Report file. The Report file can then pull the information from the Contact records, as instructed by the Report file. Confused? It is really straightforward in that the rules for creating User-defined reports are easy to grasp.

Look at the Rolodex card report definition file and see how it is put together:

1. Open the Report menu and select the Edit report item. ACT! displays the File Directory window, listing the report files (Fig. 6-2).
2. Press Escape. The cursor jumps into the File field at the top of the window.
3. Press Escape. The current file name is erased.
4. Type *.RPD and press Enter. ACT! displays the list of report definition files (Fig. 6-3).

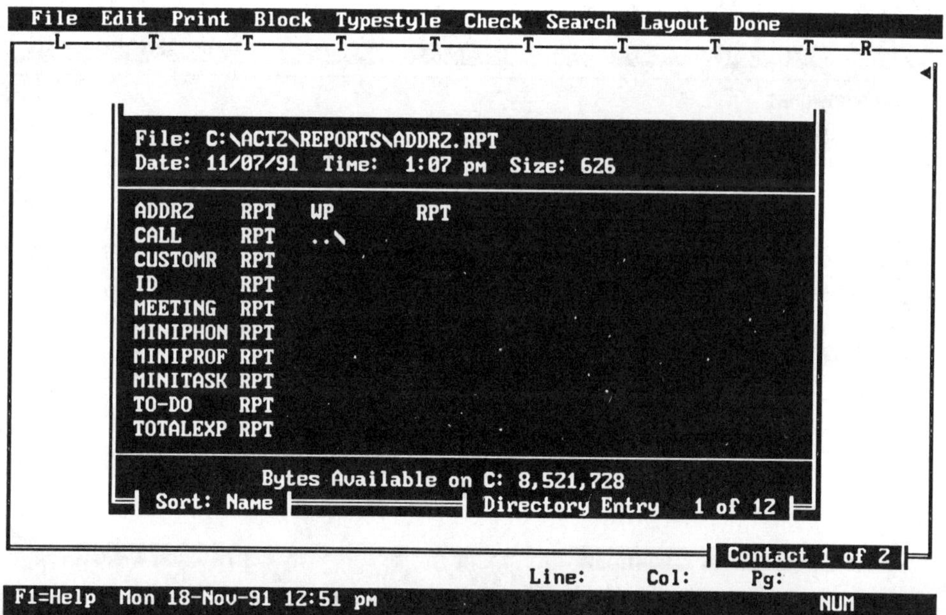

Fig. 6-2. The file directory window listing reports.

5. Position the highlight on the file ROTARY.RPD and press Enter. The ROTARY.RPD displays in the word processing screen (Fig. 6-4).

The ACT! report definition uses several code symbols to insert information from the Contact record and to define the layout of information. For example, the

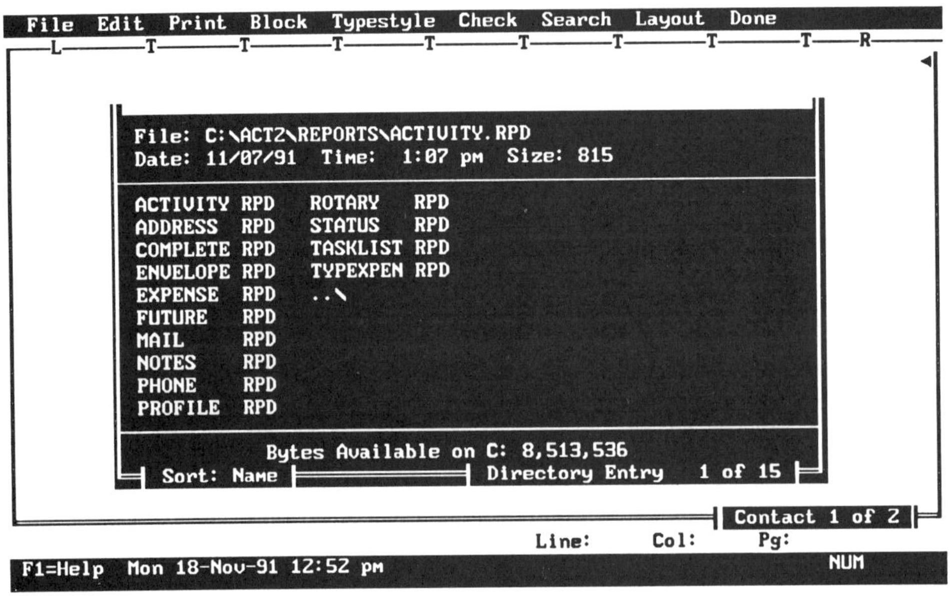

Fig. 6-3. The report definition files.

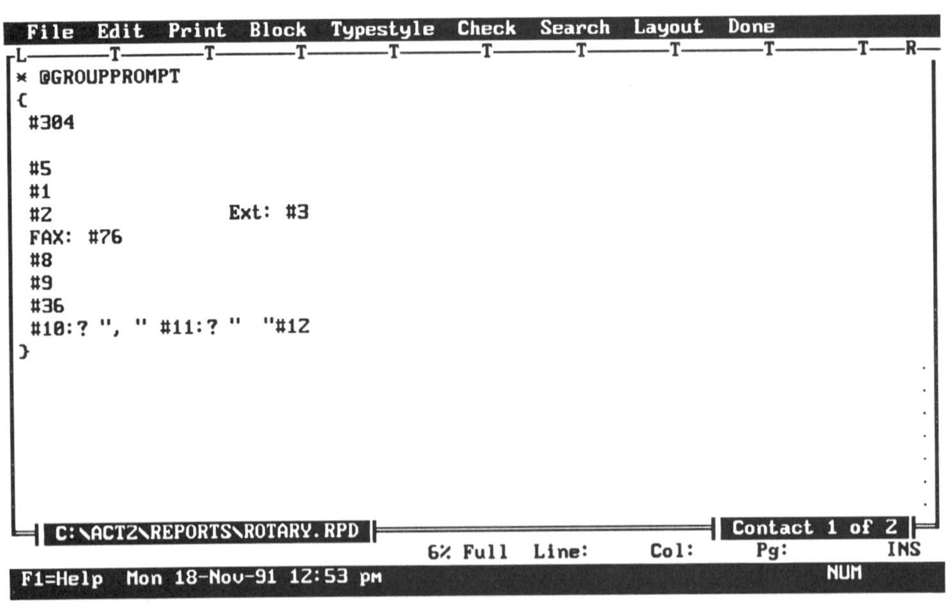

Fig. 6-4. The ROTARY.RPD report definition.

*&GROUPPROMPT at the top of the screen is the command that brings up the choice of which Contacts to use window (This Contact, Group, All) before processing the report. The leading asterisk tells ACT! that the line is not to be printed in the report. The next line down is the begin body symbol ({), which tells ACT! to print everything after the symbol, until it encounters another (}). Every field in ACT! is numbered. The #1 corresponds to the Name field, the #5 field is the Title field. You do not have to memorize the field numbers, ACT! inserts them in the report when you select the field name.

The report definition Rotary creates Rolodex-style cards. Modify this report definition to include the secretary's name, which is field #6, on the printed card:

1. Press F2.
2. Position the cursor so that it is located in line 4, column 19 (Fig. 6-5). Move the cursor to line 4, then press the space bar to move to column 19.

```
 File  Edit  Print  Block  Typestyle  Check  Search  Layout  Done
L--------T--------T--------T--------T--------T--------T--------T--------T--------T---R--
* @GROUPPROMPT
{
 #304

 #5
 #1
 #2                  Ext: #3
 FAX: #76
 #8
 #9
 #36
 #10:? ", " #11:? "  "#12
}




 C:\ACT2\REPORTS\ROTARY.RPD                                   Contact 1 of 2
                                6% Full   Line:4    Col:19    Pg:1      * INS
F1=Help  Mon 18-Nov-91   1:53 pm                                       NUM
```

Fig. 6-5. Cursor at line 4 column 19.

3. Type SEC followed by two spaces. The cursor should be positioned at column 24. *SEC* represents secretary.
4. Press F2. The list of field names displays (Fig. 6-6).
5. Press the down arrow key until the highlight is positioned on the Secretary field name and press Enter. Insert the symbol # and the number 6.
6. Add a colon and a question mark after the #6 so that the entry reads #6:?. The addition of the colon and the question mark tells ACT! to allow all the space needed to make the entry fit.

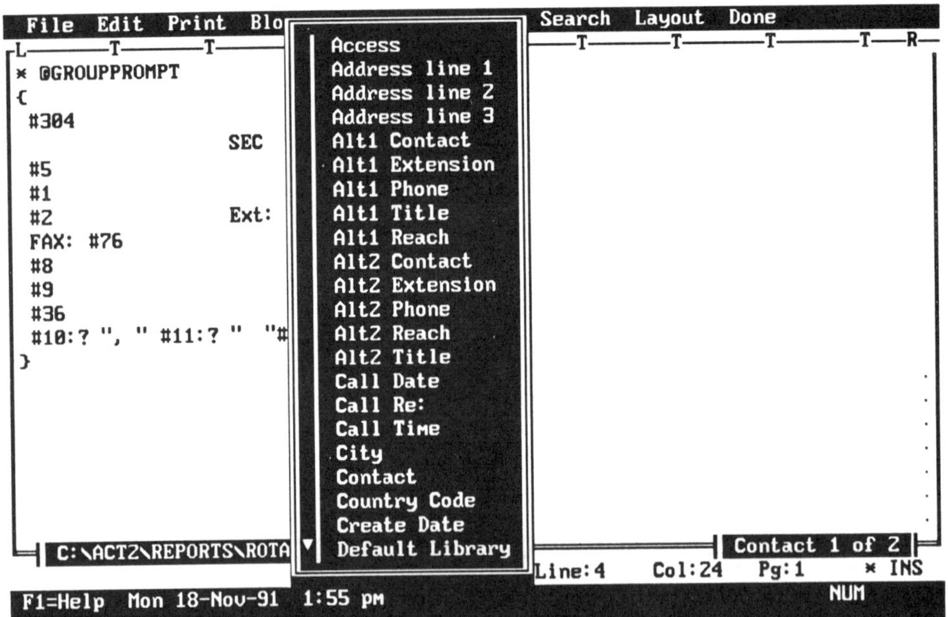

Fig. 6-6. The list of filed names window.

A further example of fitting information from the Contact record into the report definition is the last line of the report definition. There, the #10 is followed by a colon, question mark, and a comma, followed by #11, colon, question mark, and comma. The question mark tells ACT! to use the space necessary to insert the entry from field number 10 (City), followed by a comma and then start inserting the entry from field number 11 (State). The quotation marks with nothing in between tell ACT! to insert two blank spaces. Because the length of the City and State entries are not fixed, the insertion of the spaces must be flexible. So, after ACT! inserts the city and state, it immediately adds two spaces, then prints the 12 field, which is Zip.

7. Press F10 to activate the menu bar. Open File menu and select Save. ACT! displays the File Directory window.
8. The new file must have an RPT extension. Press Escape twice to erase the current file name, ROTARY.RPD.
9. Enter the new file name: ROLO.RPT and press Enter.
10. Select the Done menu name to exit the word processor.

Testing the new report

In order for this test to work, you need to have a Contact record with an entry in the Secretary field. So, either look up a Contact to find one with a secretary entry or edit the current Contact and enter a fake name.

1. Open the Report menu and select User Defined. The File Directory window appears and the newly defined report is listed.
2. Highlight the ROLO.RPT file name and press Enter. ACT! takes a few moments to compile the new report.
3. The Print To window appears. For this test, print the cards on screen.
4. Select the This Contact for printing. The Contact is printed to the screen with the secretary's name included. Follow the on-screen instructions to exit the print routine.

The report generator is a very powerful tool. With experimentation, you can create virtually any type of report you want. Take a look at a more complex report to see some other aspects of report definition files.

1. Open the Report menu and select Edit Report.
2. Press Escape twice to erase the current file name.
3. Type *.RPD.
4. Press Enter. From the File Directory window, highlight the ACTIVITY. RPD file and press Enter. The Activity Report definition appears (Fig. 6-7).

   At the top left is the entry * &GROUPPROMPT. As discussed in the previous example, the asterisk tells ACT! not to print this line, and the

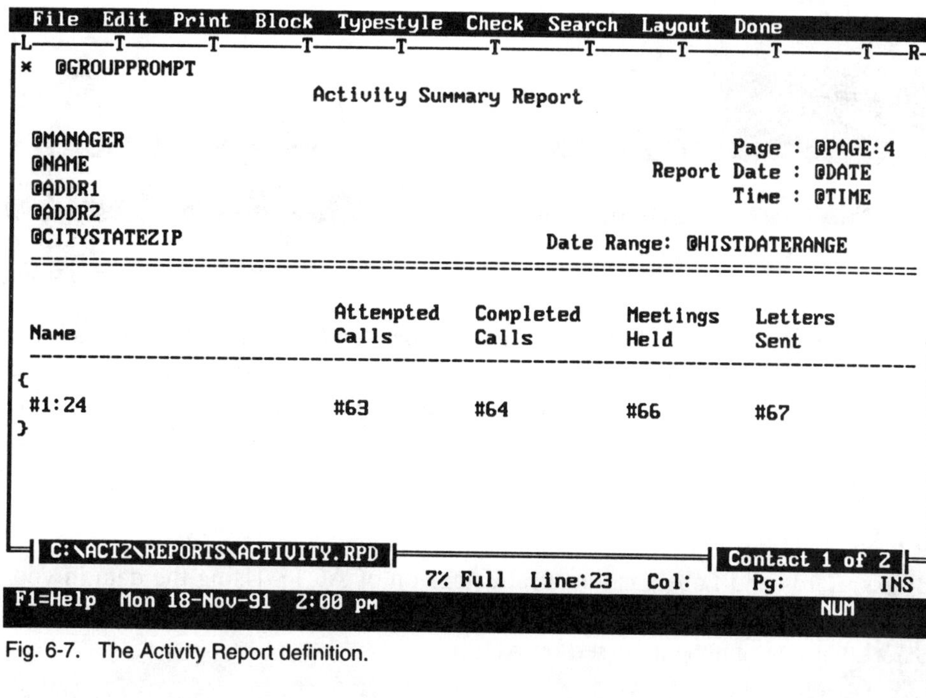

Fig. 6-7. The Activity Report definition.

&GROUPPROMPT tells ACT! to display the This Contact, Group, or All prompt before processing the report.

Next is the title to the report, "Activity Summary Report." The next lines are combinations. The &MANAGER inserts the names of the database manager. You might wonder why this entry is not denoted by a field number. Several of the fields have been automated so that they can be recovered for report purposes with a name. The &CITYSTATEZIP does not pull the contact's address, but rather inserts the Manager's City, State, and Zip. The &PAGE, &DATE, and &TIME are all special insertion codes.

5. Press F2 to go into the edit mode.
6. Press Shift and F2 to display the special Insertion code list (Fig. 6-8).

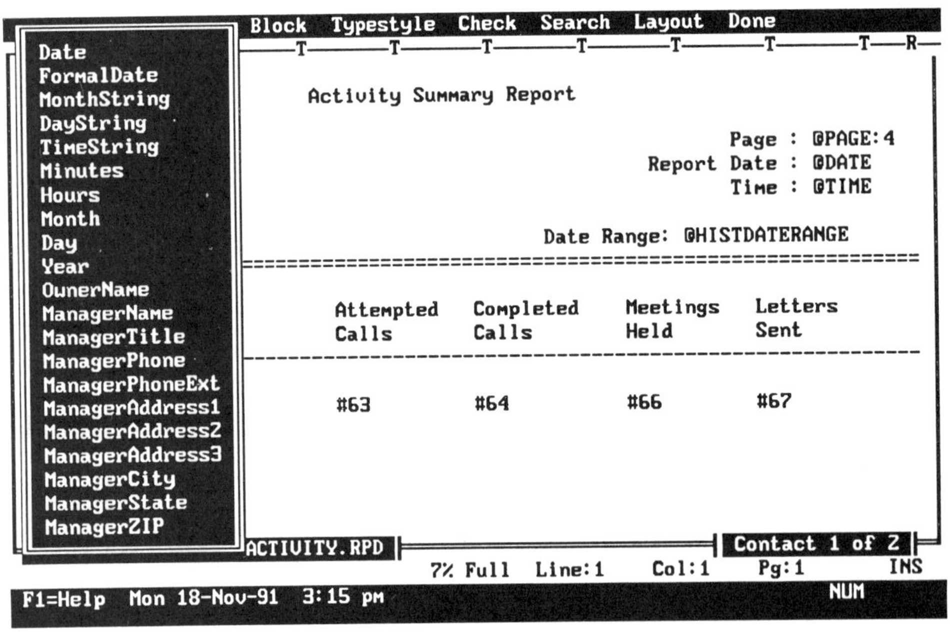

Fig. 6-8. The Insertion code list.

As you can see, ACT! offers a variety of date and time insertions, in addition to the manager information. Building your own reports is a trial-and-error process and a report can be as sophisticated as you desire. If the process is too intimidating or if the report requires extensive calculations, Contact Software will build the report for you for a price.

Books, Cards and Labels

Books, Cards and Labels is a natural extension of ACT!. Using the data in your database, BC&L can create a wide variety of output formats. You must install BC&L before it can be accessed by ACT!

Before entering BC&L, ACT! prompts as to whether you want to process the current Contact, the currently selected Group, or all Contacts. The answer to the prompt depends on what you are planning to do after you access BC&L. For example, if you plan to print a calendar of your activities for the coming week or month, it would be wise to include all contacts in the process. If, on the other hand, you plan to create an address book that contains only your personal friends, you should first use the Lookup menu to group those Contacts in the database.

To access Books, Cards, and Labels follow these steps:

1. From any Contact record screen, open the Report menu.
2. Select the item, Books, Cards and Labels. ACT! displays the window asking for input on which Contact you plan to use. Select the appropriate response by highlighting and pressing Enter. If you select Group, BC&L needs to know if you want to start with the first Contact in that group.

   BC&L prompts you as to whether or not the Contacts you are about to use have been changed since the last time you accessed BC&L. Because BC&L maintains an internal index of the Contact records, it checks if its index needs to be updated. If you have any doubt as to whether or not the index is current, select Yes. BC&L quickly reindexes the Contacts. The BC&L screen appears, as in Fig. 6-9.

The menu can be accessed in the same way as ACT! menus. You can either type the first letter of the menu name, such as S to open the Sort menu, or you can use the right or left arrow keys to position the highlight on the menu name and press Enter. Take a look at the myriad of forms that can be printed.

1. Open the Forms menu by typing the letter F or by highlighting the menu name and pressing Enter. The menu opens (Fig. 6-10). Several of the items on this menu are followed by three periods, (...) which indicate that a submenu is attached.
2. With the highlight on the item "Organizers," press Enter. The submenu appears (Fig. 6-11).

As you can see, BC&L offers you the opportunity to print your Contact in a format that you might already be using. The FiloFax has a further submenu that allows you to choose from the Pocket, Personal or Professional model.

Note: A slight difference exists between the way ACT! handles menus and the way that BC&L does. When you have opened a BC&L menu, followed by several submenus, pressing Escape completely closes the menu (as opposed to ACT!, which closes each menu in the reverse order of opening).

Printing a form

Suppose that you do want to print your Contacts in the FiloFax Pocket format and that you want to print them in a specific order:

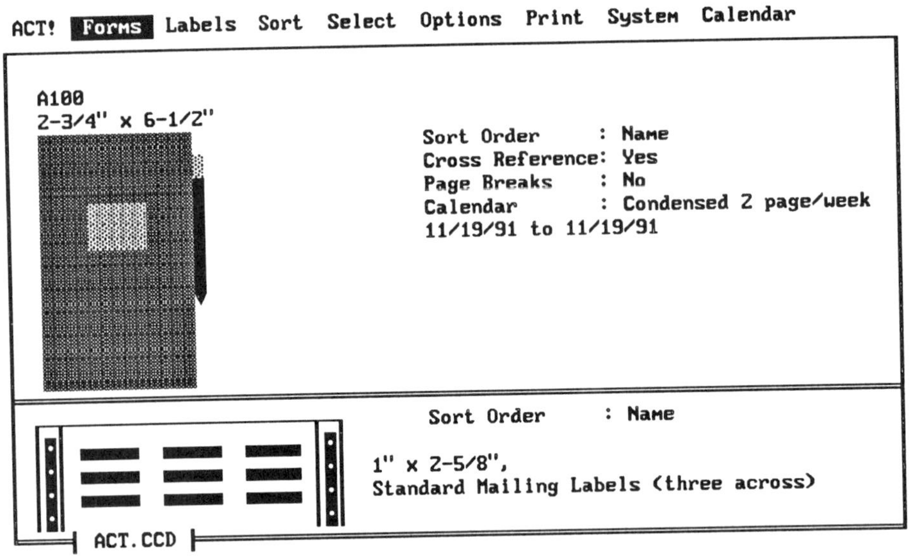

Fig. 6-9. Books, Cards and Labels Contact screen.

1. Open the From menu.
2. Select the Organizers item.
3. From the submenu, select FiloFax.
4. From the last submenu select Pocket. The menus close and BC&L displays a graphic of the form you have selected and its name.
5. Open the Sort menu (Fig. 6-12). BC&L considers an organizer a report. So,

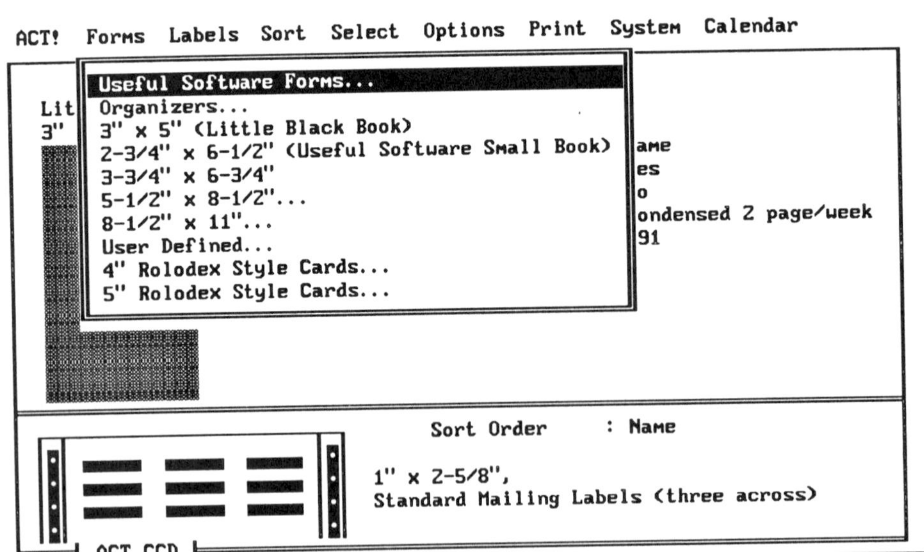

Fig. 6-10. The Forms menu.

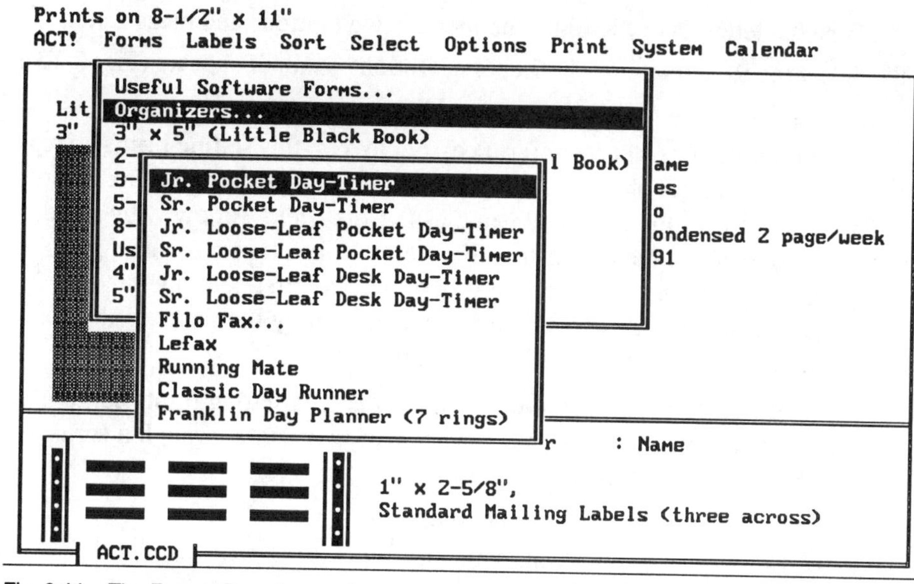

Fig. 6-11. The Forms, Organizers submenu.

you have three sort options: by name, by primary contact, or by the entry in the Status ID field.

6. Select the by Status ID item. Notice that BC&L has inserted the new sort order in the middle of the screen. Several other settings appear there. The remaining settings are accessed via the Options menu.

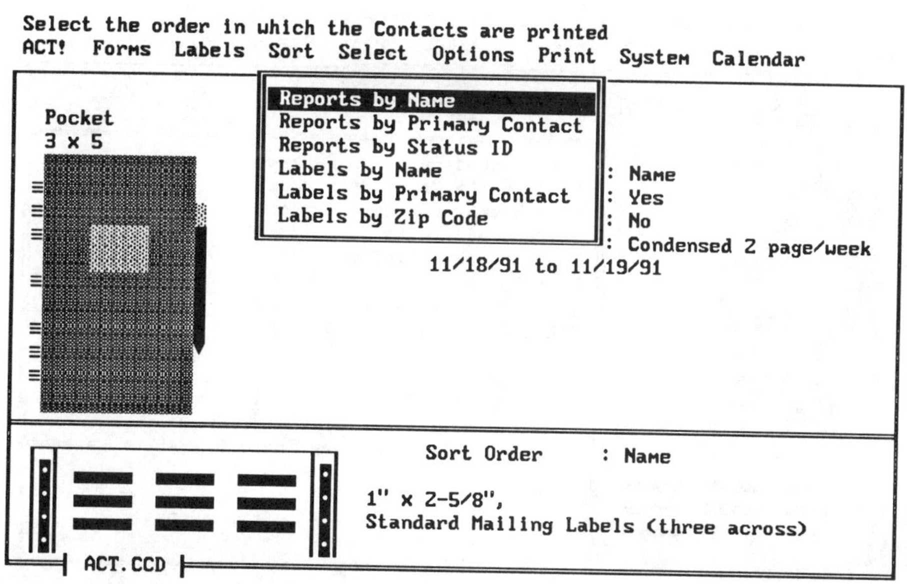

Fig. 6-12. The BC&L sort menu.

7. Type the letter O or highlight the menu name Options and press Enter.
8. Select the Reports item. The Reports, Options window appears (Fig. 6-13).

Each of the settings are discussed below:

Print standard cross reference Set to Yes, this setting prints a cross reference list after printing the report. In this example, the FiloFax records are printed with the company name as the first field, followed by the primary contact and the rest of the information. The cross reference prints in tabular format, one Contact record per line. The first column contains the primary contact, followed in the second column by the name of the company, the Status ID, and finally the company name.

Print extra cross reference Set to Yes, this setting prints additional cross references. By pressing the space bar, you rotate through a series of letters that represent the following:

T Prints city and state
S Prints state and city
Z Prints zip code
C Prints city and zip code

The cross-reference setting works in conjunction with the Include addresses setting. In order for the cross referencing to work, BC&L must have access to the information in the address fields. You can print a single cross reference by entering an N in the Print Standard Cross Reference field and then selecting T, S, Z, or C.

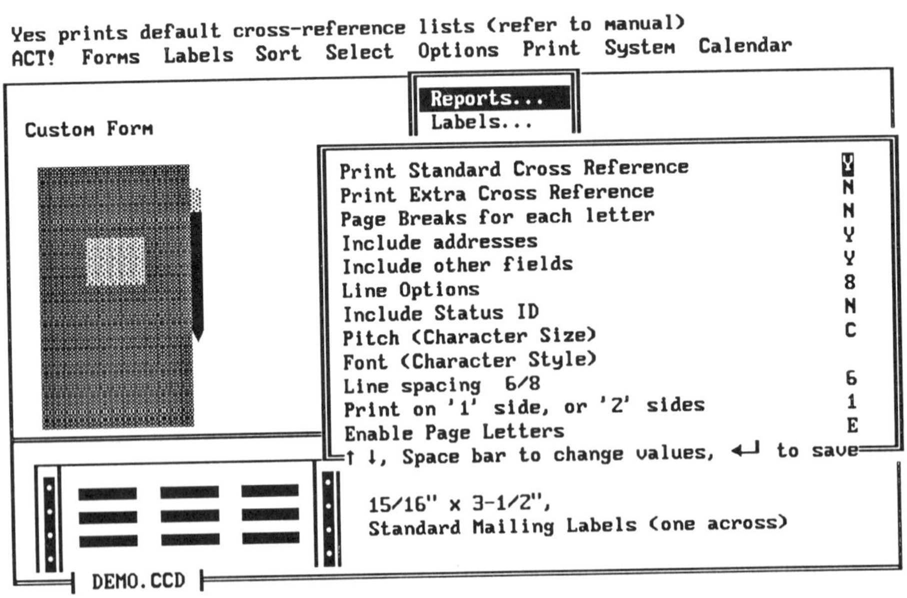

Fig. 6-13. The Options, Reports window.

Page breaks for each letter This setting causes BC&L to print on a new page when it encounters a different letter in the sort field. For example, when Name is used as the Sort field, and the entry in the field changes from *Adams* to *Burke*, BC&L prints the Burke record on a new page.

Include addresses To print the entire address, set this to Yes.

Include other Fields By entering Yes in this field, BC&L prints the information in the Referred by and User 1 through User 8 fields. In chapter 7, the means to customize the User Fields is described.

Line options BC&L has 4 formats for separating Contact records, numbered 2, 4, 6 and 8. Setting 2 prints an underline, setting 4 leaves no space and does not print anything between the records, setting 6 inserts a blank line between records, and setting 8 inserts a blank line and prints an underline between records.

Include Status ID Yes prints the information from the Status ID field with the record.

Pitch You have three options, Condensed prints 17 characters per inch, E prints 12 characters per inch, and P prints 10 characters per inch. Press the space bar to rotate the choices.

Font Select from B for bold, 2 for bold and italic, I for italic. A blank entry (space bar) prints in Roman.

Line spacing Select 6 or 8 lines per inch.

Print on 1 or 2 sides You can print some of the reports on both sides of paper. With laser printers this operation can be tricky; once paper is put through the printer, it does not behave as well as the second time.

Enable Page Letters Set to E for enable, prints the letter that matches the Contact records on that page.

9. Press Enter to save the new settings or Escape to negate the changes.
10. Open the Print menu and select Reports.
11. At the begin printing prompt, read the screen and then select Yes.

Determining which record prints first

On the Print menu, one of the items is *Position*. If you have already sorted your database by the entry in the Name field or Contact BC&L prompts you to enter a Name or Contact as the first record to print. Type in the information and press Enter. BC&L begins printing the report or label starting with the record you specified.

Installing a different printer

BC&L has the capability to install a printer different from the one installed in ACT!. Open the System menu, the single item is Printer Definition. BC&L provides a list of printer manufacturers and their respective models for your selection.

Depending on the type of printer selected, BC&L might guide you through an exacting process to correctly align the printer with its formats.

More and more labels

If you can find a label format that BC&L does not support, you are using an odd-ball label. When you select a label format, the graphic at the bottom of the screen changes to match the format. The graphic attempts to represent the way the labels look when they are in the printer.

Printing a calendar of activities

In ACT! you can print a Task List for any time period you wish. With BC&L you can print very professional looking calendars that include your activities.

Remember, BC&L can only use the Contact records to build a calendar that you specify when you access BC&L. For a calendar of activities, you want to specify All Contacts to use. After entering BC&L, follow these steps to create a calendar:

1. Open the Select menu. The single item on the menu is Select Calendar Records. Press Enter. BC&L displays to fields in which you enter the date range to include in the calendar (Fig. 6-14). In Fig. 6-14, two dates have been entered that would cause BC&L to print a calendar that includes the entire month of December.
2. After entering the dates, press Enter. BC&L displays a message that alerts you to the number of days included in the calendar. If you want a monthly calendar and select a date range that runs across two months, BC&L prints only the dates from the first month. Press Enter again to continue if the range is correct or press Escape to quit.

   The next step is to define the type of calendar you want: daily, weekly, or monthly. The daily and weekly calendars can be printed in condensed or expanded format, and you can determine the position where the hours of the day are printed.

   The monthly format prints a calendar in either portrait or landscape style, depending on your printer. On a laser printer, BC&L always prints in landscape style; you cannot select a different format from the Froms menu. On a dot-matrix printer, the calendar is printed in portrait style. If you have a 132-character dot-matrix printer, you can print calendars in landscape style.
3. The final step is to specify the Form of the calendar. Open the Forms menu and select one of the prebuilt forms or use the User-defined item to create your own form layout.
4. Open the Print menu.
5. Select Calendar. BC&L prints the calendar.

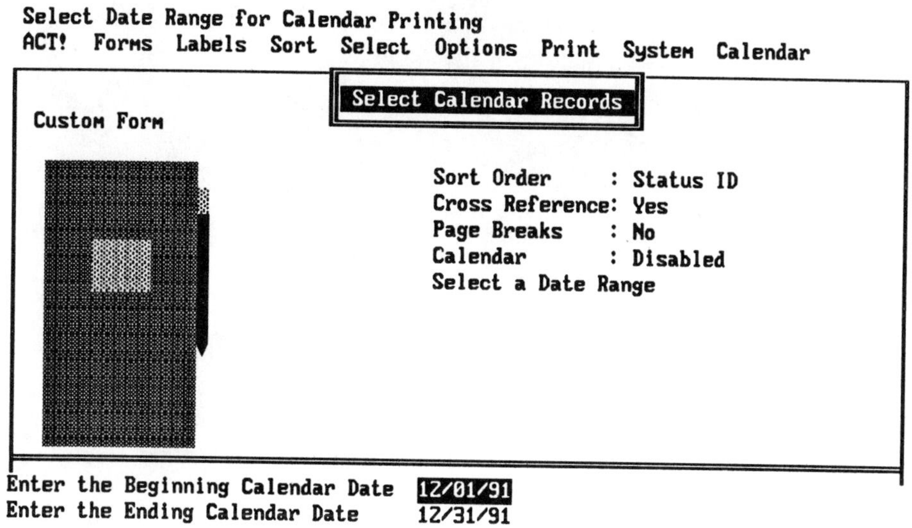

Fig. 6-14. The Calendar date range fields.

Returning to ACT!

With menus closed, pressing Escape opens a prompt that asks whether or not you wish to return to ACT!. You can also highlight the ACT! menu name and press Enter, and press Enter again.

Summary

ACT! offers a report for almost every instance: from printing your list of tasks for the coming week to compiling your activities with a particular client. In addition, you can create new or modify existing reports in order to satisfy your particular needs. With version 2.1, you can exquisitely customize address books, labels, Rolodex cards and calendars, using Books, Cards and Labels.

"Life is an instinct for growth, for survival,
for the accumulation of forces, for power."

FRIEDRICH NIETZSCHE

7

CHAPTER

Customizing ACT!

"If you pick up a starving dog and make him prosperous, he will not bite you. This is the principal difference between a dog and man."

SAMUEL CLEMENS

Some of the field labels, Name, Contact Title, etc. can be changed to better reflect the data you enter. The field label, the field prompt, the type of data that can be entered, and the type of recording that occurs when the entry is in the field can be changed. The internal field numbers cannot be changed however, because ACT! needs them to generate reports, mailing labels, and word processing forms.

The ACT.DEF file

When you start ACT!, it opens several files, one of which contains your Contact records, named ACT.CCD, another is ACT.DEF which contains all of the field attributes that you have established for the database. It also contains the entries in the Popup menus. So, if you have made modifications to the Popups, they are loaded with the specific database. This points up another attribute of ACT!—the ability to create specific definitions for different databases. Creating new DEF files for other databases is covered later in this chapter.

Editing the label

To begin editing a field label, look at the default definition for the Name field:

1. At any Contact record, press F2.
2. With the highlight on the Name field, press and hold the Control key, then press F2. The Field Name definition screen appears (Fig. 7-1).
3. Press F5. The entire field label Name is erased. This field label can only be eight characters in length.
4. Type Business and press Enter. The highlight moves to the Prompt field.

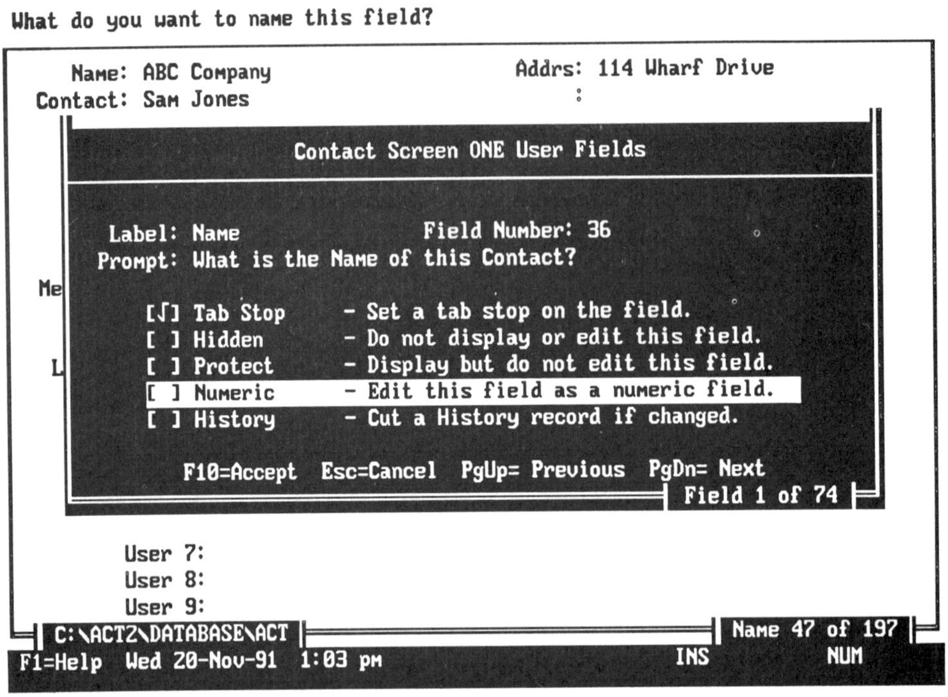

Fig. 7-1. The Field Name definition screen.

The prompt is the text that appears at the top of the screen when you have highlighted a specific field. The prompt text serves as a guide as to what should be entered in that particular field.

5. Press F5 and type Enter the name of this business.
6. Press F10. ACT! saves the new label and prompt. Press F2 and the Contact screen displays (Fig. 7-2). Notice the new field prompt.
7. Press Escape, then open the Lookup menu, which appears (Fig. 7-3).

The change in the field label is carried over into the Lookup menu, as you can see. Some ACT! users prefer this label to Name because the first field in the database is used for entering the contacts' business name.

To restore the field label:

1. Press F2.
2. With the highlight on the Business field, press Control and F2.
3. Press F5 to erase the current field label. Type Name and press Enter.
4. In the prompt field type What is the Name of this Contact?
5. Press F10. The default settings for this field are restored.

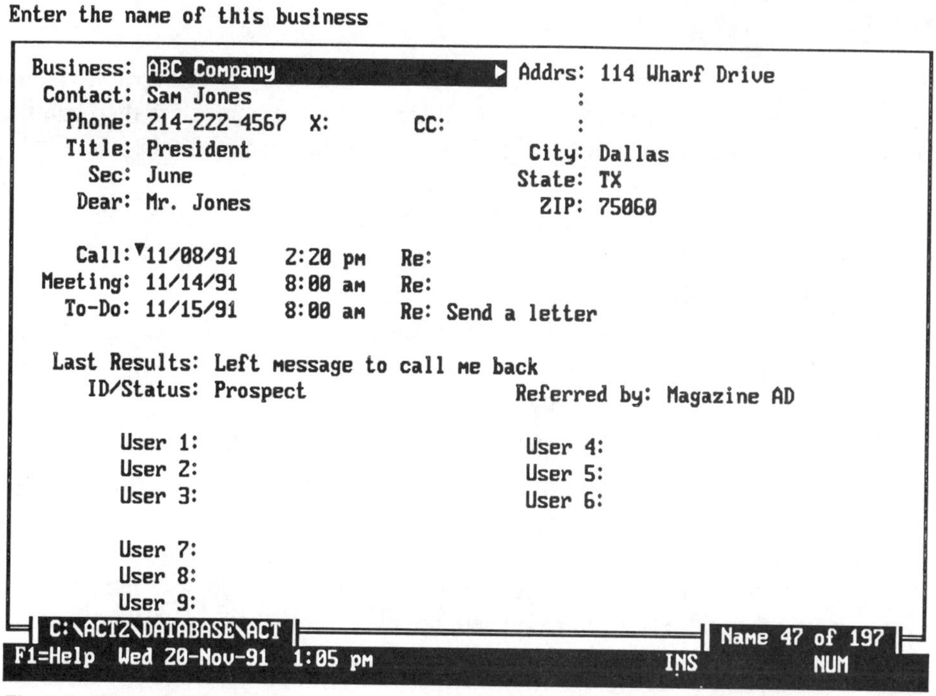

Fig. 7-2. The edited Contact screen.

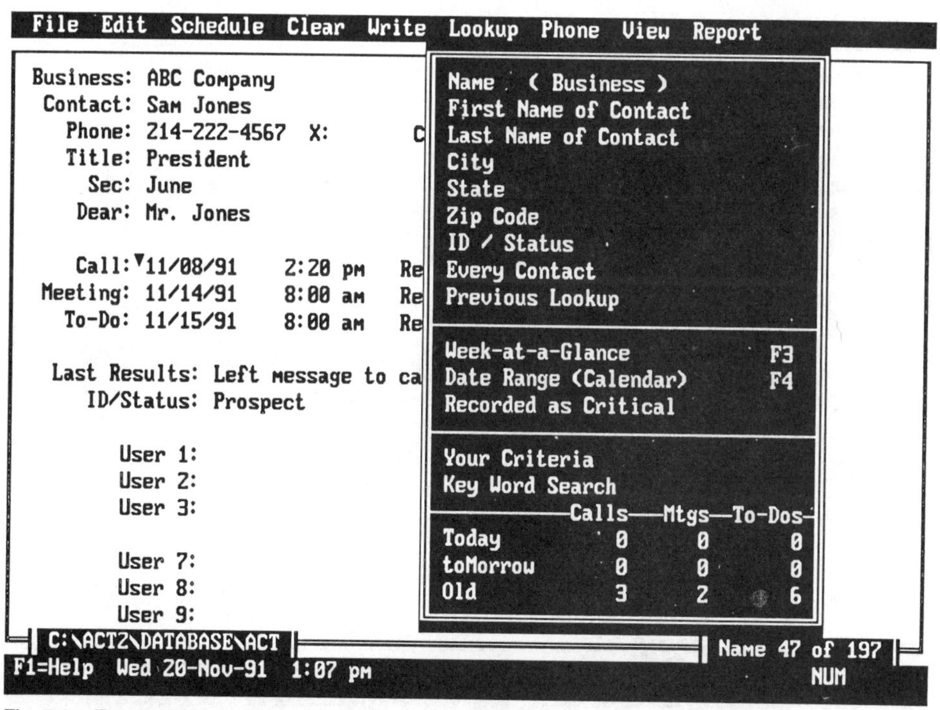

Fig. 7-3. The Lookup menu including the new field label.

Field lengths

The length of each field in ACT! is fixed. That is, it can only hold a specific number of characters. However, some of the fields hold more characters than can be seen on screen. Take a quick look at the Name field to understand this.

1. At any Contact, press F2 to begin editing. In Fig. 7-4, the Name field is highlighted. Look at the far right side of the field. A small triangle pointing to the right appears.
2. Press and hold the T key until ACT! beeps. In the field, you can see 33 t's, but in actuality 50 t's have been entered. The triangle now points to the left, indicating that you are at the end of the field.
3. Press the Home key. The cursor jumps to the beginning of the field.
4. Press the End key. The cursor jumps to the end of the field. Many of the fields in ACT!, particularly the User fields, have this attribute. If no triangle appears at the far right of the field when you highlight it, then the length of the field is exactly what you see on screen. When you print letters or reports, the entire field entry is used, not only the characters seen on screen.
5. Press Escape to erase the changes you have made.

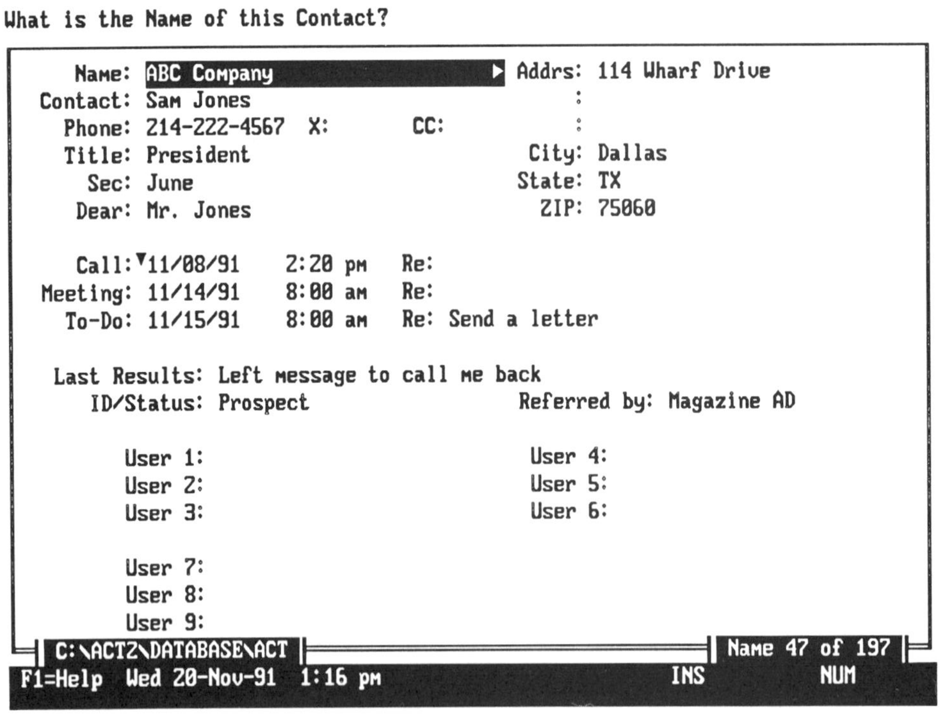

Fig. 7-4. Highlighted Name field.

Editing User fields

The User fields at the bottom of screens 1 and 2 are intended for your modification. In this example, you can change the User 1 field so that it can be used to search for birthdays of contacts. If you are in a business where it pays to know the birthdates of your contacts, such as insurance, you need to be able to find your contacts for the purpose of sending birthday cards and perhaps policy review dates.

A User field is modified in exactly the same way as the prebuilt fields. You do have more flexibility in that you can use fields for calculations and creating History file entries.

1. In any Contact, press F2 to begin editing.
2. Press the TAB key four times. The User 1 field has been designated as a TAB stop, so the highlight is positioned there.
3. Press Control and F2. The Contact Screen ONE User Fields window appears.
4. Press F5 to clear the current field label.
5. Type Birthdate and press Enter. The highlight moves to the Prompt field. You cannot modify the Field Number, nor would you want to. ACT! uses the field numbers to build reports and forms in the word processor.
6. Press F5 to erase the field. Type Enter birth date MM/DD/YY.

   The rest of the options for a field are:

   TAB Stop A checkmark in the leading parentheses sets a tab stop for the field. In this example, the User 1 field already has a checkmark and therefore, when you pressed tab, the highlight jumped to the field. To insert the tab stop, move the highlight to the item and press the space bar. To remove the checkmark, highlight the item and press the space bar again.

   Hidden Use this item to erase the User field from the screen.

   Protect Use this item to enter a permanent entry in the field.

   Numeric Use this item to force number entries only in the field.

   History Use this item so that edits to the field entries are recorded as part of the contact's History file.

   F10 Accepts the modifications.

   Esc Cancels the modifications.

   PgUp Displays the field label previous to the current field. For example, when User 1 is on screen, pressing PgUp displays Referred By field attributes.

   PgDn Displays the field label down from the current field. For example, when User 1 is on screen, pressing PgDn displays User 2.

You might conclude that because you plan to enter dates in the User 1 field, it should be modified as a Numeric field. Not so. If the field is designated as Numeric, ACT! automatically inserts a decimal point, followed by two zeros at the far right of the field.

7. Press F10 to save the new modifications. Figure 7-5 shows the new label with a date entry.

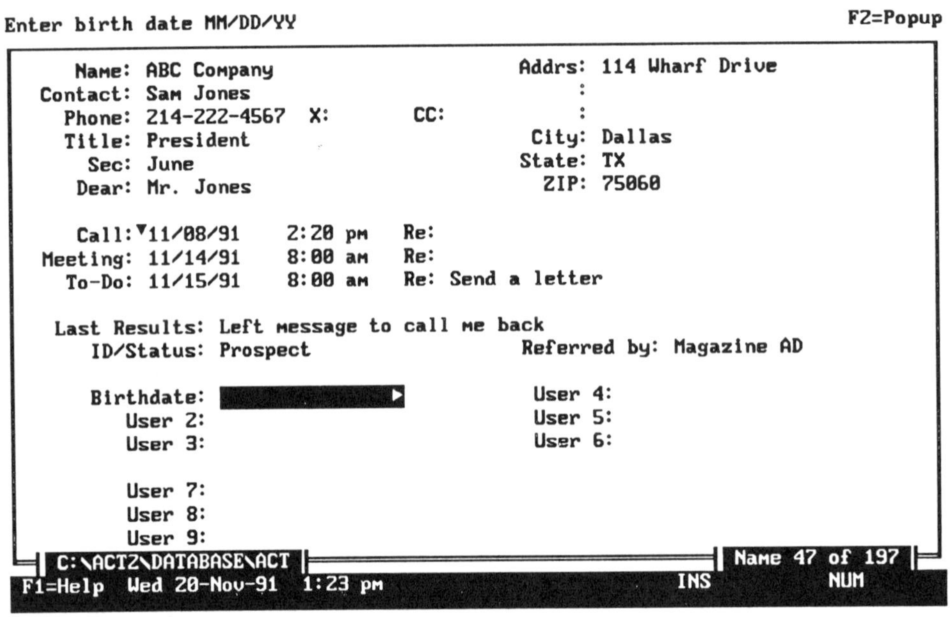

Fig. 7-5. The Birthdate field label.

User fields in searches

Now suppose that you want to print a list of contacts whose birthdays are in the month of June. This type of lookup is a Boolean search; you want to find the contacts that have a birthdate greater than May 31 and less than July 1.

1. Open the Lookup menu and select Your Criteria.
2. Select the Query menu. The Boolean screen appears. If a previous query appears, select the Clear menu to erase the query.
3. Press F2 to begin editing. Insert an open parenthesis.
4. Under the Field heading, press F2. The list of field labels appears. Scroll the highlight down the list until Birthdate appears.
5. Highlight Birthdate and press Enter. In the Op field, enter a greater than (>) sign.
6. In the Value field, type 04/30/00 and press Enter. Close the query line with a).

7. Press F10 to save the first line of the query.
8. Press Insert to begin a second line.
9. Insert a (. Under the Field heading, enter Birthdate again.
10. In the Op field, enter <.
11. In the Value field, type 06/01/00 and press Enter. Close the query line with a).
12. Press F10 to save the query line.
13. Select the Go menu. ACT! searches the contacts and finds those with May birthdates.

Adding user fields to a report

In the previous example, a group was created using the birthdates as the search criteria. Suppose that you now wish to print the names and addresses of the group so that you can send each a birthday card. You could simply open the Write menu, use the Print option, and print a list of mailing labels. However, that would not include the birthdate itself. You could print a Contact report, which would include both the address and the birthdate. Why not edit the envelope report definition to include the Birthdate field?

1. Open the Report menu and select the Edit Report item.
2. Press Escape twice. Type *.RPD and press Enter. ACT! displays the list of report definition files.
3. Position the highlight on the file ENVELOPE.RPD and press Enter. The definition appears (Fig. 7-6).

   The ENVELOPE definition includes the following fields:

   #304 Contact. The 300 is added to 4 to swap on a comma if one is encountered in the Contact entry. For example, if you entered a contact as "Smith, John," ACT! recognizes the comma and prints the name on the envelope as John Smith.
   #5 Title
   #1 Name
   #8 Address line 1
   #9 Address line 2
   #36 Address line 3
   #10 City
   #11 State
   #12 Zip

   Because you probably will not use mailing labels for birthday cards, you can safely add a line to the definition to include the birthdate.
4. Press F2.

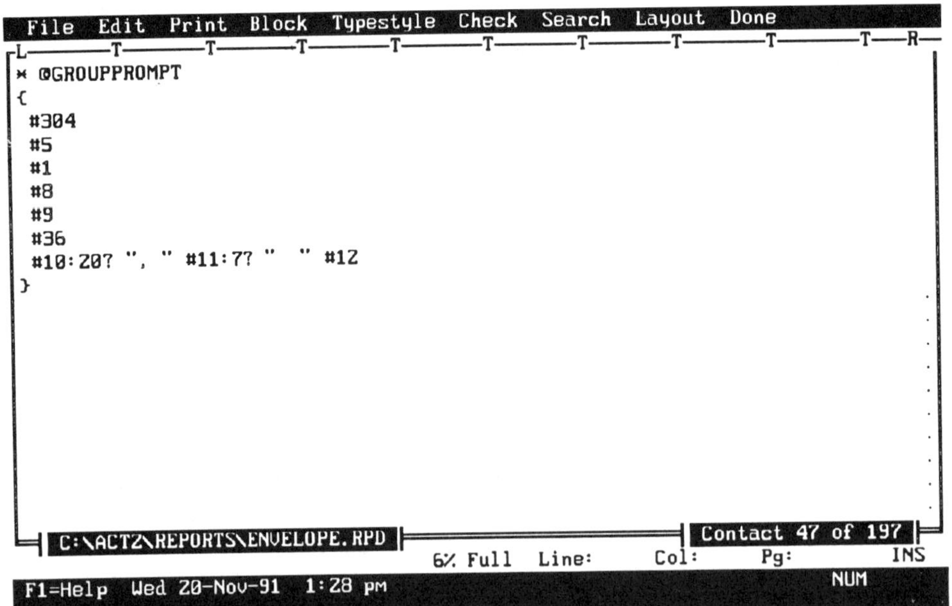

Fig. 7-6. The ENVELOPE report definition file.

5. Position the cursor at the end of the city, state, and zip line. Press Enter.
6. Press the space bar once so that the new line does not start in column one.
7. Press F2. ACT! displays the list of field labels.
8. Highlight the Birthdate label and press Enter. ACT! enters the number sign and the field number, 24.
9. Press F10 to activate the menu bar. Open the file menu and select the Save item.
10. Press Escape twice. Type the new file name, BIRTHDAY.RPT, and press Enter. Remember, the file must have an RPT extension!

The report is finished. Now, if you have completed your lookup query to group the contacts, you need only to open the Report menu and select User Defined, then from the File Directory window, select the BIRTHDAY.RPT. ACT! compiles the report, asks where to print it, then asks if it should be for the current contact, the current group, or for all contacts. Select Group and the names, addresses, and birthdates print.

Creating multiple databases

If you have several business activities that do not overlap, you might want to keep separate databases for each business. This gives you the opportunity to create separate definition files for each database.

To create a new database:

1. Open the File menu and select New. ACT! opens the File Directory window and lists the currently available databases.
2. Type a name for the new database. It can only be eight characters in length, so do not include an extension.
3. ACT! then prompts as to whether or not you want to add password protection to the new database. If you do, type the new password and press Enter. If you do not, just press Enter. If you typed in a password, ACT! verifies it by asking you to type it again. If they are not identical, including capitalization, ACT! does not accept the password, and asks you to try again. ACT! begins creating the files needed for the needed database. In a moment, you will be working in a blank database.

Note: In version 2.0 of ACT!, use the File menu, then select Retrieve. Press Escape twice and enter the new database name. Do not include an extension. Press Enter and ACT! prompts you as to whether or not you want to create a new database with the name supplied. Answer Yes and ACT! creates the new database files.

Using passwords to protect databases, version 2.1

In the previous example, adding a password to a new database was explained. But what happens if you already have a database and wish to protect it, or change the password, or eliminate the password?

To make such a change, you must execute a small program called *ACTPASS.EXE* from the DOS prompt. Unless you have created a database and stored it in a location other than the one suggested by ACT!, all of your databases are going to be in the ACT2\DATABASE subdirectory.

Suppose that you want to eliminate the password to the ACT.CCD database:

1. If you are in ACT! exit the program.
2. You should be at the DOS prompt and it should read C:\ACT2, or if you have installed ACT! on drive D, D:\ACT2. If you are using a menu program on your computer, exit from it and type: CD\ACT2, then hit Enter.
3. At C:\ACT> type: ACTPASS C:\ACT2\DATABASE\ACT.CCD"". Be careful to include the spaces between the ACTPASS and the path and file name. The double quotation marks eliminate the current password.

To add a new or change the password to ACT.CCD:

1. If you are in ACT! exit the program.
2. You should be at the DOS prompt and it should read C:\ACT2, or if you

have installed ACT! on drive D, D:\ACT2. If you are using a menu program on your computer, exit from it and type CD\ACT2, then hit Enter.

3. At C:\ACT> type ACTPASS C:\ACT2\DATABASE\ACT.CCD WOLF.

Be careful to include the spaces between the ACTPASS and the path and file name, and after the ACT.CCD and the new password. The word WOLF at the end of the line becomes the new password. When the password is successfully changed or eliminated, the screen message *Password Set* appears.

Opening a different database

ACT! includes two databases when it is shipped, the ACT and DEMO databases. When you start ACT!, the ACT! database is automatically loaded as the default database. To load a different database:

1. Open the File menu and select Open.
2. Position the highlight on the database you want to use.
3. Press Enter. The database is loaded onto the screen.

The foregoing directions assume that all of the databases you want to open are in the ACT\DATABASE\ subdirectory. If your database is in a different directory, you must press Escape to erase the path in the File field at the top of the File Directory window, then enter the correct path.

Deleting a database

You can do it if you need to, but I never recommend deleting a database unless it has been copied to a floppy disk, where you can open it later. At the time you decide to delete a database, you might be convinced that you will never again need the information contained therein. Hard experience of my own and other ACT! users proves otherwise.

To delete a database:

1. Open the File menu.
2. Select the Delete item. ACT! opens the File Directory window.
3. Highlight the database you want to delete.
4. Press Enter. ACT! displays a prompt warning you that you are going to permanently delete the database. Highlight the Yes answer and press Enter. Saving a database to disk is covered later in this scene.

Attaching a setting file to a database

When you have created different menu popup options, user field labels and attributes, you are modifying the DEF file that is part of an ACT! database. When you create a new database, a companion definition file is also created. For example, if you create a database named *TEST*, ACT! simultaneously creates a definition file named *TEST.DEF*.

Suppose that you have customized a database and now have decided to create a new database. You want to use the customized popups and field modifications in the new database, too.

To attach a setting file:

1. Retrieve the database that you want to use.
2. Open the File menu and select the Attach option. ACT! displays the list of DEF files.
3. Highlight the definition file you want and press Enter.

The user field names and other attributes are attached to the database.

Using the View menu

ACT! is a database program with some unique characteristics. However, as is true with other databases, there are two ways to look at the records in the database. One way, the way you are familiar with, is seeing a single Contact record on the screen at a time. The second method is called a *list view*. In this form, part of each Contact record is displayed with other records in list format.

To see a list of the Contact records in the database:

1. Open the View menu (Fig. 7-7).
2. Select the List item. A list appears (Fig. 7-8).

The menu choices in List view are:

Select Displays the highlighted Contact in form view.

Edit Allows you to edit only the information seen in the list view of the Contact record. Move the highlight to the Contact you want to edit and press Enter.

LastLookup Executes a lookup based on the previous lookup you executed and displays the contact(s) in list view.

Calls If you have selected a Date Range before opening the View menu and selecting List, ACT! displays the list of Contacts from the current group with whom you have scheduled Calls. To select a Date Range, open the Lookup menu, and select the Date Range item. ACT! displays its calendar. Press F7 for all dates, or press the period (.) to anchor the highlight and use the cursor keys to highlight the dates that you wanted included, then press Enter. Open the View menu and select List. When you select the Calls menu, Contacts with calls scheduled in that date range are listed.

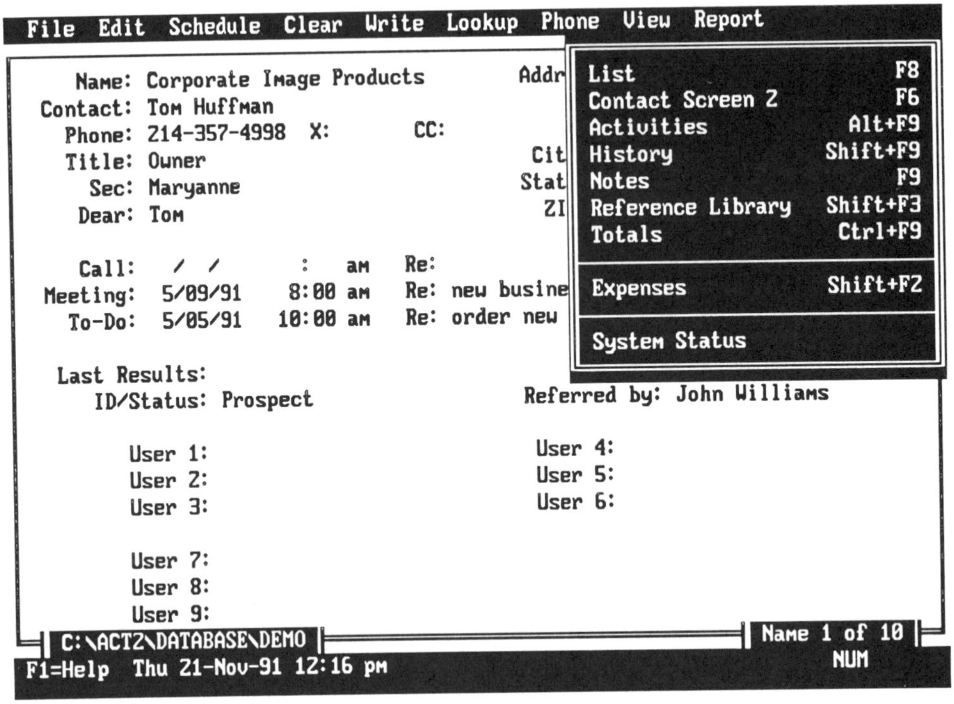

Fig. 7-7. The View menu.

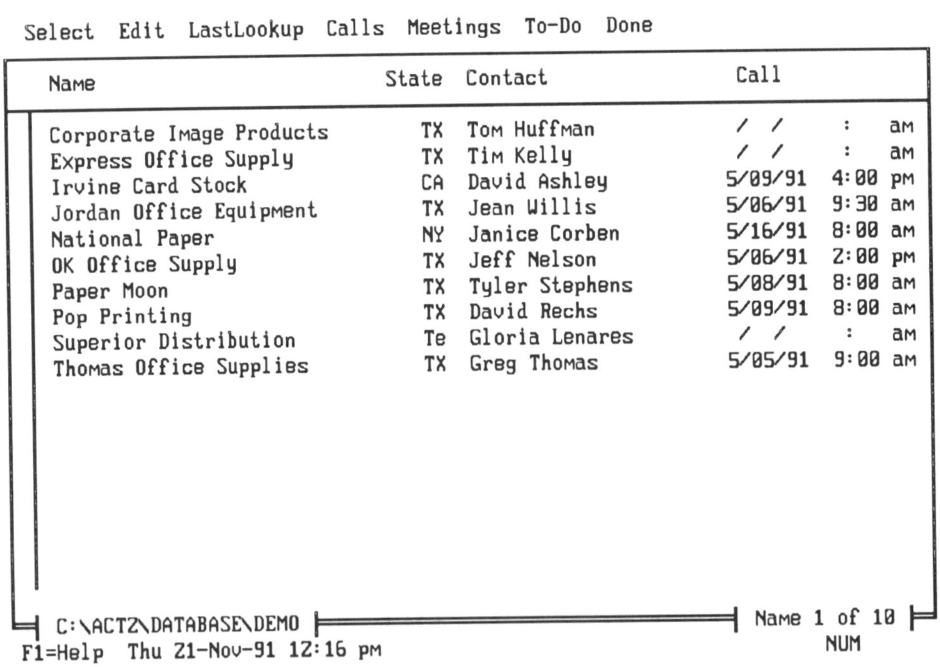

Fig. 7-8. An example of the List View.

Meetings Displays the list of contacts from the current group, with whom you have scheduled Meetings, but only if you have selected a date range prior to accessing the List. Read the explanation under Calls to set a date range.

To-Dos Displays the list of contacts from the current group with whom you have scheduled to-dos, but only if you have set a date range prior to accessing the List. Read the explanation under Calls to set a date range. Press Escape to restore the screen to form view. You can scroll the list by pressing the Page Down and Page Up keys.

Maintaining your database

As the number of Contacts in your database grows, and as you delete Contacts, you need to tune up the database. Deleting Contacts, in particular, requires that you run the Compress and Reindex item more often. You cannot harm your database by running maintenance operations, so lean toward more frequent maintenance, rather than less.

To compress and reindex your database:

1. Retrieve the database you wish to work on.
2. Open the File menu and select Maintenance. The submenu appears (Fig. 7-9).

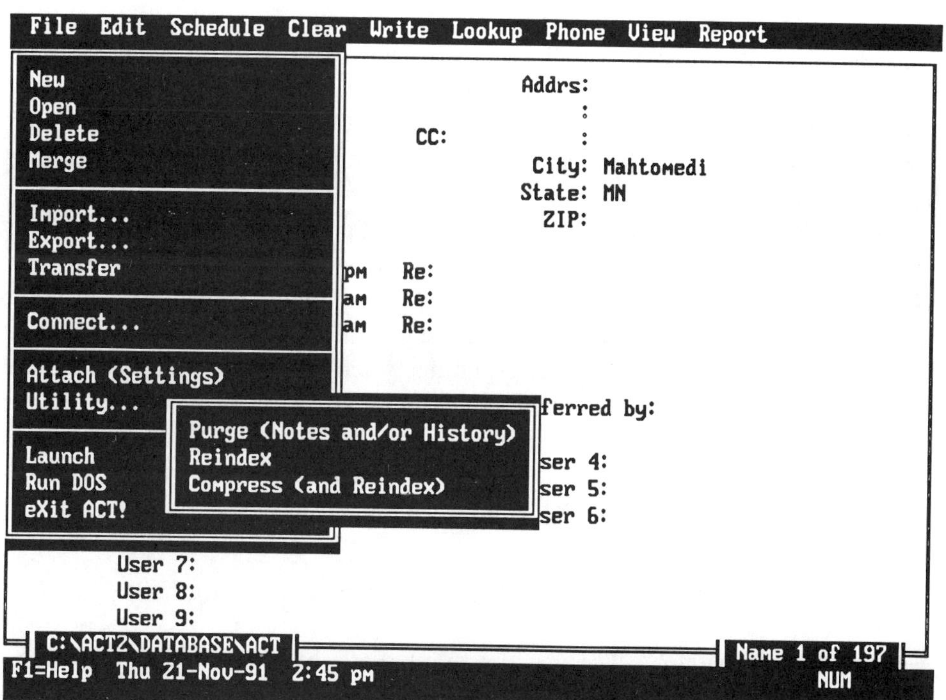

Fig. 7-9. The Utility submenu.

The utility items are:

Purge The Purge option deletes selected Notes and/or History entries. Before using this item, use the Lookup menu to select the Contact(s) that you want to affect. When you select Purge, ACT! prompts you to determine whether you want to delete the Notes, History, or both for the selected Contact(s). Make your selection, ACT! displays the Calendar, and prompts you to select a date range for the purge. To delete the entire Notes or History file, press F7. Select a range of dates by pressing the period to anchor the highlight on the first day you want to purge, then use the arrow keys to highlight the other days. When you press Enter, ACT! executes the purge. If you press Escape before pressing Enter, the operation is canceled.

Reindex The Reindex item should be selected if you have gotten an error message while working in ACT! or notice that the program seems to be operating slower than normal.

Compress/Reindex The Compress/Reindex item does exactly as it reads; it compresses the database to take advantage of space created when you deleted Contacts, then it reindexes the database.

Backing up your database

It is crucial that you copy the files, on at least a weekly basis, that compose the ACT! database. When your hard disk goes bad, you can always reinstall the ACT! program files, but your databases could be lost forever. I also recommend that you create a DOS system disk (including the DOS RESTORE program) so that you can start (boot) your computer from a floppy drive, if your hard disk crashes. Learn to back up your data and you'll sleep easier.

Backing up the files is accomplished by using the DOS copy command. If you are unfamiliar with DOS commands, you should learn them as soon as possible. The following steps will copy the files needed. The problem is that the files might be too large for a single floppy disk. Therefore you might need to copy the files one by one on several disks. Several programs, such as Norton Commander or XtreePro, can make the process much easier.

1. Insert a formatted floppy disk in either drive A or B.
2. Type CD\ACT2\DATABASE and press Enter. The DOS prompt should read C:\ACT2\DATABASE>
3. Type COPY ACT.*A: (or B: if that is where your disk is located).

DOS begins copying all of the files that begin with *ACT!*. If you get a message that the disk is full, you must copy the remaining files, one at a time. The files are:

ACT.NCI	ACT.HCD
ACT.NCD	ACT.HCI
ACT.DEF	ACT.CCD
ACT.CCI	ACT.ACI
ACT.ACD	

To copy a single file:

1. At the C:\ACT2\DATABASE> prompt, type COPY ACT.NCD A: and press Enter.
2. Repeat the process (ACT.DEF, ACT.ACD . . .) until the disk is full. The file that you were copying when DOS gave you the file full message has not been copied. So, insert a new formatted disk in the drive and start copying with that file.

Copying a single file that is too big for a disk

In the foregoing section, the instructions to save your database files were either en masse or one by one. However, one file, the ACT.CCD file grows so large that you cannot copy it to a floppy disk. For example, if your disk drive has 1.4 megabytes of capacity and the file is 2 megabytes, you cannot copy it to the disk. If you have a program, such as FastBack or Norton Backup, then split the files that are too large so that they can be copied to a floppy disk.

DOS provides another way to copy files that are too large for a single floppy:

1. Exit ACT!. Format several floppy disks in the drive you plan to copy to so that you have plenty available during the BACKUP process.
2. Change to the directory that holds your DOS files by typing CD\DOS and pressing Enter.
3. At the DOS prompt type BACKUP C:\ACT2\DATABASE*.* A:

DOS warns you that all of the files in the root directory of the floppy disk, in this case in drive A, will be deleted. If you do not want that to happen, press and hold the Control key, then the Break key. Pressing any other key starts the process.

All of the files in the ACT\DATABASE subdirectory copy to the disk(s) in drive A. If you wish, you can copy just the files ending in .CCD by substituting *.CCD for *.* in the command. Or, if you want to copy to the B drive, substitute that letter for A.

DOS copies the files, but not in the normal manner. If you asked for a directory of the disks, only two file names appear, BACKUP and CONTROL. DOS numbers the disks so that you can later restore the files in the proper order. So, as you make the disks, number them on the label. To learn more about using the DOS BACKUP command, consult your DOS manual.

Restoring files saved with DOS BACKUP

If you have stored the files using the DOS BACKUP command and your hard disk has crashed, follow these steps to get your data back:

1. Change to the DOS directory on your new hard disk by typing CD\DOS. Insert the disk that you numbered as the first disk in the A drive.
2. Type RESTORE A: C:\ACT2\DATABASE*.* This command tells DOS to take the files from the backup disk in drive A and to copy them to the subdirectory ACT2\DATABASE on drive C.

Note: the path that you used to back up the files must be used to restore the files.

DOS prompts you to insert the subsequent disks in drive A as it restores the files. Whew!

Recovering your database using reindex

If you or an associate accidentally shuts off the computer before exiting ACT!, the next time you try to start ACT!, you will get a message, such as File Error # 36 Cannot open ACT.CCD. Reindex the database.

When the computer was turned off, ACT! did not have the opportunity to reset the indexes that it uses for the database. The indexes are reset every time you exit ACT! properly. Without an index, ACT! cannot find anything. Fortunately, ACT! does have a file name, REINDEX.EXE, which attempts to repair the indexes.

After getting the Error message, follow these steps:

1. If you are not in the ACT! directory, switch to it by typing CD\ACT2 (or whatever you have named the directory).
2. Type REINDEX C:\ACT2\DATABASE\ACT. ACT! should begin reindexing. If you get further error messages, check that you are directing the reindex program on the correct path. The reindex process takes some time, depending on the number of Contacts that you have in your database. A screen message alerting you that the reindexing is finished appears.
3. Type ACT. If you are lucky, the program will start and no data will be lost.

Copying from the backup files

With luck, you have regularly been making backup copies of your database. The following steps outline the procedure for restoring the files from a floppy disk. The amount of information you will lose depends on how often you back up the database. If you do so weekly, you will have lost as much as one week's worth of histories, scheduled activities, notes, and any other aspect of ACT! that you might have added or deleted since the prior backup.

To copy the backup files, follow these steps:

1. Type CD\ACT\DATABASE to move to the ACT! database subdirectory. Your DOS prompt line should read: C:\ACT2\DATABASE>.
2. Insert the disk with your backup files into a floppy drive.
3. Type COPY A: *.* and press Enter. Substitute B: in this command if the disk containing the backup files is in drive B. DOS copies the files over the top of the files on your hard disk, including the index files.
4. Type CD.. and press Enter. The DOS prompt line should read ACT2.
5. Type ACT.

Restoring without backups

Okay, so you are really in trouble; you corrupted your database, the reindex procedure did not restore it, and you did not make backup copies. This is a last gasp attempt at a partial restoration. First, copy the corrupted files to a floppy disk. Then, exercise a trick that makes ACT! think you are importing the corrupted files to another database. The problem is that when you do this, you will not get the Notes and Histories for each Contact. You might only get the basic name and address information, but that is more than you have at the moment.

Because of the size of the ACT! database files, you might have to copy them individually to disks. For example, the ACT!.CCD file is the largest and it could fill the entire 1.2 megabyte disk itself. Copy all 11 files to floppy disks.

ACT! is shipped with two databases, ACT.CCD and DEMO.CCD. The trick is to import the ACT! Contacts into the DEMO database. When you start ACT!, it automatically tries to open the ACT! database, unless you specify otherwise at the DOS command line. The following steps start ACT! and tell it to open the DEMO database, rather than the ACT! database.

1. Type ACT DEMO. The DEMO database should open.
2. Open the File menu and select Import. The File Type submenu opens.
3. Select the ACT!/1stACT! item. The File Directory window appears. It is looking for a file with an extension CCX, which is an ACT! export file.
4. Press Escape twice.
5. Type ACT.CCD and press Enter. If the ACT.CCD database was not corrupted, the names and addresses of your Contact field should start appearing on screen.

This process takes some time, depending on the number of Contacts you have. As I mentioned, no Histories, Notes, or Activities accompany the Contacts, but at least you save the names, addresses, and phone numbers.

One other thing to try is to run the reindex program on each of the files that you copied to the floppy disk. This procedure worked once for me when the reindex would not work on my hard disk. I suspect that the problem might have been a bad sector on my hard disk, which prevented the repair.

Exiting temporarily to DOS

When you need to format a disk, copy a file, or run a different program, you can do so with the DOS shell without exiting ACT!. ACT! version 2.1 requires only 10K of memory when you use this facility.

1. Press and hold the Shift key and press F10. ACT! is saved where you left it onto the hard disk. The DOS prompt line reads Type EXIT to return to ACT.
2. After completing your tasks, type EXIT at the DOS prompt. ACT! is loaded at the place where you exited.

Importing files

If you are a new user of ACT!, you might want to import files from other database programs, such as dBase or Paradox, or from another Contact Management program. ACT! can import ACT! version 1.0 files, ACT! 2.0 files, Comma Delimited files, and Standard Data Format files. Version 2.1 of ACT! includes an improved facility to import dBase III files.

To import files from ACT! 2.0 or 1stACT!, you must first create the export file, as described in exporting files. To import from either ACT! 2.0 or 1stACT!:

1. Retrieve the database into which you want to import files.
2. Open the File menu and select Import. The submenu appears (Fig. 7-10).
3. Select ACT!

The File Directory window opens. If the files to be imported are located in a different directory, press Escape to clear the File field and type the DOS path. For example, if the files to be imported are on a disk in drive A, you would type A: followed by the file name. ACT! looks for a file with the extension CCX, the extension created when the export file is created by ACT!.

When you import files, use a database that you have created for that purpose. When you are satisfied with the import, you can use the transfer option to bring the imported files into your working ACT! database. That way, if the imported files are not what you expected, you do not have to delete them from your working database.

Importing comma delimited or SDF files

The trick to successfully importing files from these two sources is the correct order of data vis-a-vis the ACT! internal field structure.

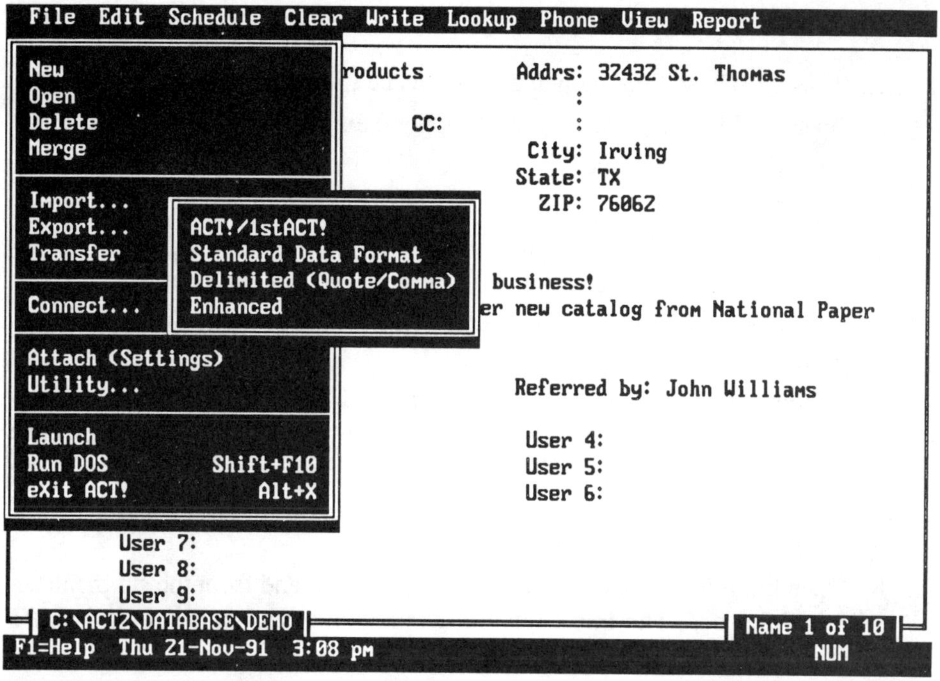

Fig. 7-10. The Import submenu.

When you create the export file, use the list of fields found in the ACT! manual's appendix E (appendix G for 2.0 users) as your guide to length of fields and the offset.

Before importing the files, set up a database expressly for importing. That way, if the importing does not go well, you can delete the imported data and try again.

1. Retrieve the database that you plan to import the files to.
2. Open the File menu and select Import, then select the Standard Data Format or the Delimited (Quote/Comma) item. ACT! opens the File Directory window. ACT! looks for the SDF extension for Standard Data Format files and TXT for Delimited (Quote/Comma) files.
3. If the file is not in the ACT2\DATABASE subdirectory, press Escape several times to enter the DOS path and file name. After the name is entered, press Enter and ACT! begins to import the files.

Importing dBase III files

Importing dBase III files requires that you create a conversion script file. A sample conversion script file is included with ACT!, which you can use as the basis for creating a script that is tailored to your database. Experience with dBase is a perquisite for creating the proper script file.

To open the sample conversion script:

1. Press SHIFT and F3 to open the Reference Library.
2. Open the File menu, and select the Open item.
3. Press Escape three times.
4. Type *.IPT
5. Press Enter. The File Directory window displays a list of the ACT! subdirectories and four files with the .IPT extension (Fig. 7-11).
6. Highlight the file ACT2.IPT and press Enter. The conversion script file appears (Fig. 7-12).

   Your task is to match the fields from the dBase file with the field structure in ACT!. For more guidance, open the other .IPT files or look on page E-10 of the ACT! User's Guide.
7. After creating the script, save the file with a new name, with an .IPT extension in the C:ACT2\ directory.
8. Open the File menu, and select the Import item, and from the submenu select Enhanced. The File Directory window opens a listing of all the .IPT files.
9. Highlight the .IPT file you have created and press Enter.
10. ACT! runs the .IPT script, prompting you for an input file name. (Remember to include a path if the file is not located in the ACT2 directory.) Type the name of the DBF file that you intend to import. ACT! then

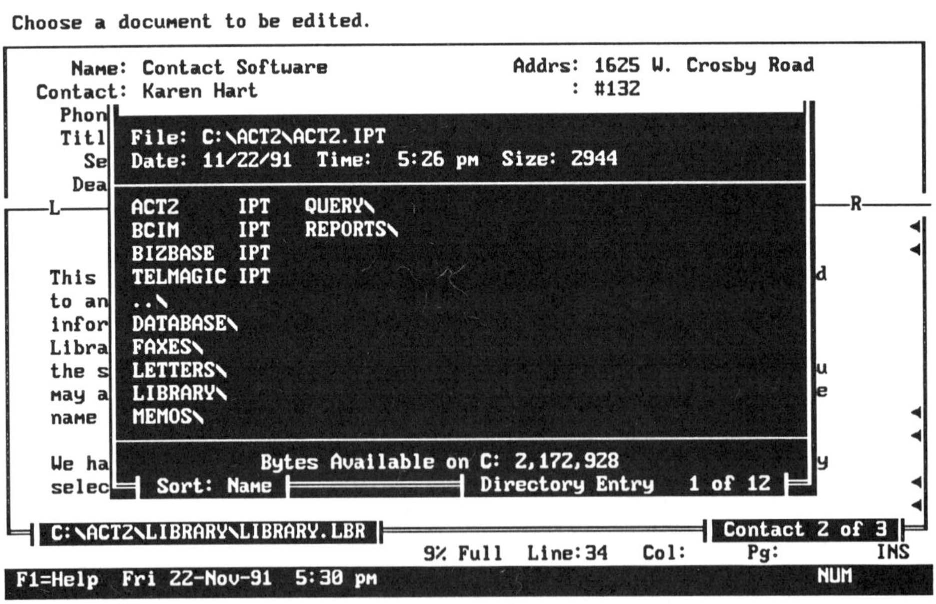

Fig. 7-11. The list of subdirectories and IPT files.

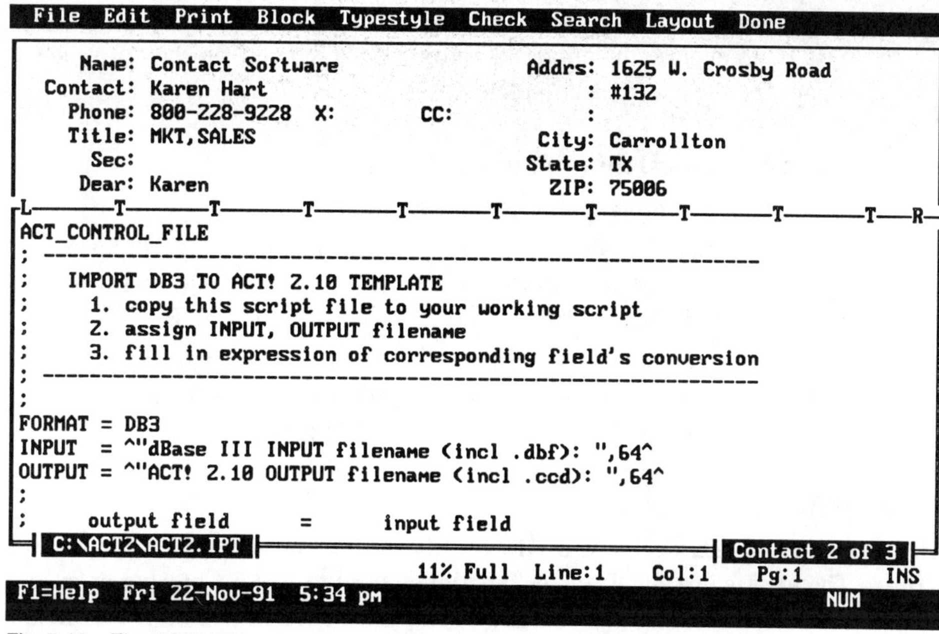

Fig. 7-12. The ACT2.IPT conversion script file.

prompts you for an output file name. Type the output file name, and press Enter.

ACT! compiles the file and returns to ACT!. The final step is to use the import item to bring the information into an ACT! file.

Exporting files

You can export ACT! files to ACT 2.0 or 1stACT!, to Standard Data Format, Comma Delimited files or to dBase III files. When you export to the ACT! 2.0 format, four files are created with the extensions: CCX, NCX, HCX, and ACX.

Exporting to ACT! 2.0 1stACT!

1. If you want to export only specific Contacts, use the Lookup items to group the Contacts.
2. Open the File menu and select the Export item.
3. From the submenu, select the Export file you want to create. ACT! then displays a prompt, asking if you want to export the current Contact or the Group. Make your selection. Next, ACT! displays the File Directory window.
4. Press Escape to clear the File field and enter the DOS path and the file name. Do not add an extension.

5. ACT! prompts you as to the date range of edited Contacts to be exported. Press F7 to export all Contacts. A progress bar appears on screen. When it disappears, the export is completed.

Exporting to Comma Delimited or SDF files

1. Open the File menu and select the Export item.
2. Select either Standard Data Format or Comma Delimited. ACT! opens the File Directory window. Press Escape to clear the File field and enter the DOS path and file name. ACT! adds the extension for you. Press Enter.
3. ACT! prompts you as to whether you want to export the user fields. Answer the prompt, after which ACT! displays a progress bar at the bottom of the screen. When the bar disappears, the file is completed.

Transferring contacts

Many new ACT! users get confused as to the distinction between *Transfer* and *Export*. The idea is that the Transfer function is used to move Contacts from one database file to another on the same computer system. When you have completed the Transfer, ACT! asks if you wish to delete the transferred Contacts from the source database. When you export Contact records, it is usually to a disk for use on a different computer.

From a business standpoint, suppose that you are the sales manager and that you have a master list of customers. You want to give your salespeople a database of customers with which to work. You could use the Lookup to define a geographic territory and export the Group of Contacts to a file. The salesperson then has his customers and you retain the master list. As the sales manager, you should use either the ID/Status field or a user field to identify which Contacts have been exported to whom.

To transfer Contacts to another ACT! database:

1. Use the Lookup menu to group the Contacts.
2. Open the File menu and select Transfer. ACT! displays the File Directory window listing other ACT! databases.
3. Highlight the database you want to transfer the Contacts to and press Enter.

ACT! begins the Transfer process. When completed, ACT! prompts you as to whether you want to delete the Contacts from the source database.

Merging databases, version 2.1

In the preceding section on transferring contacts, the scenario of a sales manager maintaining a master database while distributing Contacts to the salespeople was supposed. Let's further suppose that the sales manager wishes to update the master database with information from the salespeople. This update can be tricky, because both databases contain the same Contacts with only slight variations, perhaps in the Note or History file or a single field such as Last Results. So, ACT! presents you with a series of choices regarding how to merge the two databases.

1. To begin, use the File menu to Open the source database. For example, if the source file is on a disk in drive A:, you must start with that file open. That is the database from which you wish to merge the information. If you want to merge only a specific Contact or a specific group, use the Lookup menu to make the selection.
2. Open the File menu and select Merge.
3. Select the database into which you want the information to be merged. This becomes the target file. ACT! displays the Merge Settings window (Fig. 7-13).
4. Press F2 to edit the settings.
5. Press F2, to open the Matching Record Treatment submenu, as seen in Fig. 7-14.

   The options for merging are:

   Newest Contact Data Remains Select this option when you want the matching record that has the newest information to be copied to (or remain in) the Target database.

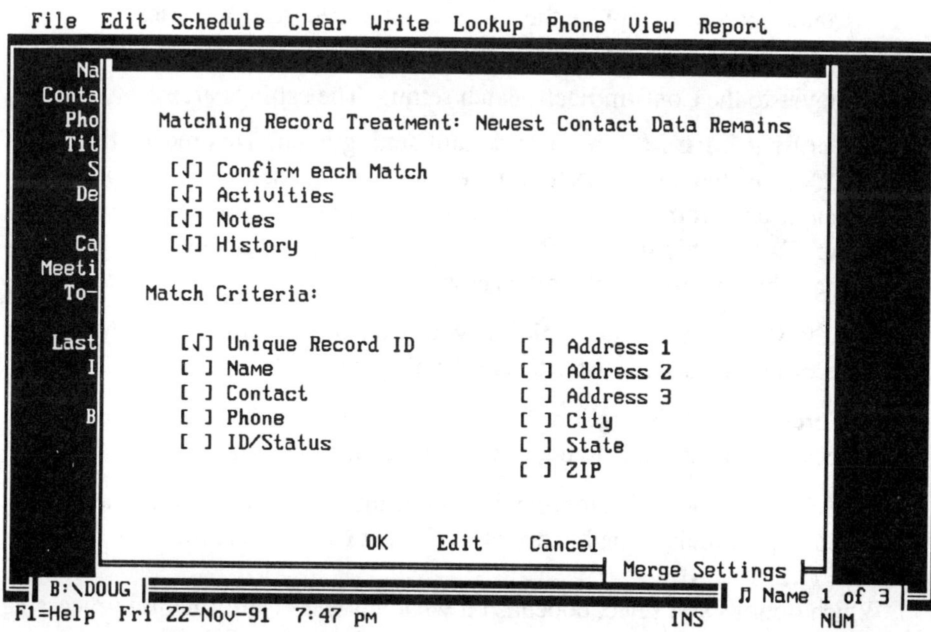

Fig. 7-13. The Merge Settings window.

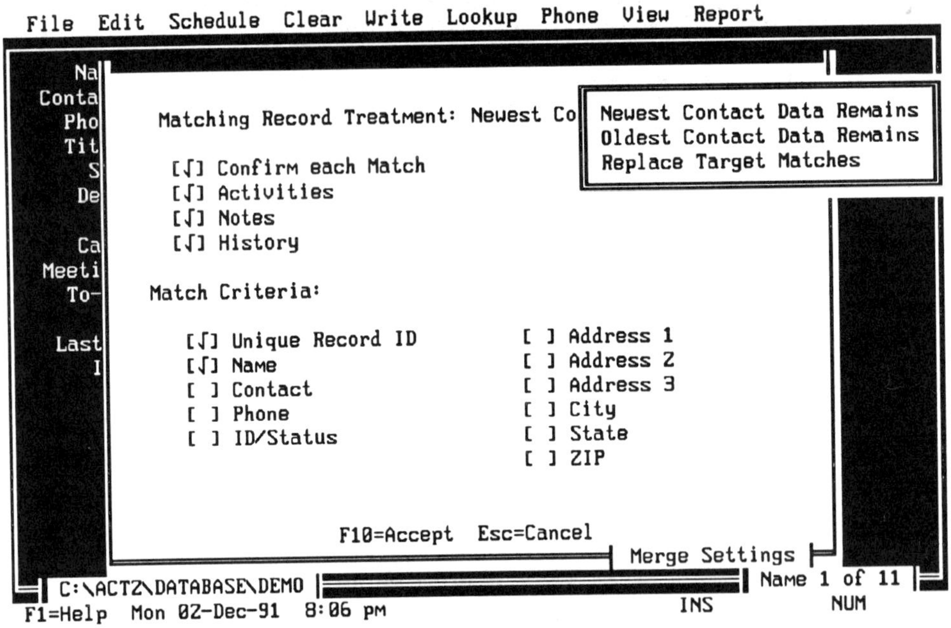

Fig. 7-14. The Matching Record Treatment submenu.

Oldest Record Replaces Select this option if you want the oldest Contact record to remain when a match is found.

Replace Target Matches Select this option if you want the Source Contact record to replace the Target Contact record in all cases.

6. Select the matching solution you want and press Enter. The highlight moves to the Confirm Each Match setting. The settings are:

   Confirm Each Match The default setting is on. This means that when ACT! encounters a matching record in both the source and target file, it pauses and prompts you to indicate whether or not to allow the merge to occur. To turn this setting off, so that ACT! does not prompt you, press the space bar and the checkmark is erased.

   Activities Select this option if you want the activities from the Source record to replace the activities of the Target record.

   Notes Select this option if you want the notes from the Source Contact record to replace the note in the Target Contact record.

   History Select this option if you want the history from the Source Contact to replace the history of the Target Contact record.

Which options you select depends on what amount of information processing occurs in the Target (master) database. For example, if the sales manager only examines the master database after the merge or then prepares reports, you would probably want the Source Contact record to overwrite every aspect in the Target (master) database file. If the sales manager annotates the history file, you would want to shut off the merging of the history from the Source to the Target. Looked at another way, the sales manager would probably want to see the activities scheduled and their resolution for each of his salespeople. In that respect, he would want the Source History file to go into the master database for tracking.

Match criteria

In version 2.1, ACT! includes a unique record number with every Contact record that is created. Part of the unique record number is a time/date stamp. So, no two Contact records can ever be confused as identical.

As an example, suppose that the sales manager creates a Contact record in the master ACT! database. When he does, the record is assigned a unique record number and time/date is stamped. Next, he exports the record to the salesperson who is assigned to that account. The salesperson adds activities, notes and a history is created. When the sales manager asks for the salesperson's database and merges it with the master database, ACT! looks at the unique record number and matches it. At that point, the merge settings take over.

Another consideration is the case where the master database has a Contact record that is not exported to the salesperson, but the salesperson creates (not knowing that the master database already has one) on his own. Because the records were created at different times, the unique record number and time/date stamp would not produce a match if that was the only match criteria selected. To avoid a spurious duplication, you can select other match criteria; just move the highlight to the criteria you want to use and press the space bar, which inserts a checkmark. To remove the checkmark, press the space bar again. The default match setting is *Name*.

Note: If you do not set any Match Criteria, the merge process adds all of the source records to the target database, but it does not overwrite the target database records.

Press F10 to begin the merge process. ACT! prompts you to determine which Contact records are to be merged, the current Contact or the selected Group. If you have set the Confirm Each Match to on, when ACT! finds a match it displays a window to confirm the merge. When completed, ACT! asks if you want to delete the Contact records from the Source database.

From laptop to desktop and back

Many ACT! users have two computers. A laptop or portable that they use while in the field and a desktop that is located in the office. ACT! 2.1 includes an easy means for communication between the two computers called *direct link.* To use direct link, both of the computers must have a free serial port, and you must have a *null modem cable*, which is a serial cable that any computer store stocks. When the ACT! file is transferred, it is stored in a file named TEMP_DB.

1. Connect the cable between the two computers. On the computer from which you want to send the files, open the database you want to send and use the Lookup menu to select a specific Contact or group of Contacts. If you do not use a lookup, all Contact records are sent.
2. On both computers, open the File menu and select Connect. From the submenu, select Options.
3. On both computers, from the options submenu, select Direct Link Options. ACT! displays a window with two settings: the communication port to which the cable is connected and the Baud Rate at which you intend to transfer the data.

   Enter the communication ports you intend to use by pressing F2 and selecting the port. If you are using a mouse on your desktop, it is likely that the mouse is using Comm 1. If you also have a modem, it is further likely that the modem uses Comm 2. So, your desktop might have to be set to Comm port 3.

   Set the baud rate so that it is identical on both computers. The suggested baud rate is 19200.
4. Press F10 to save the settings. From the sending computer, open the File menu and select Connect and from the submenu Direct Link, followed by send. ACT! displays the window that prompts as to which Contacts you want to send.
5. At the computer receiving the file, open the File menu and select Connect, Direct Link, and Receive.
6. At the sending computer, decide which Contacts you want to send and press Enter.

ACT! compresses the selected Contacts into a file, then sends them. If the wrong Comm ports were selected, ACT! displays a message to that effect. When completed, ACT! displays the *Transfer Completed* message.

The file that was sent is stored in the ACT2\DATABASE\ subdirectory under the name TEMP_DB, in a noncompressed format. Now that the Contacts have been transferred, you have the option of merging them into an existing database (as already discussed) or using the File, Transfer item to bring them into another database. The key is to do something with the file soon; if you do not and then send a second Direct Link file, the first file is overwritten. Only one TEMP_DB can be in ACT! at any one time. You might have to test this process by sending several files and checking their integrity before you find the optimum baud rate.

Creating expense records

Every salesperson I know hates to fill out expense records, but if you want to be reimbursed, you must do it. If you are self-employed, this way is good to track tax deductible mileage and other expenses.

To create an expense record:

1. Open the View menu and select Expenses. You can also access the expense screen by pressing Shift and F2 together. The expense entry form is shown in Fig. 7-15.
2. The highlight is on the File menu name. Press Enter.
3. Select the Expense Screen item.
4. Enter the information. The date entry can be made by pressing F4 to display the Calendar and then highlighting the date and pressing Enter. Other fields have Popups, also.
5. Press F10 to save the expense. ACT! displays the total of all expenses in the upper right corner of the screen.

The following file items are used:

Odometer Use this menu to enter your beginning odometer reading and the end reading. ACT! calculates the miles driven and the cost.

Field Defaults Use this menu item to enter a permanent value in any of the ex-

```
 Edit  Report  Lookup  Done

           Date: 11/23/91                    Total Expenses: $             0.00
           Type:
         Amount:             0.00
        Payment:
      Charge to:
        Purpose:
          Where:

           Name:
        Contact:
           City:
          State:
         User 1:
         User 2:
         User 3:

      Bill Time:    0.00         x $      35.00   per hour  =              0.00

 Begin Odometer:             0
   End Odometer:             0
 Total Distance:             0   x $      0.210   per km/mi =              0.00
   DATABASE\EXPENSE                                               Date 1 of 1
F1=Help  Sat 23-Nov-91   3:20 pm                                       NUM
```

Fig. 7-15. The Expense entry screen.

pense fields. For example, if you only record one type of expense, you can enter that once.

Default Rates Use this menu item to enter your normal charge for hourly billings and odometer reimbursements.

Field Labels Use this menu item to modify the field labels and the field attributes. For example, if you want the User 1 field to be used for entering the name of the project to which the expense should be charged, you could rename the field "Project."

The following Report menu items are:

Date Range The Date Range report can be printed to a printer or to the screen. ACT! displays the Calendar, in which you can select a date range by highlighting the dates you want or by pressing F7 to include all reports.

Type of Expense The Type of Expense report prints the expense records by the date of the expense and then by the type.

User Defined You can create your own style of expense report. To understand how to create a User-defined report, see chapter 6 on reports.

The following Lookup menu items are:

Date Range Finds expenses in a specified date range.

Type of Expense Finds expenses by the entry in the Type field.

Every Expense Makes all expenses available for reports.

Name Finds expenses by the entry in the Name field.

Contact Finds expenses by the contact's name.

City Finds expenses by city.

State Finds expenses by state.

Checking the System Status

The System Status window gives you important information on the amount of RAM available, hard disk space, and the version of ACT! and DOS that is installed on your computer. One of the key indicators is the Memory Available number. If you have any problems with the word processor, particularly when you attempt to spellcheck a document, check this number to determine if 80K is available. If you have less, you will have to remove some of the RAM resident programs.

To see the System Status, open the View menu and select System Status. The window appears (Fig. 7-16). You cannot make any entries in the window; it is for

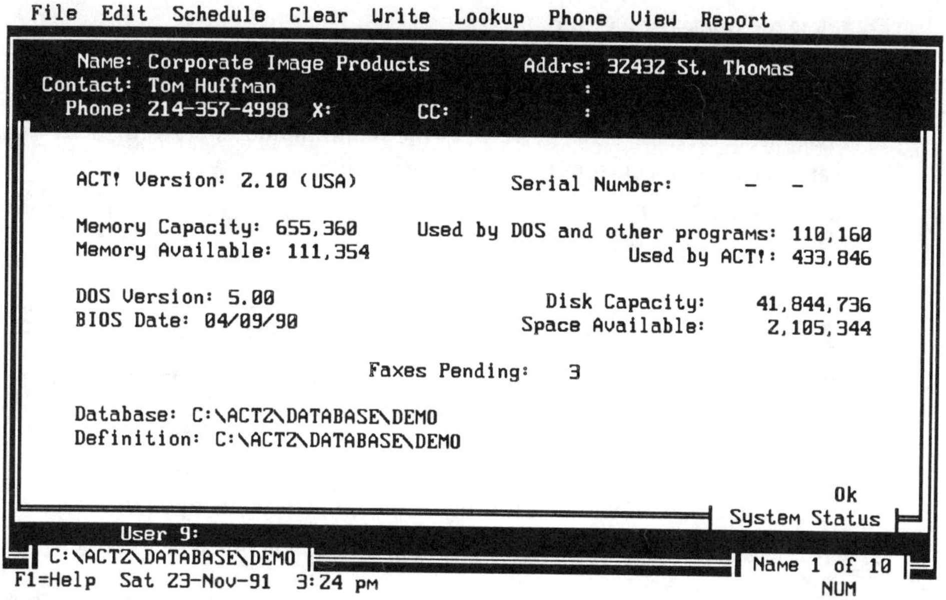

Fig. 7-16. The System Status window.

information purposes only. Version 2.1 includes a status of the number of faxes that you have pending, if any.

Editing groups

From time to time, you might need to make an edit that affects many of your contacts. For example, if a zip code is added to an area, many of the contacts in the old zip must be updated. Rather than using the lookup to find each Contact individually and then making the edit, ACT! can change each zip code (or area code) as a group.

1. Use the Lookup to create the group of Contacts that need an identical edit.
2. Open the Edit menu and select Group. ACT! displays the Contact record with blank fields.
3. Move the highlight to the field that must be changed. Type in the new entry.
4. Press F10. ACT! updates all of the Contacts with the information that you entered.

Deleting Contacts

Most ACT! users never permanently delete a Contact, but use the Transfer item on the File menu to move the Contact record to a different database. See the next section on transferring Contacts to do so.

To delete a Contact or a group.

1. Use the Lookup menu to find the Contact(s).
2. Press the Delete key. ACT! verifies the deletion and checks to see if you want to delete the current Contact or the group.
3. Select either This Contact or Group. ACT! verifies the deletion once more. If you select Yes, the Contact(s) are deleted.

Using the Calculator to enter numbers

One of the more useful tools that ACT! has is the Popup calculator. With it, you can enter numbers and perform calculations. When finished, the total can be inserted into the Contact record, a Note, or an expense.

1. Position the cursor where you want the calculated value to be inserted.
2. Press and hold the Shift key, then press F4. The Calculator appears (Fig. 7-17).

Enter numbers from the keyboard just as you would into a normal calculator. The following keys execute arithmetic operators:

+	Addition
–	Subtraction
*	Multiplication
/	Division
=	Total
Enter	Total

Insert Inserts the number in the display into the Contact record at the cursor position.

Escape Exits the calculator without inserting any number into the Contact record.

Clear Type C to clear the total in the left window and in the register, if you have not already pressed a function key.

Print Type P to print all the numbers from the tape in the left window.

Tape Type T to clear the contents in the tape window.

F3 Clears value in memory.

F4 Recalls the value in memory to the display.

F5 Adds the value in the display to the value in memory.

F6 Subtracts the value in the display from the value in memory.

F7 Multiplies the value in memory by the value in the display.

F8 Divides the value in memory by the value in the display.

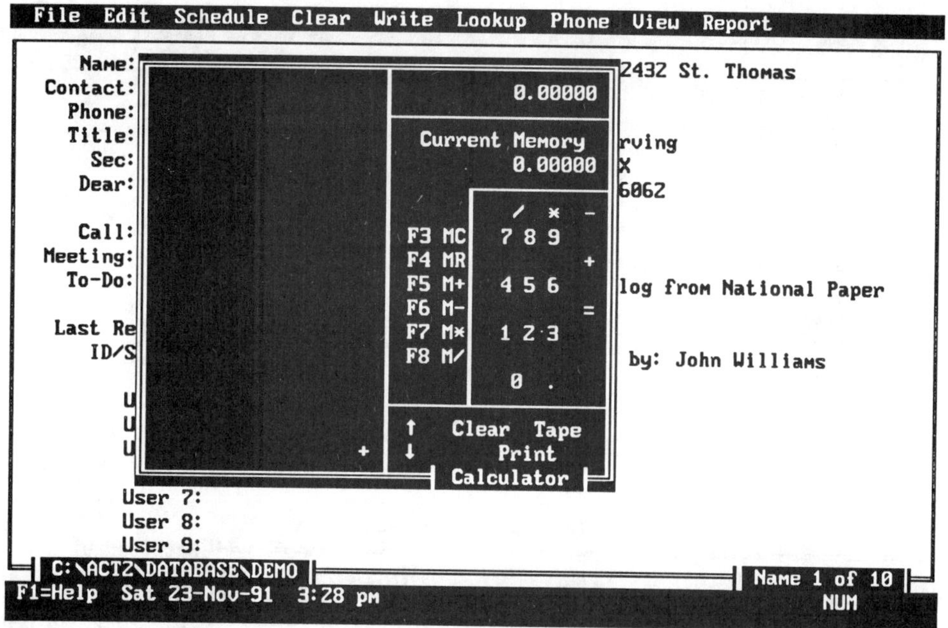

Fig. 7-17. The Calculator.

If you have entered more figures that the window can display, press the up arrow or down arrow to see the remaining figures. If you want to move the position where the calculator displays when you press Shift and F4, press the scroll lock and use the arrow keys to position where you want. Press the scroll lock again to begin calculations.

Setting path defaults

When you installed ACT! it automatically set up a series of subdirectories for storing Databases, Letters, Memos, Faxes, Libraries, Reports, and Queries. In addition, it assumes that ACT! is the default database to open when you start ACT!. You can change the start-up database and the "path" for any of the subdirectories.

1. Open the Edit menu.
2. Select the Options item.
3. From the submenu, select Path Defaults. The Default Directory Information screen appears (Fig. 7-18).

The first field at the top of the screen is labeled *Database Directory*, and the entry in the field is DATABASE. This label tells ACT! that the databases are located in the DATABASE subdirectory. Because ACT! is installed in the ACT2\ main directory, it assumes that the database is in the ACT2\DATABASE subdirec-

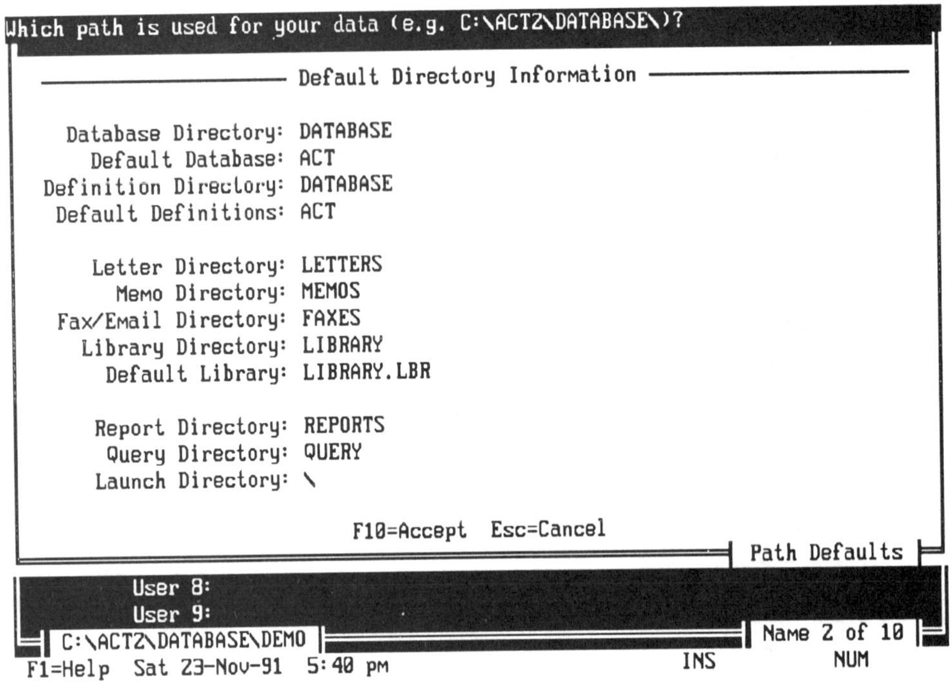

Fig. 7-18. The Default Directory Information screen.

tory. If you wanted to, you could enter a different subdirectory name and ACT! would then attempt to open the ACT! database from that location. Before that would work, you would first have to use the DOS command MKDIR to create the subdirectory.

The second field is labeled *Default Database* and has the entry ACT. This entry tells ACT! to open the ACT! database when the program starts. If you have created a different database that you want ACT! to open at start-up, enter the name of the database here.

The last field is labeled *Launch Directory*. The entry in the field is "\", which means to look in the root directory for files that end in .BAT. So, when you open the File menu and select the Launch item, ACT! displays the contents of your root directory (Fig. 7-19).

As you can see in Fig. 7-19, two files end with .BAT. The first one is the AUTOEXEC.BAT file. This is the file that DOS runs when you start your computer. An AUTOEXEC.BAT file is very handy; for example, you could use it to start ACT! every time you turn on your computer. Another BAT file is named, *QPRO.BAT* and I use it to launch Quattro Pro. When I am finished working in Quattro Pro, ACT! automatically takes control and returns me to ACT!. So, I can access other programs, do some work, and return to ACT! very easily.

Note: do not attempt to load memory-resident software with the Launch item. They must be loaded prior to starting ACT!.

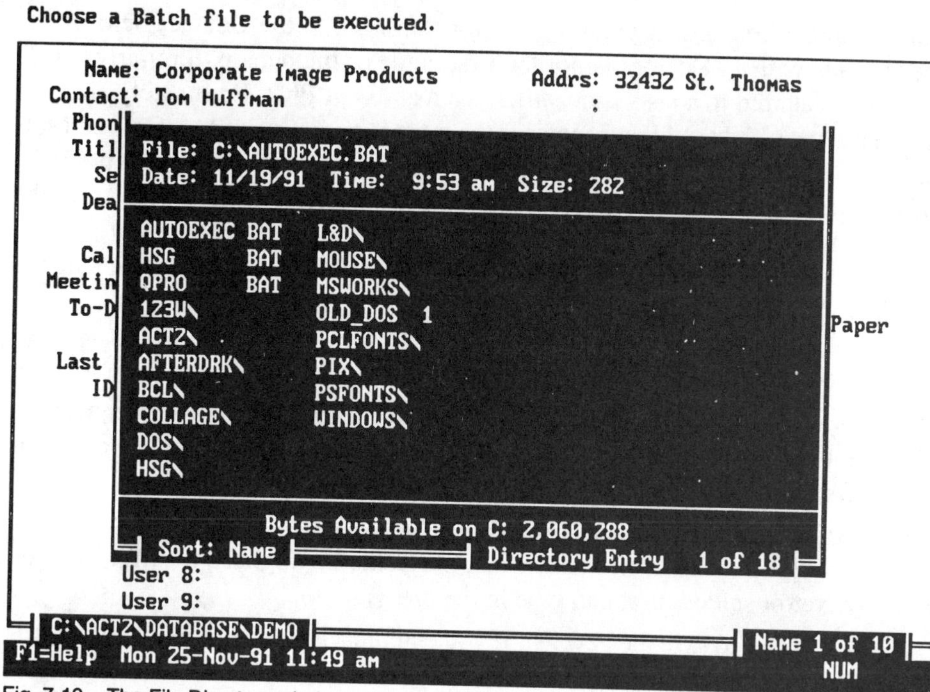

Fig. 7-19. The File Directory window of the root directory.

Field defaults

Act! allows you to define entries in fields in order to save you time and eliminate errors. For example, if your contacts are primarily located in Texas, you shouldn't have to enter the TX abbreviation in the State field every time you insert a new Contact.

To insert default field entries:

1. Open the Edit menu and select the Options item.
2. From the submenu, select field defaults. ACT! displays a blank Contact record screen. Move the highlight to the field into which you want to insert a default entry. If, for example, you want TX to be inserted in the State field when you begin inserting a new Contact, move the highlight to the State field and type TX.
3. Press F10 to save the new field default. You can enter as many field defaults as you want. When you actually insert a new Contact, you can edit the field defaults that you set up, just in case the contact is not from Texas.

Defining name separators

The names of the people with which you do business might be of a specific form. For example, if you are in the medical instruments business, the majority of your contacts might be MDs. If you type Doctor Van Lom in the Contact field, ACT! needs to know that "Doctor" is not the first name of the person. Similarly, ACT! needs to be alerted to a last-name suffix, such as JD or PhD. Fortunately, the programmers at ACT! have already entered the most commonly used prefixes and suffixes; therefore you do not have to do anything. However, if you use a prefix or suffix that ACT! does not expect, it assumes that the prefix or suffix is part of the contact's name.

To see the list of first name prefixes, last name prefixes, or last name suffixes which ACT! already expects:

1. Open the Edit menu and select the Options item.
2. From the submenu, select Name Separators. From the next submenu, select the appropriate separator. For this example, selecting the Last Name suffixes opens the Last Name suffixes window (Fig. 7-20).
3. ACT! automatically recognizes all of the suffixes you see in the list. If you use a suffix that is not on the list, move the highlight to a suffix that you never or seldom use, and type in the one you use.
4. Press F10 to save the new list. If you entered a new suffix, ACT! disregards it when Looking Up by Last Name. Check the other lists to verify that a first-name prefix or last-name prefix that you used is on either list. If it is not, add it (as described).

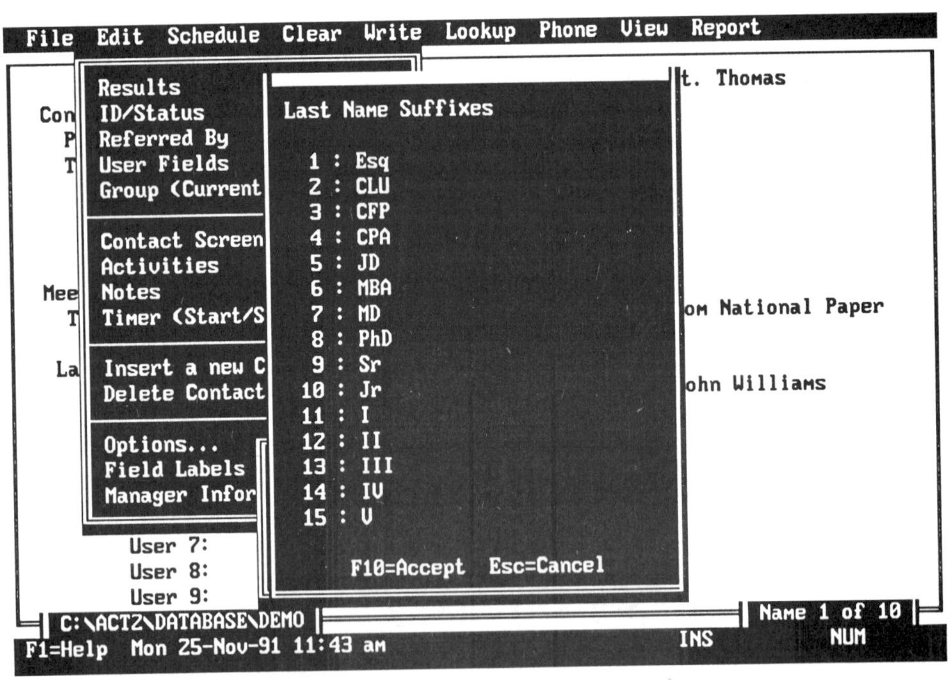

Fig. 7-20. The Last Name suffixes window.

Creating ACT! macros, adjusting the mouse

A *macro* is a series of recorded keystrokes that can be replayed by pressing a combination of two keys, called *HotKey*. For example, one of the tasks that you should undertake at day's end is to update, usually by moving them to the next business day, the calls and to-dos that you have not accomplished. The procedure for doing so was described earlier. The first macro is a simple one that inserts a message in the Last Results field. The second macro outlined here updates the Calls and To-Dos that you had scheduled for the current date and reschedules them for the next day.

1. If you are already in ACT!, you must exit.
2. At the DOS prompt, type ACTMOUSE. This does two things, if you have a mouse connected to your computer properly, the mouse activates and the macro program is loaded.

    After ACT! is loaded, create a new Contact that is to be used just for creating and testing macros. I use a Contact named *Macro Inc.*, and the Contact person is *Guinea Pig*. Enter data into most of the fields so that when you run a test, you can see the effect the macro has on the intended fields.
3. Press the Left Shift key and the Control keys together. ACT! displays the Control Panel (Fig. 7-21).

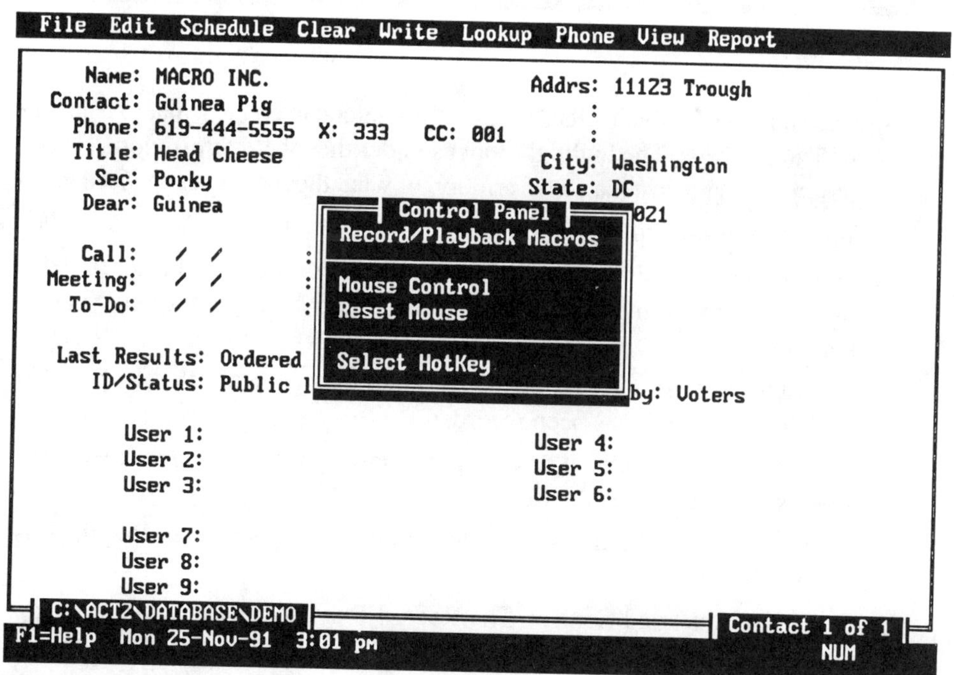

Fig. 7-21. The Control Panel.

4. With the highlight on Record/Playback Macros, press Enter. The Record/Playback macros window appears (Fig. 7-22).

   You can create up to 10 different sets of macro files of 10 macros each, which gives you a total of 100 possible macros. However, you can only have one macro file loaded into memory at a time.

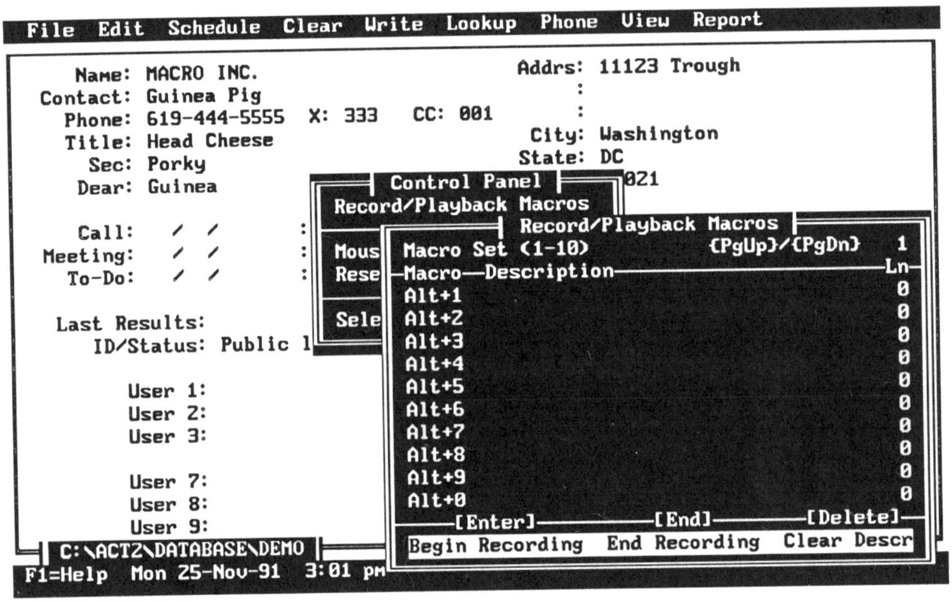

Fig. 7-22. The Record/Playback macros window.

5. Press number 1, which tells ACT! that you intend to create a macro using the ALT and 1 keys. The highlight moves under the label *Description*. The description field is just that, a description of what the macro is supposed to do.
6. Type: Left Message in Last Results.
7. Press Enter. ACT! is now in record mode. It is best to use the access letter method for recording macros so that the macro clearly interprets your intentions.
8. Open the Edit menu by typing E. ACT! emits a beep after each keystroke so that you know it has been recorded.
9. Type: R to edit Results. The Popup window appears and the screen highlight is in the Last Results field.
10. Type L. The entry "Left Message to Call me back" is entered into the Last Results field.
11. Press Left Shift and Control. The Record/Playback macros window reappears.
12. Press End.

Testing a macro

The macro is now saved and can be replayed by pressing the ALT and number 1 keys together. Test the macro in the Contact record you have created for this purpose. First, erase the contents of the Last Results field by pressing E to open the Edit menu and R for the results field. Then, press B to blank the Results field.

Press ALT and 1. As the macro replays, the screens flash by as the same keystrokes that you pressed are repeated. The message is inserted into the Last Results field. If your macro does not work, repeat these steps and try again.

Accessing more macros

Each macro file can contain a total of 10 macros that are assigned from ALT 1 to the ALT 0. After you have created 10 macros, you must start working in a new macro file.

1. Open the Control Panel by pressing Left Shift and Control.
2. ACT! opens Macro Set 1. Look at the top left of the Record/Playback window. A number is displayed, which alerts you as to which file is active.
3. To go to another macro file, press PgUp or PgDn. The number changes in the top left corner as you press the key.
4. When you find the file you want, press Escape until the Control Panel is closed. The file that you were on is now the active file.

Deleting a macro

If a macro does not work properly, it cannot be edited. Instead, you must start over from scratch.

1. To open the Control Panel, press Left Shift and Control.
2. Move the highlight to the HotKey for the macro, ALT 1 to ALT 0.
3. Press Delete.

Mouse settings

1. Highlight the item and Mouse Control, and press Enter.

   The Mouse Control submenu appears with the following settings:

   Motion Sensitivity Enter a number from 1 to 10, 10 being very sensitive, 1 being very insensitive to determine the response to the horizontal movement of the mouse.

   Vertical Speed Adjust Enter a – (minus sign) to slow down the vertical movement of the highlight in a menu, or enter a + (plus) to speed up the movement. The vertical movement is adjusted in relation to the number you entered for the horizontal movement. If the horizontal value is 6, and you enter a minus sign, then the vertical is reduced to 3. If the horizontal value is 6 and the plus sign is entered, then the vertical movement is set to 12. An equal sign keeps the vertical number the same as the horizontal number.

Both Button Delay When you press the far left and far right mouse buttons together, ACT! displays the Macro Record/Playback Macros window. If you enter a number such as 500, you must hold both buttons down for a longer time to display the window. If you enter a low number, press both buttons quickly to display the window.

Default Settings If you want to return to the default mouse movement settings, select this item.

2. Press Enter to change a setting.
3. Press Escape to return to the Control Panel main menu.

Resetting the mouse

Use this item to reset the mouse after you have used the File menu and Launch item to load a different application.

Selecting new hotkeys

One of the items on the control panel is *Select Hotkey*. If you load a *TSR* (*terminate and stay resident*) program, the keystrokes to activate that program might be in conflict with the keystrokes that are used to activate the ACT! control panel. If this has happened to you when you tried to access the control panel, you have to exit ACT! and reboot your computer or use the commands that come with the TSR to remove it from memory. If the TSR is loaded in your AUTOEXEC.BAT file, you must use the ACT! Reference Library editor to load the file and modify the file so that the TSR does not load. An easy way to do this is to put the letters REM at the beginning of the line that loads the TSR. That way, after you modify ACT!'s Hotkeys, you can go back and reload the AUTOEXEC.BAT file and delete the REM letters.

1. Assuming that you have shut off the conflicting TSR, press Left Shift and Control.
2. The Control Panel opens. The Select Hotkey window opens (Fig. 7-23).
3. Highlight the keystroke combination that you want to use to access the control panel.
4. Press Enter. The checkmark on the right moves to the new key combination.
5. Press Escape to close the window.

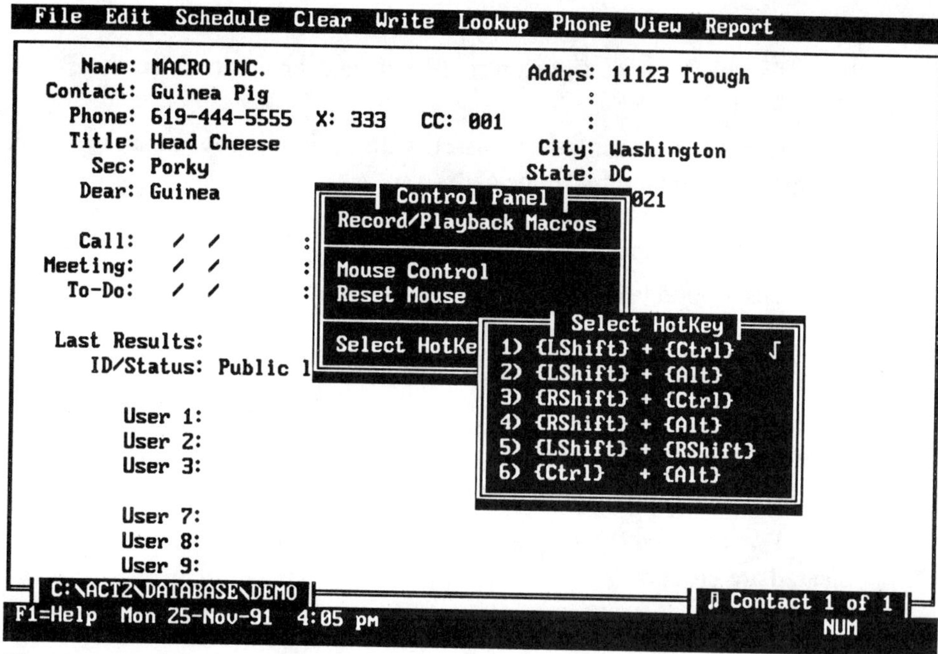

Fig. 7-23. The Select Hotkey window.

A combination macro

Let's run a macro that stops and waits for your input so that you can replay a second macro to finish the task. This macro is designed to be executed at the end of the business day. It groups those Contacts for which you had a call scheduled, but did not make. After you enter a new date to make the calls, a second macro is replayed that repeats the steps to update the to-dos.

1. Open the Control Panel and select the Hotkey.
2. In the description field enter *Updating Calls.*
3. Press Enter.
4. Type L to open the Lookup menu.
5. Type T to select the Today item.
6. The Task List appears and the highlight is in the Calls column. Press Enter. All of the Contacts with Calls set for Today that were not cleared are grouped.
7. Type E to open the Edit menu.
8. Type G for group.
9. Type Tab twice. The second tab stop (if you have not changed it) is in the Call field. At this point you need to enter a new date, so this macro ends.
10. Press Left Shift and Control.

11. Press End.
12. Press Escape to close the Control Panel, and again to close the Blank Group Edit.

When you replay this macro, the Contacts with Calls are grouped, and you can enter a new date on which to make the calls.

1. Open the Control Panel and select the Hotkey.
2. In the description field enter *Updating to-dos.*
3. Press Enter.
4. Type L to open the Lookup menu.
5. Type T to select the Today item.
6. The Task List appears and the highlight is in the Calls column. Press the Right Arrow key twice, so that the highlight is in the to-dos' column.
7. Press Enter. All of the Contacts with to-dos set for Today that were not cleared are grouped.
8. Type E to open the Edit menu.
9. Type G for group.
10. In the blank Contact screen, press Tab twice and the down arrow six times so that the highlight stops in the To-Do field.
11. Press Left Shift and Control.
12. Press End.

The second macro is finished! At the end of your working day, you can press two hotkeys, one for calls and one for to-dos and rest assured that the activities that time declared impossible to finish are scheduled for another day.

Summary

This chapter covered the many aspects of ACT! that can be customized to the individual user or company. Several new features of version 2.1 were discussed, including creating macros, sending data from a laptop to a desktop, and merging those files.

"I cannot give you a formula for success,
but I can give you the formula for failure: Try to please everybody."

HERBERT SWOPE

8
CHAPTER

Mapping your Contacts

The 2.1 version of ACT! is designed to take advantage of several software products. In chapter 7 you were introduced to Books, Cards, and Labels, a software product that enhances output of ACT!. This chapter is devoted exclusively to MAPLINX, a software product that you can purchase to link directly to your ACT! database files and create graphic representations of the location of your contacts and much more. MAPLINX comes in two versions, MAPLINX PRO and MAPLINX BASIC.

The main difference between the two versions is the inclusion of zip code polygons in the Pro version. When you look for contacts, MAPLINX finds them a specific zip code area (or areas), the polygons are drawn on the screen. These polygons are the boundaries of the zip code areas, as designated by the United States Postal Service.

To order MAPLINX, and I recommend that you do, call them at 214-231-1400.

After you install MAPLINX, the ACT! Lookup menu is modified to include the Map item. MAPLINX includes a sample file that you can import into an ACT! database. The MAPLINX manual steps you through the various output features.

When you start MAPLINX, a map of the entire U.S. is presented with small dots designating the location of your contacts. If you are using the professional version, you can load any of the U.S. zip codes, or just the zip codes of a specific region of the country. If you load only a regional set of zip codes and if some of your contacts are outside the region, MAPLINX tells you via a screen prompt that XX number of contacts are not within the limits of the map. If you have a mouse connected, MAPLINX activates the mouse driver, even if you did not use the

ACTMOUSE start-up command. Figure 8-1 shows the opening screen of MAPLINX.

One of the View menu items is *Zoom in*. With it, you can select two points on

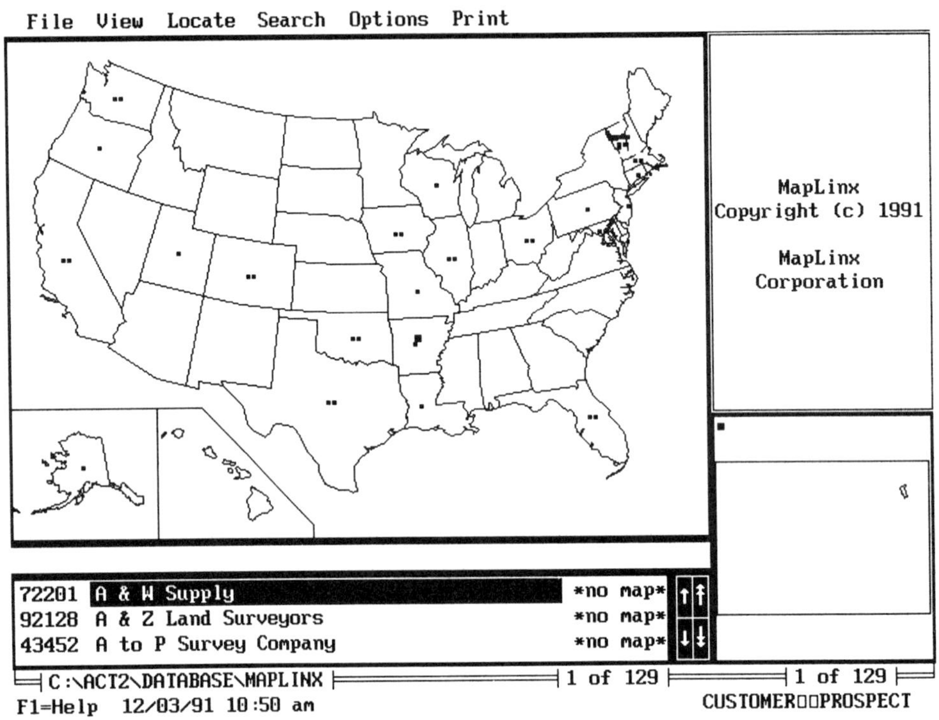

Fig. 8-1. The Opening Map with Contacts.

the map, creating a box, which MAPLINX zooms. In Fig. 8-2, a portion of San Diego County is zoomed. MAPLINX displays the zip code polygons. One of the items on the Options menu is *Places*. When Places is selected, MAPLINX inserts the name of the major cities on the map. Notice in the lower right corner of the map is the larger map showing you which area of California is zoomed.

Selecting the Zoom in item again, and MAPLINX displays the number of contacts in each zip code polygon, not including the names of cities. By pointing and clicking each polygon with a contact, the zip code appears (Fig. 8-3).

What else can you do with MAPLINX? To explain all of the attributes of MAPLINX would require another book. The highlights of what you can do are:

- Create a base map that can be saved and becomes the default map when you open MAPLINX.
- Locate a contact by the entry in the Name field.
- Locate a place by entering the city name.
- Find contacts, based on a rectangle you draw on the map.
- Find contacts by a polygon you draw on the map.

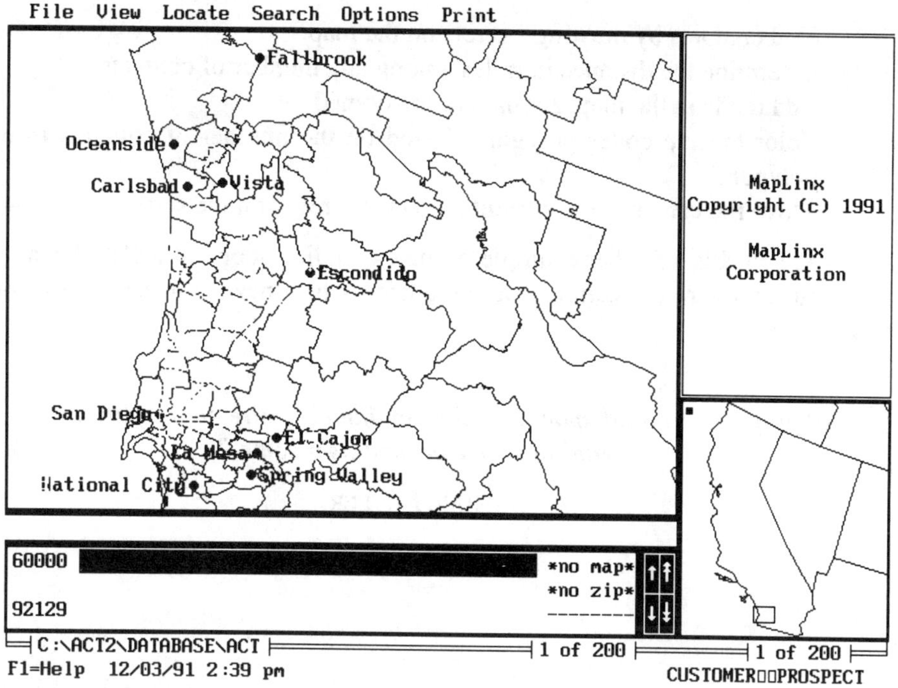

Fig. 8-2. San Diego county zip code polygons and cities.

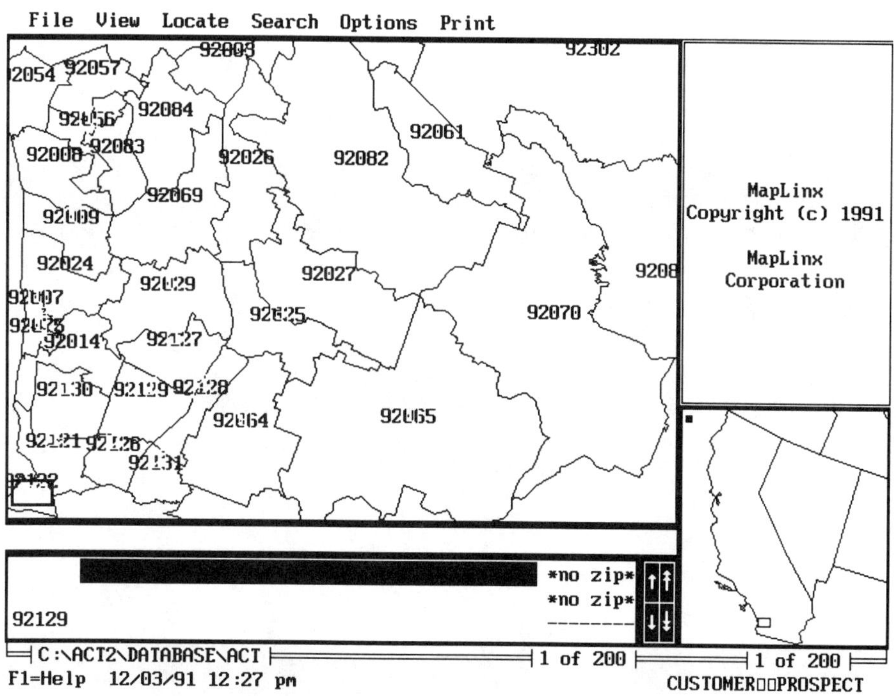

Fig. 8-3. Polygons with zip codes.

- Find contacts by drawing a circle on the map.
- Determine the distance in miles among any number of contacts.
- Add roads to the map, zoomed or unzoomed.
- Color the zip codes polygons, based on the number of contacts in each polygon.
- Move the center of the current map to wherever on the screen you want.

MAPLINX is a further example of the expanding scope of ACT!. By adding it to your software collection, you have access to a new dimension in Contact management.

"All progress is based upon the universal innate desire on the part of every organism to live beyond its income."

SAMUEL BUTLER

Index

H

I

K

L

Other Bestsellers of Related Interest

STACKER®: An Illustrated Turorial —2nd Edition—*Dan Gookin*

Turn your single hard disk into two with this professional guide. Updated through Stacker 3.0, it contains information not found in the manuals. You'll use such features as Express or Custom Setup for Windows and DOS; Windows Stackometer™—a set of real-time gauges showing hard disk capacity, compression ratio, and fragmentation levels. Plus, you'll use Unstack™, a time-saving utility that decompresses files and automatically returns systems to their original state. 208 pages, 50 illustrations. **Book No. 024010-8, $19.95 paperback only**

THE HANDS-ON GUIDE TO NETWORK MANAGEMENT—*John Mueller, CNE, and Robert A. Williams, CNE, CNI*

Here's a toolbox of power-packed network management scripts, batch files, menus, and strategies for the optimum care and feeding of your network. Mueller and Williams, both Certified Netware Engineers, explain how to customize workstations, prepare documentation, increase efficiency, design corporate databases, assign and monitor network responsibilities, run different applications and operating systems on a network, and more. 368 pages, 135 illustrations. **Book No. 043968-0, $26.95 paperback, 043967-2, $39.95 hardcover**

SUPER VGA GRAPHICS: Programming Secrets—*Steve Rimmer*

Programming advice isn't generally considered witty, whimsical, or fun—except when it's from Steve Rimmer. In the latest of his computer graphics books, he not only provides the tools you need to make Super VGA graphics modes work for you, he makes them enjoyable, too. With very little math, indirect addressing or exponential notation, the examples Rimmer uses will let you access the Super VGA Graphics modes of most of the popular display cards, display pictures, print graphics, manage a mouse, use clickable buttons, draw graphic primitives, and more. 592 pages, 100 illustrations, 3.5" disk. **Book No. 053000-9, $36.95 paperback, 052999-X, $49.95 hardcover**

SAVING WATER IN THE HOME & GARDEN—*Jonathan Erickson*

Regardless of whether or not your clients live in drought-prone areas, new federal, state, and local restrictions to reduce water consumption will soon make saving water everyone's business. This book shows you many water conserving products you can incorporate in your work, including the use of low-flush toilets and low-flow showerheads, the design of "gray water" systems, the installation of efficient sprinkler systems, and much more. 160 pages, 125 illustrations. **Book No. 019705-9, $12.95 paperback only**

VISUAL BASIC™ FOR DOS —*Namir C. Shammas*

Program effectively with Visual Basic for DOS With this user-friendly, hands-on reference and accompanying 3.5" disk by verteran computer author Namir C. Shammas. Designed so that you can develop professional looking DOS applications quickly and easily, this book contains 17 information-packed chapters on a wide range of Visual Basic topics. For easier access and comprehension, topics are logically organized into introductory, intermediate, and advanced sections. 360 pages, 218 illustrations, 3.5" disk. **Book No. 056860-X, $29.95 paperback only**

PARADOX® PROGRAMMING —2nd Edition—*Patricia A. Hartman and Cary N. Prague*

With more specific programming solutions than any other book, this guide details all of 4.0's new features—the Windows-like interface, drop-down menus, PAL extensions, memo fields, and enhanced query performance. You'll cover database management techniques, from simple data entry and screen design to more complex functions like generating reports, sorting databases, and querying databases. Plus, you'll review PAL programming and script creation, screen design for data entry, multifile database systems, and more. 576 pages, 502 illustrations. **Book No. 026978-5. Book No. $29.95 paperback only**

MS-DOS® BATCH FILE PROGRAMMING —4th Edition—*Ronny Richardson*

Reviewers praised Richardson's previous books: "*Exhaustive and exhilarating guide. . . . Give this book an A+ for utility.*" **—Computer Shopper**

Find command-by-command batch file explanation tables, complete DOS command summaries, and a library of practical batch file programs included on disk in this book/disk package. Updated for DOS 6.0, this book has been extensively revised to make it even more helpful to beginning and intermediate-level DOS users. 432 pages, 59 illustrations, 3.5" disk. **Book No. 052366-5, $32.95 paperback, 052371-1, $39.95 hardcover**

BUILD YOUR OWN LOW-COST POSTSCRIPT® PRINTER AND SAVE A BUNDLE—2nd Edition —*Horace W. LaBadie, Jr.*

LaBadie shows you how to assemble your own inexpensive laser printer, as well as how to upgrade, or replace a chip. You'll learn how to convert stock Canon CX and SX laser engines to full PostScript printing capability. Plus, you'll discover how to find, purchase, and assemble components. You'll understand engines, controllers, interfaces, power supplies, cabling lasers, toner cartridges, fuser mechanisms, memory upgrades, and more. 232 pages, 130 illustrations. **Book No. 035887-7, $19.95 paperback only**

LAN PERFORMANCE OPTIMIZATION —*Martin A. W. Nemzow*

Resolve your most stubborn network performance problems with this practical resource for LAN managers and consultants. This book-disk package will help you locate and eliminate bottlenecks in local area networks quickly. The diagnostic tools provided are equally effective with Banyan Vines, Novell Netware, UB Access One, Unix, Sun NFS, IBM LAN Server, Microsoft LAN Manager, Ethernet, Token Ring, and FDDI network operating systems. 230 pages, 90 illustrations. 5.25" disk. **Book No. 024629-7, $29.95 paperback only**

WRITING DR DOS® BATCH FILES —*Ronny Richardson*

Boost the performance and increase the efficiency of the DR DOS operating system with this first and only book/disk package on batch file programming for DR DOS. After a complete batch file programming tutorial, you'll discover how to create your own batch files using DR DOS commands and the batch file utilities included on the FREE 3.5" companion disk. A screen compiler, a batch file utility kit, and a quick-reference summary of the DR DOS command language round out this thoroughly practical, easy-to-follow guide. 464 pages, 79 illustrations. **Book No. 052364-9, $32.95 paperback only**

NETWORKING WITH LANtastic® —*Michael S. Montgomery*

With this instructive book you'll have an easy-to-read alternative to the program documentation—a comprehensive guide to setting up and running an efficient, high-performance LANtastic network. The author describes proven techniques for sharing files, printing, and using peripherals. Focusing on ways to configure LANtastic to meet specific needs and ensure maximum productivity, he shows you how to plan and design networks, install LANtastic software, use program functions and menus, and more. 632 pages, 199 illustrations. **Book No. 042907-3, $22.95 paperback, 042906-5, $34.95 hardcover**

BUILD YOUR OWN 486/486SX AND SAVE A BUNDLE—2nd Edition—*Aubrey Pilgrim*

This hands-on guide makes it possible for you to build your own state-of-the-art, 100% IBM-compatible PC for about one-third the retail cost or less with little more than a few parts, a screwdriver, and a pair of pliers. So don't shell out huge sums of money for a PC at your local retail outlet. This book will allow you to enjoy the speed and power of a 486—and still put food on the table. 256 pages. 58 illustrations. **Book No. 050110-6, $19.95 paperback, 050109-2, $29.95 hardcover**

UPGRADE OR REPAIR YOUR PC AND SAVE A BUNDLE—3rd Edition
—Aubrey Pilgrim

Why replace an old PC or PS/2 with an expensive new one when a few simple upgrades would do the trick? The third edition of this popular guide covers motherboards, CPUs, floppy and hard disk drives. BIOS and RAM chips, graphics cards, displays, printers, modems and faxes, memory boards, giving you the latest hardware and software options, prices, and sources. You can save from $900 to $1,500 in less than an hour—the amount of time it takes to replace a motherboard. 272 pages, 77 illustrations. **Book No. 050112-2, $19.95 paperback, 050111-4, $29.95 hardcover**

WINDOWS® BITMAPPED GRAPHICS
—Steve Rimmer

Stocked with ready-to-run source code in C, and illustrated with many fine examples of bitmapped output, this complete programmer's reference gives you all the practical information you need to work effectively with Windows-compatible graphics formats, including Windows BMP, TIFF, PC Paintbrush, GEM/IMG, GIF, Targa, and MacPaint. You get a toolbox of portable source code designed to help you integrate these standards into your Windows applications plus an hole lot more. 400 pages. 82 illustrations. **Book No. 052996-5, $26.95 paperback, 052995-7, $38.95 hardcover**

Rx PC: The Anti-Virus Handbook
—Janet Endrijonas

This timely guide and its companion 3.5" disk are an effective prescription for the prevention of computer viruses. Your lesson in preventive medicine starts with a brief intorduction to what computer viruses are, where they come from, and how they can harm your computer. You'll discover how to install the proper virus protection software and how to perform regular system monitoring, maintenance, access control, and file backup—all of which can significantly reduce your risk of losing data to viral infection. 208 pages, 100 illustrations, 3.5" disk. **Book No. 019624-9, $29.95 paperback, 019623-0, $39.95 hardcover**

ALL THUMBS GUIDE TO COMPACT DISK PLAYERS—*Gene B. Williams*

Keeps your CD player running smoothly and save money in the process. This easy-to-understand guide offers clear illustrations and step-by-step instructions for cleaning, lubricating, and repairing virtually any CD player. You'll discover how to do maintenance and repairs without harming your CD player, your discs, or yourself. 144 pages, 163 illustrations. **Book No. 070587-9, $9.95 paperback**